CORPORATE LENDING AND SECURITIES

Chris Parry
Mark Largan
and
Dr Iain MacNeil

The Royal Bank
of Scotland

The Applied Diploma in Corporate Banking was developed in association with
The Royal Bank of Scotland.

Financial World Publishing
IFS House
4–9 Burgate Lane
Canterbury
Kent
CT1 2XJ
United Kingdom

T   01227 818649
F   01227 479641
E   editorial@ifslearning.com
W   www.ifslearning.com

Financial World Publications are published by The Chartered Institute of Bankers, a non-profit making registered educational charity.

Typeset by John Smith

Printed by IBT Global, London

© Chartered Institute of Bankers 2002

ISBN 0-85297-673-9

CONTENTS

1

INTRODUCTION TO THE FINANCIAL STRATEGY OF CORPORATES

1.1 The Finance Function in Corporates

The following sections refer to the finance functions in corporates, however, they apply equally to the function of the finance director in a limited company and the principal with financial decision-making responsibilities within a partnership or sole trader.

1.1.1 The Finance Function

The finance function within a corporate covers a large number of activities which will include the following matters.

– Co-ordination of commercial strategy

– Corporate finance policy

– Dividend policy

– Acquisitions and divestments

– Resource allocation and monitoring of financial targets which will include capital management (debt and equity), dividends, taxation, exposure management and all aspects of treasury operations

Any one of these items can have a tremendous impact on the corporate's profitability and capital structure, and ultimately on the maximisation of shareholders' wealth. Ultimate responsibility lies with the board of directors in a corporate but in many corporates day-to-day responsibility falls to the finance director who takes initial responsibility for the above matters by co-ordinating information and papers on relevant topics to the board or to a finance committee of the board.

1.1.2 Group Financial Strategy

The net result will be the construction of a group financial strategy within the business strategy of the corporate. The implementation of this strategy will be delegated to the various section heads such as the financial controller, the group treasurer and the tax manager with overall responsibility lying with the finance director. The financial strategy will have a common theme which is likely to comprise the following:

– corporate finance policy by establishing the optimum capital structure in terms of the right balance between debt and equity;

– funding management – managing the right type and structure of debt;

– exposure management strategy; and

– tax strategy.

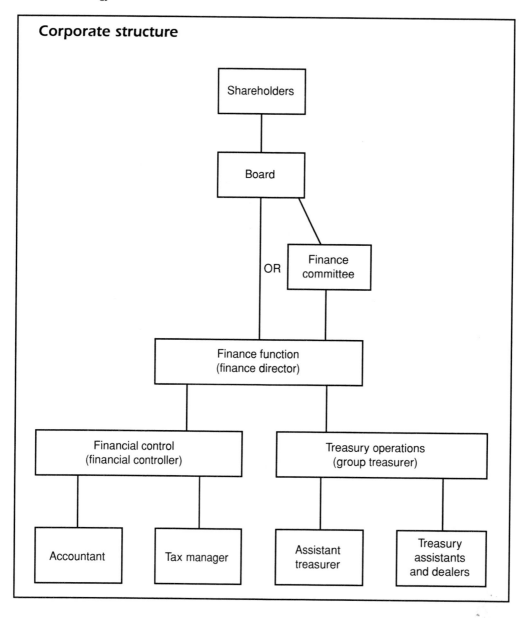

Corporate structure

1.1.3 The Role of the Finance Director

- Ensuring the finance function operates in accordance with the parameters that the board has set.

- Implementing and establishing overall financial strategy.

- Implementing acquisition, investment and divestment policies.

- Implementing dividend policy

- Co-ordinating all finance activities.

1.1.4 The Role of the Financial Controller

- Responsible for producing management accounting information.

- Responsible for producing financial and statutory accounts.

- Preparing budgets and forecasts.

- Implementing management information systems.

1.1.5 The Role of the Tax Manager

- To set a formal tax strategy

- To ensure compliance with tax legislation.

1.1.6 The Role of the Accountant

- It is the internal accountant who assists the financial controller in the discharge of his duties.

1.1.7 Functions of the Group Treasurer

- Maintenance of and ongoing management of banking relationships.

- Working capital management.

- Cash management – efficient use of cash.

- Exposure management.

- Funding or debt management.

- Overseas or trade finance.

- Transmission or payment methods such as cheques, BACS, CHAPS, etc.

- Taxation (in conjunction with the tax manager).

1.2 Strategy: Why do Corporates Require Finance?

- Return – making profit. Long-term projects may be in operation for several years before a positive cash flow is generated

- Financial capital expenditure/expansion

- Financial working capital – short-term, daily requirements, eg funding stock purchases

- Strategic – hedging; tax planning

  The key issue is the maintenance of an appropriate mix of debt finance

The corporate treasurer needs to avoid bunching, this is where repayments of various facilities or funding instruments should not be repaid closely to one another. Despite this being a tenet of Corporate Treasury, witness the restructuring of First National Bank in 1991 for this very reason; adequate maturity profile. Future cash flow forecasts required to meet specific needs, ie day-to-day; short-term; medium-term; long-term.

1.3 Objectives of the Corporate Treasurer

The corporate treasurer has the following objectives:

- Balance of equity and debt (see further 7.2.2)

- UK tax and overseas tax management

- Covenants on lending not set at restrictive levels

- Interest gearing level – very important

- Interest cover

The treasurer will try to:

- Ensure access to committed funding on a contingency basis or in case of need.

- Try to match foreign currency-denominated assets by borrowing foreign currency which is knownas translation hedging.

- Mix of fixed and variable debt. This is also known as smoothing.

Reason for financing: financial return, expansion, working capital, strategic.

1.4 Issues to Consider in Raising Finance

Reasons for financing: return, expansion, working capital, strategy.

Factors affecting growth:

1.   Average rate of return earned on invested funds

2.   Depends on level of distribution to shareholders

Investors look at: security, maturity and flexibility but in equities they should also look for growth. SECURITY, CAPITAL GROWTH, YIELD.

Banks look at: return, ability to repay, possibly security. Also balance of debt/equity.

1. Debt/Equity.

2. Purpose.

3. Amount – restrictions; equity is too costly for small amounts of less than, say, £20m.

4. Sole/Syndicated/Bilateral.

5. Source/Availability – some markets are very liquid, others are not.

6. Currency.

7. Fixed/Floating – instruments available to protect interest rate exposure.

8. Maturity – adequate maturity profile.

9. Repayment – should ensure this fits in with the cash flow forecasts.

10. Revolving/Non-Revolving – revolving is for working capital purposes; non-revolving is for specific purposes, ie term loans.

11. Committed/uncommitted. Committed facilities give assurance to the corporate that finds will be made available – subject, of course, to any terms/conditions contained in the legal agreement. An uncommitted facility has no assurance or obligation by the bank to lend.

12. Costs – fees; commitment fees.

13. Interest.

14. Documentation – restrictive clauses.

15. Security.

16. Complexity – money market lines; simple.

17. Public/Private. Public means that the financing is made public, eg a rights issue on the stock exchange. Private is when the finance is not made public.

18. Exposure management – interest/exchange rate management; hedging.

19. Balance sheet – impact of debt on gearing/interest cover.

20. Taxation – debt tax deductible.

21. Borrowing vehicle – special purpose vehicles are used for securitisations.

22. Image – high profile.

23. Timing – are funds needed urgently?

1.5 Banking Relationships

A large corporate will generally have several banking relationships and banks in recent years have been competing strongly to offer corporates their services. This, coupled with the sophistication of the corporate treasury function, has enabled a company's treasurer to negotiate the keenest pricing on a transaction-by-transaction basis. This has represented a move away from the traditional single relationship where one bank supplied the majority of a corporate's requirements. Banks now realise that they must co-ordinate and focus their services to meet the corporate's requirements. In order for them to do so, there must be a thorough understanding of the corporate's business, achievable only through a trusting and sustained relationship between the bank and the corporate; banks do not necessarily have to compete on price as the corporate will have a number of criteria upon which they will assess a bank. These include reputation and expertise, the quality of their research, the speed of their decision making and follow up combined with chemistry and communication of the human relationship.

From the bank's point of view, the relationship with its customers may be viewed as relationship- or transaction-based, the differences being summarised as follows:

	Relationship	*Transaction Banking*
Objective	Profitability of total Customer relationship	Profitability of specific transaction
Strategy	Increase business with existing customers, cross-selling of all banking products and services.	Create new business, selling individual products and services.
Marketing	Emphasis on matching customer's needs and bank's products.	Emphasis on knowledge of bank's products.

Whilst small corporates and other businesses may not have such strong negotiating positions with the bank, the above principles still apply, given the competitive nature of the UK banking sector.

1.6 The Lending Environment

You need to be aware that any bank that is in the market for corporate lending is in a competetive market and so the following factors will influence the corporate lending market. You should consider these factors before turning to the Porter model which is discussed later.

1. Competition amongst banks is very high for the business of lending to corporates.

2. Sophistication amongst corporate treasurers.

3. Technology – corporates demand speed, efficiency and accuracy of information.

4. Innovation – package a deal that is competitively priced.

5. Specialisation – ensure specialist staff available to meet sophistication required.

6. Globalisation – 24-hour markets around the globe.

7. Disintermediation – traditional bank role of a lender reduced, whereby corporates go directly to the financial markets and not directly to the banks;

    credit standing of banks

8. Deregulation – the single European Market.

9. Regulation – impact of capital adequacy provisions.

1.6.1 Canons of Lending

The purpose of the canons of lending is to provide a professional and structured approach to the assessment of propositions before the bank and to undertake a full risk appraisal. The canons allow the lender to assess all aspects of the proposition, thereby enabling a balanced decision to be made. The canons of lending are used for personal and small business customers. For corporate lending, lenders should refer to principles of good lending practice, as outlined below.

1.7 Financial Strategy

Corporate strategy is beyond the scope of this book but it is useful to have an understanding of the way in which large corporates evolve and the strategic issues that affect them. Growth can be organic in other words by natural causes and is achieved by

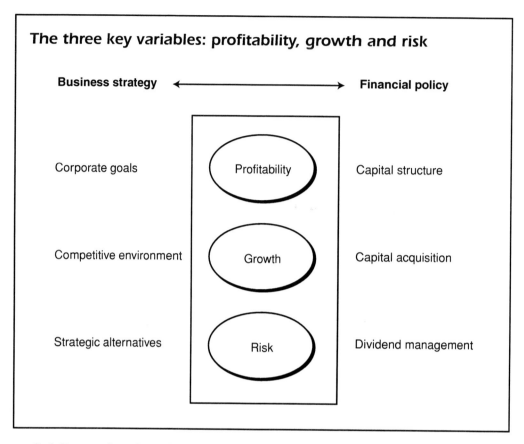

The three key variables: profitability, growth and risk

Business strategy ⟵⟶ Financial policy

Corporate goals	Profitability	Capital structure
Competitive environment	Growth	Capital acquisition
Strategic alternatives	Risk	Dividend management

profitability, product diversification, market diversification and new locations. The other forms of growth are acquisition and mergers.

There are three key variables of profitability, growth and risk which straddle the business strategy of the corporate and its financial policy.

A corporate that has high profits may be exposing itself to unnecessary risk. On the other hand, those corporates who espouse growth may be sacrificing profit.

In terms of business policy all corporates have goals such as market share or growth but these must be seen in the context of its competitive environment. A corporate can pursue these goals through various strategic alternatives such as mergers, acquisitions, joint ventures or organic growth.

Whatever business strategy a corporate adopts must be adequately financed and this is the financial policy. The key financial policy is getting the right capital structure in terms of debt and equity. Another key financial consideration is the capital allocation that a corporate makes between its different subsidiaries and operating units. Capital allocation is the process of where the capital expenditure is going to be made throughout the corporate. Finally, a corporate has to pay its shareholders through dividends and a key question a corporate must make is what level of dividend should be paid.

A corporate banker in any analysis of the corporate must focus on the business strategy and evaluate whether the financial policy is adequate. A banker must ask whether the corporate is taking too much risk in terms of either its business or financial policy in that it may be over-geared, or the corporate may be sacrificing profitability for growth or market share.

Understanding the strategy of the corporate is as, or more, important than the financial statements because if the strategy is wrong or flawed it eventually feeds into the financials.

Just think of the examples of Marks and Spencer or Marconi whose business strategies have gone awry. The business strategy was geared up for growth into certain markets which never came and the financials suffered as a consequence. The lesson of this is that the lender must appraise the business strategy of any corporate it is considering lending to.

1.8 Swot and Pest Analyses

It is essential as a first step to any credit assessment that the lender should understand the business dynamic, how it operates and what are the internal and external environments in which it has to operate on a day-to-day basis. For businesses, and especially corporate borrowers, a greater degree of information and precision can be expected when weighing up whether to lend. Usually for corporate customers a lender would expect to see up-to-date accounts, management accounts, agreed lists of both debtors and creditors, and for larger lending, business plans. This is essentially a qualitative overview of the business, giving details of the management team, the product range, the current trading position and projections of the expected outcomes if the loan facilities requested are granted. It is common practice now for a business plan to contain both SWOT and PEST analyses that provided a detailed picture of the business within defined parameters. If a business seeks facilities without having prepared these, it could be considered best practice to "insist" that they are prepared as a condition of sanction.

A SWOT analysis looks at the following aspects of a business.

1.8.1 Strengths
It is useful for a business to correctly ascertain what its main strengths are. This section should consider internal strengths (management, cash flow, location, etc) and external strengths, ie what does the business do better than its competitors?

1.8.2 Weaknesses
As important as discerning the strengths of the corporate is discovering and acknowledging the weaknesses – again both internal and external. The primary reason being to formulate a strategy for dealing with them. A chain is only as strong as its weakest link; similarly a business is only as strong as its weakest area. Examples of internal weaknesses might be in cash flow management or marketing skills. Once identified, these can often be overcome by hiring people who possess the requisite skills.

An external weakness might be that the corporate is sited in a poor location compared with a competitor. This might mean that transport costs (and delivery times) are greater than the competitor's. Once identified, a number of solutions should be considered. These could be moving – drastic but perhaps necessary – or consideration of alternative transport methods (rail as opposed to road).

The essential issue in considering weaknesses is that they are not to be ignored. It may be that no changes are made due to cost/benefit analysis considerations but the inaction should be based on decisiveness, not ignorance. It is almost certain that competitors will be analysing the weaknesses within competitors and seeking strategies to exploit them.

The failure to have identified weaknesses is in itself a weakness, and should be viewed with scepticism. It would suggest a weakness in management competence.

1.8.3 Opportunities

Often, it is the identification of business opportunities that will have been the catalyst for the requested facility. The option to buy the shop unit next door might be an opportunity for this business to expand its selling space cheaply. The business will need to show that utilizing the opportunity will be financially viable.

1.8.4 Threats

These are elements that might harm a business. For example, changing fashion tastes is a major threat to a dress manufacturer. For an established financial institution, the current threat is the growth of financial services offered by companies such as Sainsburys, Marks and Spencer and Virgin.

The table below is neither complete nor extensive. Different businesses will have different types of SWOTs.

Possible Strengths	*Potential Weaknesses*
Competent management	Out-of-date production techniques
Good financial resources	Poor management
Good brand awareness	Narrow product range
Acknowledged product superiority	Under-capitalization
Good marketing skills	Poor staff relations
Advanced technical skills	Poor distribution network
Opportunities	*Threats*
Complacency of rivals	New rules and regulations
New technologies	Business cycle
Export possibilities	Changing taste of customers
Flexible technology	Demographic changes

While a SWOT analysis looks at the internal concerns of a business a PEST analysis looks outward. The acronym stands for:

Political Factors

Economic Factors

Sociocultural Factors

Technological Factors

1.8.5 Political Factors

Political factors have a huge influence upon the regulation of businesses. Consideration needs to be given to the following:

1.   Is the political environment stable?

2.   What is the government's policy on the economy?

1.8.6 Economic Factors

The state of an economy needs to be considered in both the short and long-term. Factors which are of concern here might be:

1.   Interest rates.

2.   The level of inflation.

3.   Average earnings per head.

1.8.7 Sociocultural Factors

The Sociocultural influences on business are immense and vary from country to country and, indeed, within regions of a country. A business will ignore them at their peril. It is very important that such factors are considered. It may be necessary to consider:

1.   Religion

2.   Dominant language

3.   Is there cultural reluctance towards specific products or services?

4.   Age demographics.

1.8.8 Technological Factors

In many instances it is technical advantage which drives a business and gives rises to competitive advantage. Consider the following:

1.   Can technology allow products to be made more cheaply/to be of a higher standard?

2.   Does the technology offer innovative products, eg Internet banking?

An extra E for ecological or ethical factors may be added to the PEST analysis. Many businesses are becoming increasingly aware of their responsibilities along these lines. Indeed, many of our largest companies now have policies on social awareness. While it is good for a company to be aware of these issues and their effects, being "ethical" or "eco-friendly" does not make a proposition less risky.

1.9 Porter Model

In 1979 Michael Porter outlined a simple model to help companies formulate strategies to cope with a competitive situation they faced in their market sector. Understanding what a corporate can achieve in its sector is a useful guide as to what a company may achieve in the future. It is also important for the corporate banker to understand the variables and the issues that the corporate faces in any evaluation of it from a lending perspective.

Porter observes that potential profitability in a sector is determined by five factors:

(a)   the case in which new entrants can join the sector;

(b)   the bargaining power of the sector's consumers;

(c)   the bargaining power of the sector's suppliers;

(d)   the availability of alternative products and services which could meet the needs currently met by the sector's output; and

(e)   the behaviour of existing players in the sector.

Put very simply, Porter suggests that the aggregate level of potential profits in a sector will depend on how easy it is for aspiring competitors to join the sector. The level of profits that remain within the sector will be influenced by the ability of suppliers or customers to capture a share of the potential profits through the price at which they do business with the sector. The price of substitute products and services which meet the same needs as the sector's products or services will act as a cap on the sectors prices and hence the industry's profit. Finally, Porter observes that the aggregate level of profits may be influenced by the behaviour of players within the sector; if there are a limited number of players it may be possible for them to act cooperatively to maximize the aggregate level of profit. Such co-operation may of course be deemed to be a cartel, an act not in the public interest.

The five forces model is a useful tool that corporate bankers can utilize to think about the market position and the competitive variables that a given corporate faces.

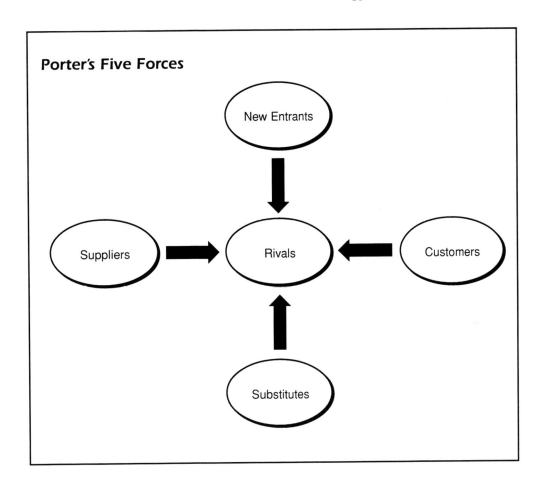

2

TYPES OF BORROWER

2.1 Sole Trader Borrowers

A sole trader is a person who is running a business as its sole owner. In many cases he or she will work alone and employ no staff. However, he or she may employ three or three hundred people. If the sole trader is solo, the mandate will be reasonably simple. If, however, he or she is an employer, it may well be necessary for the mandate to reflect the fact that one or more employees will have the right to sign cheques, etc, on the trader's behalf. Does this mean that such an employer partakes in the liability for any debts incurred? No. The ability to sign on behalf of the employee does not imply joint liability. The employee is distinct from the business. In some cases the sole trader himself makes a distinction between his business and personal affairs. This is, however, incorrect. As far as the law in the UK is concerned, the business is indistinguishable from the individual even though many sole traders will differentiate between their business and personal affairs by adopting a business or trading name. In this respect the sole trader does *not* have the protection of limited liability. For example, Joe Bloggs may run a business trading as Bloggs Car Services. In practice there will be two accounts opened:

- Joe Bloggs   Personal Account

- Joe Bloggs trading as Bloggs Car Services   Business Account

As far as the law is concerned, any money lent to Bloggs Car Services is in fact lent to Joe Bloggs and Joe cannot avoid the debt on the grounds that the debt was incurred by the business. In practical terms the only difference between the two accounts is in the area of account charges. Most financial institutions levy limited charges on personal accounts when the account is using borrowing facilities. With regard to the accounts of a sole trader the financial institution charges either a quarterly fee or a turnover fee to reflect the extra work and expertise involved in providing services to business customers.

There are no legal requirements to follow in setting up as a sole trader.

2.2 Other Non-corporate Borrowers

2.2.1 Partnerships – Including Limited Partnerships

The oldest definition of a business partnership is where two or more people join together to carry on a business-in-common with a view of profit.

Since 1890, a business partnership is deemed to exist if the definition above could be applied to the business.

Under the terms of the Partnership Act 1890, partnerships are defined as being either trading or non-trading partnerships.

Trading partnerships are limited in numbers to 20 partners and can be groupings of skilled tradesmen such as painters, mechanics, etc.

Non-trading partnerships, in contrast, which include, for example, accountants, solicitors and dentists, are not restricted to a maximum of 20 partners. In general we would consider these to be professionals. As a general rule of thumb, professionals are those who have, by a process of experience and education, been granted membership of a professional body whose rules of conduct, behaviour and competence they become subject to. Those who conduct themselves in a manner at odds with the professional body will be struck off.

Professionals often seek high levels of borrowing. Much professional business (especially accountancy and legal work) is done on credit and many large, successful and profitable practices have large amounts owed to them by clients – and equally large overdrafts.

Generally, banks like to lend to professionals, both sole traders and partnerships, as a general rule they have higher earning capacity (hence borrowing capacities) and are held to be better credit risks than non-professionals. While this *generalization* is probably true it should not obscure that *principle* that every proposition should be viewed on its own merits.

Normally the partnership will consist of general partners. Each partner will take an active part in the business and management of the business. Each general partner will have contributed funds into the business and will be entitled to a proportion of the profits. Importantly he or she, jointly with other partners, will be jointly and severally liable for the debts of the partnership.

Occasionally the partnerships may contain:

- *limited partners:* these, as the name suggests, have only limited liability for the debts of the partnership. This amount is the amount of the capital injected. Limited partners cannot participate in the day-to-day running of the business, neither can they withdraw their financial investment in the course of everyday events. They will also have a limited share of the profits;

- *sleeping dormant partners:* this type of partner receives a share of the profits but takes no part in the day-to-day business or management of the business. Sleeping partners are also fully liable for debts;

- *salaried partners:* this type of partner receives a salary in lieu of profit share but is not liable for the debts of the partnership.

The Partnership Act 1890 also gives the power to the partnership to:

1. *own assets.* Both types of partnerships are permitted to own assets. An asset is considered to be owned jointly by the partners provided it is bought with partnership money or brought into the partnership when the partnership was formed. The use of a property owned by a partner does not make that property partnership property; and

2. *borrow.* Trading partnerships have implied powers to borrow and pledge security. Non-trading partnerships do not have an implied authority to borrow, although the partners can take this power either via a partnership agreement or through the bank account mandate.

2.2.1.1 Joint and Several Liability

Obviously if the partnership is borrowing and defaults, the question arises, "who is responsible for the debt"? The key to the answer lies in whether a partnership is a separate legal entity distinct from the partners. The answer, in English law, is a resounding no! Liability for the borrowing, therefore, rests with the partners jointly. Financial institutions have, however, long utilized mandates that expand this joint liability to joint and several liability. As with joint accounts, this means that each partner is fully responsible for all the partnership debts. Lenders, should therefore, be sure of the identity of all the partners and the practice of credit references, etc, is indispensable.

The partnership may trade under a name other than that of the partners.

For example, Bloggs and his new partner Mr J Ames may decide to continue to trade under the name Bloggs Car Services (and benefit from the reputation of the business) rather than trade as Bloggs and Ames. In this case the account, and any subsequent borrowing, will be in the name of J Bloggs and James trading as Bloggs Car Services.

The mandate used when opening the account of a partnership is of vital importance. As already mentioned, the mandate will create joint and several liability and will specify the signing instructions. Unlike the joint account of Mr and Mrs Smith, which will have an either-to-sign mandate, the mandate of a business partnership may contain several levels of authority. For example cheques of up to, say, £150 may be signed by any of the partners. Cheques in the range £151 – £250 by any two, and cheques over £250 by all partners.

If one of the partners enters bankruptcy that partner loses the right to engage in business.

The partnership account must, therefore, be stopped immediately. Some partnership agreements acknowledge that bankruptcy might happen and allow for it. Normally the bankrupt partner sells his or her share of the partnership to a third party or the remaining partners. The proceeds are paid to the trustee in bankruptcy. If a partnership agreement does not exist or does not cover this aspect, the partnership is automatically dissolved even if the remaining partners are not bankrupt. In all likelihood the remaining, non-bankrupt, partners will open a new account in the name of a new partnership.

It is of course possible that the partnership itself could become insolvent. This may or may not mean the bankruptcy of all the partners and great care would be needed to ascertain the actual type of insolvency. If the order were made under the Insolvent Partnerships Order 1994 (in relation to a partnership with a principal place of business in England and Wales) then the insolvency would apply only to the partnership and not to the individual partners and so only the partnership account would be stopped. Otherwise the partnership account and the personal (and joint) accounts of any partner also held by you would be stopped.

2.2.2 Clubs and Associations

These are groupings of people who share a common aim or purpose. This might be related to a common sporting interest or other pastime. In these circumstances the group usually formalizes the arrangement by forming a club. This formalization is often evidenced by the collection of annual subscriptions, the appointment of officers and the opening of a club, or association, bank account. This can present a few problems to the financial institution. In practice, when the club is formed the first treasurer often opens the account with his or her own bankers and so the identity of at least one of the officers is established. However, the club mandate normally requires more than one officer to sign instructions to the bank. Does the bank take references on the other officers? If it is prudent, yes. The first problem arises when, as regularly happens, the original officers leave the club or relinquish office and their replacements, in all probability, are not known to you. The mandate should be amended immediately to reflect the new signatories on the account but the question arises – do you know any of the new officers? If not, do you need to prove their identity? Some financial institutions do not bother, relying on the implied introduction of the outgoing officers, whereas others make basic account-opening enquiries to clubs.

2.2.2.1 Lending to Clubs and Associations

If the club or association's account always operates in credit, the lender need not worry about the responsibility for debts as there are enough moneys in the account to cover debts presented to the bank. However, if an overdraft is requested, then the lending bank should identify a person or persons to bear the liability for repayment. As unincorporated associations, clubs and associations have no legal identity and therefore cannot be sued for the recovery of a debt (this protects the club/association's members from having to repay debts). Under *Bradley Egg Farm Ltd v Clifford* (1943) an appointed person could be liable for any borrowing which has been authorized by the club/association's committee under any rules which may govern its operation.

The bank may request third-party security in the form of a guarantee indemnity – under which the person providing the guarantee will assume primary responsibility. Such an indemnity should be in the form of a charge to be effective.

2.2.3 Trustees

Trustees are personally liable for any borrowing, but are only jointly liable (ie they are liable for an equal share of the borrowed moneys) unless agreement to joint and several liability is obtained. The lender would need to be satisfied with the financial standing of the trustees before lending against the trustees' undertaking to repay.

Although trustees have no implied power to charge their assets, they will be able to do so:

(a) when authorized to do so under the terms of the trust;

(b) under the Trustee Act 1925, when, by the terms of the trust, or by statute, the trustees have power to pay or apply capital money for any specific purpose, and the charge is to secure moneys raised for that purpose;

(c) when trustees with no original power to charge trust property are authorized to do so by the beneficiaries.

Where borrowing is effected by virtue of the provisions of the trust deed, those provisions must be strictly construed. Where lending is granted under the Trustee Act, this may not, however, protect the banker where the borrowing is ultra vires, see further 2.3.1.1.1.

Advances to trustees should be made on loan account when secured by trust property, but can also be made by way of overdraft when granted against the personal liability of the trustees.

Charity trustees may, subject to the trusts of the charity, confer on any of their body (being not less than two in number) a general authority or an authority limited in such manner as the trustees think fit to execute assurances, deeds and other instruments. On its ordinary construction, the word 'instruments' includes cheques.

Unless the trust deed specifically gives the power to borrow then the power does not exist.

Lending may be made available to a trustee who is seeking to sell the business of a deceased person. It makes sense that the business is sold as a going concern because this will generate the greatest benefit for the beneficiaries. There could, perhaps, be a problem if the beneficiaries believed that the trustee had continued trading for too long (assisted by bank lending), thus losing them money.

2.3 Company Borrowers

2.3.1 Limited Companies

A limited company is incorporated under the terms of the relevant Companies Act. A company has a legal personality. It also has limited liability, which means that the members' liability for the debts of the company is normally limited to the amount unpaid on their shares. For example, if a member buys one hundred £1 shares "at par" and pays up to 50p on each share, he has paid £50. He cannot be made to pay more than another £50, as members' liability is limited, in this case to £100. If the company became insolvent, then in the example above the shareholder would only have to pay 50p per share.

The property of the company always belongs to the company and not to the individual members of that company even if virtually all the shares are owned by one person, as established by the case of *Salomon v Salomon and Co Ltd* (1897).

The formation of the company is effected by promoters. A promoter was indirectly described by the Companies Act 1985 as a person "engaged or interested in the formation of the company". The legal position of the promoter is quite clear; s/he is in a "fiduciary" position towards the company and so must act in the interests of the company about to be formed — for example, the promoter must not make secret profits from contracts s/he negotiates on behalf of the new company or accept bribes or in any other way act in bad faith. Of course, promoters are remunerated for their work, usually in the form of full-paid shares or by cash remuneration. A promoter must be a professional skilled in such matters as company formation or one of those engaged in the actual business of the potential company itself.

Promoters will also be held liable for any misstatement in the prospectus which is the document issued to the public offering shares for sale in the company. Promoters often make contracts on behalf of the company prior to the date of incorporation. The Companies Act 1985 states that, where a contract purports to be made by a company or by a person acting as its agent, when that company has not been formed, then the contract can be seen as being made by the person in his own company and he, of course, is liable accordingly.

A director of a limited company is not personally liable for debts incurred by the company – with the exception of non-payment of national insurance contributions.

2.3.1.1 The Memorandum of Association

The Memorandum is the document that defines a company's powers and regulates its dealings with the outside world. The company may only do what it is authorised to do either within the Memorandum or by reasonably necessary implication.

The contents of the Memorandum must contain the following five clauses.

- The name of the company. If the company is a public company the name must end with the words "Public Limited Company". If the company is a private company the last word of its name must be "Limited".

- Where the company is resident, ie whether the registered office is in England, Wales or Scotland. The Memorandum does not need to contain the actual address of the company, but this information must be given to the Registrar at the time of the application or within a 14-day period thereafter.

- The public limited company clause (plc) – if appropriate.

- The objects of the company, ie the purpose for which the company has been formed. The Companies Act 1989 introduced a more simplified approach by allowing the objects to be merely "to carry on business as a general commercial company".

- The limitation of the liability of the members, if the company is limited by shares or a guarantee.

- Unless the company is an unlimited company, the amount of share capital.

- The association clause.

These clauses are normally referred to as the "compulsory clauses", but other clauses are often included within the Memorandum.

The Memorandum must be signed by each subscriber (the initial shareholders or promoters) who must personally take at least one share within the company, and against their names the total number of shares they hold will be shown, and their signatures must be witnessed by at least one person. Model forms of Memorandum for the different types of company are given in the Company Regulations 1985, and these must be followed as closely as possible. The company must not use a name already being used by another company nor must it use a name of an offensive nature. Both the Companies Act 1985, the Business Names Act 1985 and subsequent case law impact in this area.

2.3.1.1.1 Objects

As we have seen, one of the compulsory clauses in the Memorandum sets out the objects of the company, ie what the company can legally do. If the company acts outside of the objects set out in the Memorandum, ie outside what it can legally do, it is regarded as having acted "ultra vires".

Acts which are considered to be ultra vires should not be confused with acts which are an abuse of a director's powers. In *Rolled Steel Products (Holdings) Ltd v British Steel Corpn* (1986) the Court of Appeal drew a clear distinction between acts which are genuinely ultra vires the company and acts which are within the company's capacity but are entered into by the directors in abuse of their powers. Acts can therefore only be ultra vires if they are acts beyond the capacity of the company.

The Companies Act 1989 amended the Companies 1985 with the intention that the new rules on ultra vires would protect third parties, ie creditors and shareholders, from being party to an ultra vires agreement which would not be enforceable. Section 35(1) of the Companies Act 1985 now states that "the validity of an act done by a company shall not be called into question on the ground of lack of capacity by reason of anything in the company's memorandum". A new s 35A was added which deals with a transaction which amounts to an unauthorized transaction entered into by the board of directors (which therefore makes the transaction beyond the company's capacity). Section 35A provides, in favour of a third party dealing in good faith, that the power of the board is free of any limitation under the company's constitution. New s 35B provides that a party to a transaction with a company is not bound to enquire as to whether it is permitted by the company's memorandum or as to any limitation on the powers of the board of directors to bind the company or authorize others to do so.

2.3.1.1.2 Alteration of the Objects

While the Companies Act 1985 only allowed alteration of the objects where justified by seven specific references, the Companies Act 1989 instituted a less restrictive approach, although a special resolution is still required for any alteration to the objects. The alterations become effective, unless an application is made to the court for their cancellation, within 21 days. A cancellation can only be made by the holders of not less than 15% of the nominal value of the issued share capital or 15% of any debenture holders. When an alteration is made to the Memorandum (or the Articles of Association) a copy must be sent to the Registrar of Companies.

2.3.1.2 Articles of Association

The Articles of Association are the regulations for the internal management of the company. They form the rules of the company, and constitute the contract between the shareholders and the company. The management of every company is governed by its Articles. The Articles are signed by the same persons who signed the Memorandum of Association, and the signatures again must be witnessed.

As with the Memorandum, the 1985 Companies Regulations specify forms of Articles for the different types of registered companies. These may be adopted in total or partially, subject to the alterations specified in the statement the company submits to the Registrar.

The Articles of Association will normally cover:

- transfer of shares;

- borrowing powers of the company;

- directors' meetings;

- voting rights;

- forfeiture of shares; and

- reduction or increasing of capital.

Like the Memorandum, the Articles may be altered by special resolutions but only if the alteration is made for the benefit of the company as a whole. Articles are always subsidiary to the Memorandum and where there is a conflict between the two, the provisions of the Memorandum will prevail.

Both the Memorandum and the Articles bind the company and the members as if they were signed and sealed by each member and as though they contained covenants by each member to observe the provisions. Both the Memorandum and the Articles must be lodged with the Registrar together with a number of other prescribed documents.

2.3.1.3 Registration

The Registrar of Companies retains and registers a company's Memorandum and Articles together with the following documents:

- the names and particulars of the Directors and the Secretary, and a consent signed by each of them to act in these capacities together with a notice of the intended situation of the company's registered office. (The list of the Directors is not required in the case of a private company); and

- a statutory declaration confirming compliance with the Companies Act, signed by a Director and the Secretary of the company.

When the Registrar is satisfied that the statutory requirements have been complied with, a Certificate of Incorporation is issued, which is effectively the company's birth certificate. Prior to the Companies Act 1989, it was compulsory for a company to have its own seal. This is no longer necessary, and any document signed by two directors (or director and secretary) has the same effect as if previously executed under the common seal.

2.3.1.4 Incorporation

The Certificate of Incorporation is issued and a registered number allocated to the company by the Registrar.

Once the certificate has been issued, a private company can begin its activities immediately. However, a public company must obtain a Trading Certificate to commence business; this will be issued when the following two requirements have been complied with:

- the nominal capital is at least £50,000; and

- a statutory declaration containing details of the nominal values of the shares, the extent to which they are paid up, the preliminary expenses paid, and to whom, and payments made to promoters is provided to the Registrar.

If a company carries on its business, including borrowing, without this certificate, it would be liable to prosecution. If a third party had effected dealings with the company during this interim period any contract made would remain valid although the directors could be personally liable for any loss or damage incurred by a third party.

The Companies Act 1985 states that the company must maintain a number of registers and documents at its registered office the major one being a Register of Members (s352 of the Act). This Register must contain the names and addresses, the shares held and the amount paid up for every member together with their date of entry in the Register, all duly indexed. The Register and Index must be open for inspection by members free-of-charge.

2.3.2 Capital Issues

A company raises its share capital in the first instance by issuing shares to people investing their money in the company. This process can be repeated as many times as required during the life of the company.

There is a very important difference between public and private companies in the raising of capital. A public company, which raises its capital from the public, is governed by many statutory provisions, designed to protect the investing public, and contained in Parts 4 and 5 of the Financial Services Act 1986 and Part 6 of the Financial Services and Markets Act 2000.

However, there are only two statutory provisions relating to private companies:

- cannot apply for its shares to be listed on the Stock Exchange; and

- cannot issue any advertisement offering shares unless agreed with the Secretary of State for Trade and Industry.

By buying shares in a company, the purchaser becomes a member of that company and so is bound by the Articles of Association.

The Memorandum of Association contains a statement as to "nominal capital", which is the maximum amount of capital which the company is authorised to issue. The whole of this amount may be issued, or perhaps initially only part will be issued. The nominal capital issued is known as issued capital. It may be that only part of the issued capital will be fully paid. If it is the amount outstanding on each share may be called up by the company at some later date, either in total or in part.

The shares in any company may all carry the same rights to attend and vote at company meetings and to receive dividends, or they can be of different types, with varying rights.

The company will then commence in raising its share capital. If it is a public company a prospectus will be issued, inviting members of the public to subscribe for shares in that company. The directors will then decide which applications to accept and allocate shares accordingly.

The prospectus must comply with the provisions of the **Companies Act 1985**, and with the **Financial Services and Markets Act 2000**, in respect of its contents and the information contained in it. Compensation is payable by the person responsible for the prospectus to anyone who acquires shares, but who suffers a loss on the basis of false or misleading information contained in the prospectus. Once a person's offer for shares has been accepted s/he becomes a shareholder, and will receive a share certificate which states the number of shares allocated and the amount that has been paid in respect of these shares.

To ensure that the shares will be taken up, even if the issue is a failure with the public, a company will normally arrange for its issue to be underwritten by an underwriter (ie a financial house which undertakes to buy shares which are not taken up by the public). If the issue is a large one, several underwriters may be used, since one alone may not be prepared to bear the risk. Underwriters make their profit by charging a commission on the number of shares underwritten. This commission is still payable even if the issue is a complete success and all the shares are bought immediately by the public, so that underwriters are not compelled to take any of them up.

2.3.2.1 Transfer of Shares

Shares can be transferred according to the provisions of the Stock Transfer Act 1963. A transfer of shares is simply a "voluntary assignment" and occurs when a shareholder sells his or her shares to another person. The person wishing to transfer the shares signs a stock transfer form containing particulars of the shares being sold, and the name of the person to whom the shares are being transferred. Often transfer is made by nominees of the beneficial owner (including officers of a bank). This has become increasingly popular as it eases dealing arrangements. Sometimes the right to transfer shares is limited by the Articles of Association, so the directors have discretion to refuse to register a transfer. Of course, the company must alter its register of members to show the transfer, where it consents to the transfer.

If any shareholders transfer only part of a shareholding in a company, they will send their share certificates to the company who will endorse the instrument of transfer, returning it to the transferor but retain the share certificate; this process is known as the certification of the transfer. When the transferee (the receiver of the shares) applies to the company for registration, the company will issue two new share certificates, one to the transferor in respect of the shares s/he continues to own, and one to the transferee to cover the shares required.

If the instrument of transfer is forged this document will not have any legal effect, and can never move ownership from one person to another. If the company registers a forged transfer the true owner can apply to be placed on the register.

Special arrangements apply in relation to the transfers of listed shares. These are dealt with through a share settlement system known as CREST. CREST enables shares to be held and transferred in 'dematerialised' form, as provided by the Uncertificated Securities Regulations 1995. However, shareholders do have the option to retain proper paper share certificates. Those who do choose to participate in CREST will hold their shares within CREST computer accounts. Brokers, in particular, hold shares electronically under CREST on behalf of larger clients and institutional investors.

2.3.2.2 Transmission of Shares

This term is used to cover the situation where shares are transferred automatically on the death or bankruptcy of a shareholder. The personal representatives of a deceased shareholder may transfer the shares without becoming shareholders themselves, so avoiding any personal liability on those shares, subject to the Articles of Association.

2.3.3 Borrowing

A company's Memorandum of Association, usually contains an express power to borrow money. A trading company, however, automatically has an implied power to borrow money. The Memorandum and Articles will normally contain the extent of the company's power to borrow money and issue debentures. For example, the company may be empowered to borrow up to two-thirds of its paid-up capital. These powers are usually exercised by the company's directors.

The statutory definition of a debenture is very wide, and includes debenture stock, bonds and other securities of a company, whether constituting a charge on the assets or not. Strictly speaking, a debenture is a document while debenture stock is not. The issue of a debenture provides a method by which the company can raise money, other than by issuing shares. The debenture document provides evidence of the debt owed by the company, and the holders of the debenture become creditors of the company. The loan evidenced by the debenture is secured by way of a charge on the company's assets; this charge can be either fixed or floating.

2.3.3.1 Fixed Charge

This is a legal, or an equitable, mortgage charge over a specifice piece of property, for instance on machinery or factory premises. A fixed charge prevents a company dealing with the asset, which provides security for the loan, without the consent of the debenture holder, or a trustee appointed for that purpose.

2.3.3.2 Floating Charge

This is an equitable charge on the assets of a company, never a specific property, which may vary from time-to-time, such as with stock-in-trade. In this case, the company may continue to deal with its assets, because the charge only "crystallizes" (that is, becomes fixed on particular assets) when the company is in default of its obligations under the debenture.

2.3.3.3 Fixed versus Floating Charges

A floating charge is advantageous to the company as it enables the company to charge property which may change in the course of business and over which it may not be practicable to give a fixed charge. However, from a debenture holder's viewpoint, a floating charge has the following disadvantages:

(a)   It can be postponed to rank behind certain other interests. For instance a subsequent fixed charge over assets, which are already subject to a floating charge, will have priority unless the floating charge specifically prohibits the subsequent charge, and the subsequent fixed chargor has notice of the prohibition. Consequently any floating charge holders must ensure that details of the restriction are filed with the Registrar of Companies.

(b)   Certain items will always have priority over floating charges such as preferential creditors, eg unpaid tax, VAT and wages up to defined limits.

(c)   If the company is insolvent when the floating charge is created and winding up begins within 12 months, the charge will be void under the Act, except for cash paid to the company at or after the creation of the charge and in consideration for it.

(d)   The company can dispose of its assets which gives rise to the risk that by the time the debenture holder does intervene there may be very few assets left. The debenture-holder could overcome this by requiring periodic certificates to be lodged by the company detailing its liquid assets and liabilities.

(e)   Increasingly, suppliers of goods provide, through "Retention of Title" clauses in sales contracts, that the goods remain their property until payment has been made. If the goods are sold on before payment has been made, the sale proceeds must be held in trust for the supplier. Retention of the title clauses are also comonly known as "Romalpa clauses".

2.3.3.4 Remedies open to debenture holders

If the company defaults the debenture holders have the following rights:

(a)   to appoint a receiver. The right to do so must be contained in the debenture deed;

(b)   to bring an action for sale on those assets secured by the debenture; and

(c)   to present a petition for the winding-up of the company (this right applies *any* creditor of the company, not just a debenture holder).

Any charge should be registered with the Registrar within 21 days otherwise the charge will be void against a liquidator or creditor of the company. Registration may be effected by any person interested in the charge. The Registrar will then issue a certificate noting the registration of the charge.

2.3.4 Insider Dealing

2.3.4.1 The Criminal Justice Act 1993 and Insider Dealing

Insider dealing is the offence of acting with information which is not freely and openly available to all other participants in the market. This became an offence in 1980 and was given its own Act in 1985. In 1993 the whole Act was revised by the Criminal Justice Act.

The Act makes it a criminal offence for insiders to act on inside information. Part V of the Criminal Justice Act 1993 applies to insider dealing. It applies to all securities traded on a regulated market (including all European Community (EC) stock exchanges. LIFFE, OMLX and NASDAQ), and to all warrants and derivatives (including index options and futures) relating to these securities.

The main objective of the laws is to protect corporate confidences and to prevent persons with inside information from gaining an unfair advantage when they deal. Insider dealing can be defined as trading on the basis of unpublished price-sensitive information obtained as part of an individual's employment.

The Criminal Justice Act 1993 in effect gave more precise meaning to 'insider dealing'. The principles established in the Company Securities (Insider Dealing) Act of 1985 were extended by the 1993 Act to include a wider range of traded securities. The 1985 Act made it a criminal offence for insiders to deal in securities using confidential information and information not widely available. The 1993 Act provided a tighter definition of what constituted inside information and the point at which its use was illegal. Inside information may no longer be divulged unless in the normal course of the employee's duties. Previously, there needed to be intent to use privileged information for personal gain.

An individual who has information as an insider is guilty of an offence if they deal in these price affected securities on a regulated market or through a professional intermediary. For the purposes of the Act the market or the intermediary must be in the UK.

An individual will also be guilty of an offence under the Act if:

(a) he encourages another person to deal (whether knowingly or not) in price affected securities either through a regulated market or via a professional intermediary;

(b) he disclosed the information other than in the proper performance of the functions of her/his employment.

2.3.4.2 The FSA Code of Market Conduct

The Financial Services Authority, (FSA) has a code of Market Conduct that sets out the stance that the FSA will take towards Insider Dealing and the sanctions which the FSA will use to combat stock market abuse and the manipulation of share prices.

The FSA has powers to levy unlimited fines or to order them to disgorge their profits and compensate victims and prosecute anyone suspected of insider dealing to combat stock market abuse and the manipulation of share prices.

The Code sets out behaviour which would be unacceptable in the markets. The FSA's job is to sustain confidence in the market and to assist in the detection and the prevention of financial crime. The FSA civil fines will require a lower burden of proof than the criminal charges used against insider trading at the current time. Although the Code will not be enshrined in law a breach of it will be legal evidence of a breach of the law.

2.3.4.2.1 Duty of a firm

A firm must not effect (either in the United Kingdom or elsewhere) an own account transaction when it knows of circumstances, which mean that it is prohibited from effecting that transaction by the statutory restrictions on insider dealing. This applies to the firm and any of its associates or employees.

Every firm has a duty to ensure that it does not knowingly make a transaction for a customer if it knows it would be an offence under the insider dealing legislation. There are three exceptions where this does not apply:

(a) If the prohibition only applies because of knowledge of the firm's own intentions.

(b) If the firm is a recognised market maker with obligations to deal in the investment.

(c) If the firm is a trustee or personal representative who acts on the advice of a third party appearing to be an appropriate adviser who is not so prohibited.

2.3.4.2.2 Duty of an individual

This means that any individual with inside information:

(a) Cannot deal for himself, or on behalf of his firm or a client

(b) Should not procure or encourage another person to deal in the price affected securities (regardless of whether the other party knows the information is price sensitive)

(c) Should not pass on the information to another person unless it is a normal part of his employment.

2.3.4.2.3 Main defences to insider dealing

An individual is *not guilty* of insider dealing *if* he can show;

(a) that he did not at the time expect the dealing to result in a profit attributable to the fact that the information was price sensitive;

(b) that at the time he believed on reasonable grounds that the information had been disclosed widely enough to ensure that none of those taking part in the dealing would be prejudiced by them not having the information;

A similar series of defences are available to the charge of encouraging another to deal in price affected securities.

An individual is not guilty of insider dealing by virtue of a disclosure of information if he shows:

(a) that he did not at the time expect any person, because of the disclosure to deal in securities either through a regulated market or via a professional intermediary;

(b) that although he had such an expectation at the time, he did not expect the dealing to result in a profit attributable to the fact that the information was price sensitive information in relation to the securities.

2.3.4.3 Special Defences

2.3.4.3.1 Market Makers

An individual is not guilty of insider dealing by virtue of dealing in securities or encouraging another to deal if he can show that he acted in good faith in the course of market making.

2.3.4.3.2 Market Information

An individual is not guilty of an offence under the Act if he can show that:

(a) the information which he had as an insider was market information; and

(b) it was reasonable for an individual in his/her position to have acted in that way having inside information.

In determining whether it is reasonable for an individual to do any act despite having market information at the time the following will be taken into account:

– the content of the information;

– the circumstance in which he first had the information and in what capacity; and

– the capacity in which he now acts.

2.3.4.3.3 Definition of Market Information

For the purposes of this Act market information is defined as consisting of one or more of the following facts.

- that securities of a particular kind are to be acquired or disposed of, or that their acquisition or disposal is under consideration or the subject of negotiation;

- that securities of a particular kind have not been or are not to be acquired or disposed of;

- the number of securities acquired or disposed of or of whose acquisition or disposal is under consideration or the subject of negotiation;

- the price, or range of prices, at which securities have been or are to be acquired or disposed of or the price, or range of prices, at which securities whose acquisition or disposal is under consideration or the subject of negotiation may be acquired or disposed of;

- the identity of the persons involved or likely to be involved in any capacity in an acquisition or disposal.

2.3.4.3.4 Price Stabilization

An individual is not guilty of an offence under the Act by virtue of dealing in securities or encouraging another person to deal if he can show that he acted in conformity with the price stabilisation rules.

2.3.4.4 Definitions

2.3.4.4.1 Securities

The Act covers:

- Shares.

- Debt securities issued by the private or public sector.

- Warrants.

- Depository Receipts.

- Options.

- Futures.

- Contracts for a difference.

2.3.4.4.2 Inside Information

For the purposes of this Act inside information means any information which:

– relates to *particular securities* or to a particular issuer of securities;

– is *specific or precise;*

– has not been made public;

– if it were made public it would be likely to have a significant effect on the price of any security.

2.3.4.4.3 Price Affected Securities

A security is price affected in relation to inside information, and inside information is "price sensitive" in relation to securities if, and only if, the information were made public it would be likely to have a significant effect on the price of the securities.

2.3.4.4.4 Insiders

For the purposes of the Act a person has information as an insider *if and only if:*

(a)   he has it through:

– being a director, employee or shareholder of an issuer;

– having access to the information by virtue of her/his employment office or profession;

(b)   the direct (or indirect) source of the information is a person defined above.

2.3.4.4.5 Information made public

For the purposes of the Act information is made public if:

● it is published in accordance with the rules of a regulated market;

● it is contained in records which are open to inspection by the public;

● it can be readily acquired by those likely to deal in the securities to which the information relates;

● it is derived from information which has been made public;

Information may be treated as made public even though:

● it can be acquired only by persons exercising diligence or expertise;

● it is communicated to a section of the public and not to the public at large;

● it can be acquired only by observation;

- it is communicated only on the payment of a fee;

- it is published outside the UK.

2.3.5 Directors

The powers of management of a company are vested in the board of directors. A director is an officer of the company and is regarded as an agent of that company. The directors of private companies are often substantial shareholders – the owners of the company. The directors of public limited companies may hold shares in their company but are normally employed on a salaried basis.

A public company must have at least two directors and every private company must have at least one (Companies Act 1985). In the latter case, the director and secretary cannot be the same person.

The persons named in the statement supplied to the Registrar on the registration of the company become, upon incorporation, the first directors. At the first Annual General Meeting (AGM) all the directors retire, and at every subsequent AGM, one-third or the number nearest to this retire. Of course they can always be voted back into office at the AGM.

The Articles will normally require a director to possess a minimum share qualification, although this is not essential.

The Companies Act 1985 established that any person dealing with the company is not affected by matters of internal management, for example the obtaining of some necessary prior consent. While the directors are in office, there is very little the shareholder can do to influence the way in which the company's affairs are managed. But, if the shareholders disapprove of the method of management strongly enough, they can remove the directors by ordinary resolution at a general meeting. However, if a director is removed in this manner without his rights, he can sue for damages for breach of contract, where applicable.

The Articles of Association will normally make provision for remuneration and expenses. Restricted loans can also be made to directors by the company as long as they come within the criteria laid down under the Companies Act 1985. The exceptions under ss 332–338 of the Companies Act 1985 in which a company can lend to a director are as follows.

(a) For a relevant company a 'quasi-loan' can be made for a short-term period, providing the maximum amount does not exceed £5,000.

(b) Any company can make small loans up to a maximum amount of £5,000.

(c) Relevant companies which are money-lending companies can make loans or quasi-loans up to £100,000 to a director. The loan must be made in the ordinary course of business and on terms no more favourable than would be offered for similar facilities to the public at large.

(d) When the company is a member of a group of companies the other members of the group would be classed as 'connected persons'. However, the company is allowed to make loans or quasi-loans to other companies in the same group, or to guarantee, or to give security for the borrowing or quasi-borrowing of the other companies in the group.

(e) Any company can give a director financial assistance to enable him to carry out his duties as a director properly, provided that prior approval has been granted at a general meeting and that all details were disclosed at the meeting.

If a bank lends for any of the purposes specified above as being an 'exception', then such lending will be enforceable. If the lending is not for any of these exceptions it will be unenforceable against the company.

The board of directors, where authorized by the Articles, may appoint a managing director, who will be responsible for the day-to-day running of the company. This delegation may be made subject to conditions and may be revoked or altered. Normally the managing director is a service director with a contract, setting out his or her powers and duties and terms of employment. S/he has a dual capacity, as a director and as an employee.

2.3.5.1 Directors' duties

Directors' powers, duties and liabilities relate to all persons who fall within the definition of "director" under s 741 of the Companies Act 1985. Directors powers are conferred on them by their company's Articles of Association and the Companies Act 1985.

It is usual practice for companies to use Table A, which is ancillary to the Companies Act 1985, as the basis for Articles of Association. Table A, reg 70 and which gives a director a general power of management which is only limited by the Companies Act, the company's Memorandum and Articles or any special resolutions passed to that effect. Table A allows the directors to appoint a power of attorney to act on the company's behalf or delegate some or all of their powers to a committee comprising of one or more directors. The directors may borrow money for the company, buy or sell its assets and enter into contracts on the company's behalf. There is a general duty that a director must at all times act equitably and in good faith in the company's interests and for the purpose for which the power was given.

There are four types of duty owed by a director: statutory; common law; fiduciary and contractual.

2.3.5.1.1 Statutory Duties

Statutory duties are defined in the Companies Act and include the following:

(1) to keep accounting records, prepare accounts, disclose certain information in the notes to the accounts, and to submit accounts to Companies House (CA 1985, ss 221-262);

(2) to submit other documents and returns to Companies House such as the annual return (CA 1985, s 363), forms of appointment, change of registered office, etc;

(3) to maintain the company's statutory books and records;

(4) to display the company name correctly at premises and on documents;

(5) to declare any direct or indirect interest in any contract or proposed contract with the company (CA 1985, s 317). Such a disclosure must be made at a full board meeting. It was held in *Guinness plc v Saunders* (1998) that it is not sufficient for disclosure to be made to a committee of the board;

(6) to disclose their interests in shares and debentures of the company (CA 1985, s 324);

(7) not to enter into any arrangement to acquire from or transfer to the company a 'non-cash asset' without obtaining prior approval from the shareholders for the transaction (CA 1985, s 320(1));

(8) to convene and hold shareholder meetings when required, for example an annual general meeting (CA 1985, s 366) meetings to approve ordinary or special resolutions.

2.3.5.1.2 Common Law Duties

Common law duties, essentially, stem from the following:

(a) obedience to lawful instructions;

(b) care and skill;

(c) personal performance; and

(d) good faith.

2.3.5.1.3 Fiduciary Duties

A director of a company is invariably in control or possession of substantial company assets. As a result, duties over and above those of a mere commercial agent (ie common law duties) are imposed on him. These are called "fiduciary duties", which arise out of trust principles. These can be summarized as follows:

(a) to show and act in good faith;

(b) to act the interests of the company;

(c) not to act for an unconnected or "collateral" purpose;

(d) to show and act in good faith on a takeover.

There is also a general requirement to avoid a conflict between interest and duty. It is important to note that transactions for improper motives are voidable.

2.3.5.1.4 Contractual Duties

In most cases, a director will have a service agreement with the company (not necessarily reduced to writing) in which his relationship with the company as an employee is outlined. Such an agreement will almost certainly place duties on the director which are more extensive than those to which he is subject by virtue of his office as director, for example promoting the interests of the company, observing confidentiality and competition restrictions, etc.

2.3.5.2 Where a Director Gives Security

Frequently a bank will hold, as security for advances made to the company, a personal guarantee of the company director or possibly third-party security from a director over, eg land and buildings, to secure the company's liability. Where company facilities are secured by a guarantee from a director and subsequently security from the company itself is offered in addition or substitution to the director's guarantee, then the granting of the security by the company is a transaction in which, in view of the existence of the guarantee, the director is personally interested.

2.3.6 Financial Assistance for Purchase of Own Shares

The Companies Act 1895, s 151 stipulates that where a person is acquiring or proposes to acquire any shares in a company it shall not be lawful for the company or any of its subsidiaries to give financial assistance directly or indirectly for the purpose of that acquisition; nor can the company give financial assistance after the event for the purpose of reducing or discharging any liability incurred for the purpose of the acquisition.

A private company, or a subsidiary of a private company (which itself is a public company) can provide financial assistance for the purchase of its shares. However, the approval of the company by a special resolution is necessary and the directors must make a declaration of solvency. Private companies are given greater freedom that public companies to provide financial assistance for the purchase of their own shares or those of a holding company. However, the additional freedom is available only where the private company is not owned by a public company. A private company can give financial assistance, provided that either its net assets are not reduced as a consequence, or assistance can be provided out of distributable profits.

2.3.7 Financial Services Authority Listing Regulations

Not every company can sell its shares to members of the public. Indeed the vast majority of the companies in the UK are private limited companies who cannot do so. In the majority of cases this structure works well and is sufficient for most company needs.

Occasionally a successful private limited company will find that extra growth is possible but is being hampered by a lack of:

(a)   money; and

(b)   status.

A stock exchange listing can overcome both these drawbacks. A listing is not an automatic right nor is it granted easily. Indeed the procedure (called floating a company) is complex and time consuming:

● What percentage of the business are we going to sell?

● How many shares will this be?

● What price?

● When?

● Which market – eg full listing FTSE 100 or a listing on the smaller companies index or the Alternative Investment Market (AIM)?

It is rare for a private limited company (or a new venture) to go via the full listing route and most will list on AIM. Many will stay there but a few will eventually progress to "Footsie status". Even Microsoft was a tiddler once! In order to guide a company through this minefield they will need to appoint a sponsor, usually an Investment Bank, accountant or law firm to oversee and promote the floatation.

3

FINANCIAL STATEMENTS

The main sources of information provided to potential lenders by companies. Take the form of financial statements. There are four main statements:

1. Trading and profit and loss account.

2. Balance sheet.

3. Statement of recognized gains and losses.

4. Cash flow.

By law, large companies (generally with annual profits greater than £1,500,000) must produce these statements prepared by auditors for their shareholders and the Inland Revenue. They are published annually as "Annual report and Accounts" – the "accounts" contain the quantitative information detailed above and extra qualitative detail. The qualitative detail comprises the following:

1. Chairman's statement: a report from the CEO in the form of an overview of the year and information of the direction of the company in the coming year.

2. Operating and financial review: a qualitative summary of the financial results.

3. Board of directors: a list of directors and their areas of responsibility. Also a list of the non-executive directors.

4. Corporate governance: details of how the directors manage the company.

5. Report on remuneration: a report on how the directors are paid including salary, bonuses, pension contributions, share options, etc – the non-executives place a major part in setting the remuneration package of the directors.

6. Statement of director's responsibilities.

7. Auditors' report: the auditors seek to ensure that the financial records provide:

   A true and fair view of the state of affairs of the company as at (year end date) and of the profit of the company for the year ended and have been properly prepared in accordance with the Companies Act 1985.

   If the auditors cannot give this clean bill of health they can give other statements detailing areas of concern. Occasionally auditors will refuse to provide a statement.

Anything other than the clean bill of health, expressed above, should be of concern to a potential lender.

8. Trading and profit and loss account.

9. Balance sheet.

10. Statement of recognized gains and losses.

11. Reconciliation of net cash flow to movement in net debt.

12. Accounting policies: details of how a company treats depreciation, etc.

13. Notes to financial statements.

14. Notice of annual general meeting: the report and accounts must be presented to the AGM for approval of the shareholders.

15. Five-year record: shows how turnover, profits and earnings per share have progressed (or not) in the last five years.

16. Financial calender.

17. Advisors: bankers, auditors, financial advisors, stockbrokers, solicitors and registrars. Will also show the company's head office.

3.1 Trading and Profit and Loss Account

This trading and profit and loss account statement shows in a standard format how much profit the business has earned over a particular period. This is achieved by subtracting the cost of the goods sold and the expenses of the business from the income generated.

A standard format for a company would be:

Table 3.1 Trading and Profit and Loss account for Parry Plc for the 12 months ended 31 December 200X

Turnover		**A**
Continuing operation	B	
Discontinued operations	C	A=B+C
Cost of sales	D	
Gross profit		GP=A-D
Distribution costs	F	
Administrative costs	G	
Other income	I	
Operating profit		OP= GP-F-G-I
Profit/Loss on sale of fixed assets	J	may be nothing here
Profit on ordinary activities before interest		PBI=OP +/- J
Interest received	K	
Interest paid	L	
Profit on ordinary activities before tax		PBT=PBI +K – L
Tax	M	
Profit on ordinary activities after tax		PAT =PBT-M
Dividends paid and proposed	N	
Retained profit		RP= PAT-N

Note: the figure for profit/loss on the sale of fixed assets (J) above may not be quoted as a separate item in the accounts of a smaller company but will be disclosed in the notes to the accounts or cash flow.

3.2 The Balance Sheet

This is a snapshot of the net worth of a business at the balance sheet date. The balance sheet is based on a standard basic formula which you must be comfortable with.

The ACCOUNTING EQUATION

ASSETS – LIABILITES = CAPITAL

A standard balance sheet for a company would be:

Table 3.2 Balance Sheet for Parry Plc as at 31 December 200X

Fixed assets
Tangible fixed assets		A
Intangible fixed assets		B
	Sub total	A+B

Current assets
Stock		C
Debtors		D
Cash at bank or in hand		E
	Sub total	C+D+E =CA

Current liabilities
Creditors		F
Bank overdraft		G
	Sub total	F+G=CL

NET CURRENT ASSETS   CA-CL

Long term liabilities
Loan A		H
Loan B		I
Provisions	Sub total	H+I

TOTAL NET ASSETS   (A+B)+(CA-CL)-(H+I)

Financed by

Capital and reserves
Called up share capital		S
Profit and loss account		P
		S+P

ASSETS – LIABILITES = CAPITAL
THUS
Total net assets = Capital + Reserves
THUS- *Mathematically*

(A+B)+(CA-CL)-(H+I) = S+P

3.3 Statement of Recognized Gains and Losses

The statement of recognized gains and losses attempts to show the profit for the accounting period together with other movements in shareholder reserves.

Table 3.3 Statement of recognized gains and losses for the period ended 31 December 200X

Profit for the financial year	A
Unrealised surplus on revaluation of properties	B
Currency translation differences	C (– can be + or –)
Total recognized gains and losses	A+B+C

There are currently some concerns, within accountancy circles, regarding the value and appropriateness of SORG.

3.4 Cash Flow

This cash flow statement is a tool whose use is seen as very valuable. It shows, in a tabular form, the total movements of cash within a business. The importance of a good cash flow within a business cannot be overstated. William Buffet, the US investment guru, makes a strong positive cash flow a prerequisite for investment.

An acceptable format for reconciliation of net cash flow to movement in net debt is as follows.

Reconciliation of operating profit to net cash inflow from working capital adjustments

	Source of information
Operating profit	From profit and loss account
Depreciation charge	From profit and loss account
Profits/Losses on sale of fixed assets	From profit and loss account
Change in stocks	From balance sheet
Change in debtors	From balance sheet
Change in creditors	From balance sheet
TOTAL	xxx

Note: this is the figure will be the starting point in the "Cash flow statement" another very useful piece of data for a lender.

These changes refer to the difference between one balance sheet and the subsequent year's balance sheet, eg

	200X	*200X*
Debtors	12,000	10,000 an increase on debtors

The following rules need to be followed in reconciling.

1. The operating profit may be a loss.

2. Depreciation is added back to operating profit because, while it is deducted as an expense, it does not leave the business. All other expenses (eg wages payments) actually leave the business.

3. If a loss is made on the sale of a fixed asset this loss is added back. A profit made on the sale of fixed assets is subtracted. The reasons for this spring from ramifications of depreciation that do not need to be considered.

4. The following rules apply for changes in stocks:

	Action
Increase in stock	Subtract
Decrease in stock	Add

5. The following rules apply for changes in debtors:

	Action
Increase in debtors	Subtract
Decrease in debtors	Add

6. The following rules apply for changes in creditors:

	Action
Increase in creditors	Subtract
Decrease in creditors	Add

Let us expand on the descriptions in the balance sheet because in all probability this is what you will look at and analyze most.

3.5 Constituents of a Balance Sheet

3.5.1 Assets

The assets owned by the business are sub-divided into fixed assets and current assets.

3.5.1.1 Tangible fixed assets

The fixed assets are generally considered to be those that have an element of permanence. They can be seen as the spine of a business and are those assets that will be used by the business more than once. The fixed assets are as follows.

3.5.1.1.1 Property – land or land and buildings

Normally the place from which the business operates. If this is not owned but rented, the value of the property will not be reflected in the balance sheet unless a long lease is in operation. A business can own a property and rent it out. The value of the property would appear in the balance sheet and the rental income in the profit and loss account.

3.5.1.1.2 Plant and machinery

Used in the business to produce goods, etc. This could, for example, be a lathe or a computer.

3.5.1.1.3 Fixtures and fittings

For example, tables and chairs in a restaurant.

3.5.1.1.4 Vehicles

Any vehicle owned by the business and used for business purposes. This would include company cars provided to staff.

A quick review of these fixed assets shows they have one thing in common – they are tangible, that is they can be seen and touched. This makes them reasonably easy to value, which is important as accurate valuation is one of the cornerstones of good accounting. Does a value remain constant? If we think about our own personal assets for a moment we will realize that the answer is no. We will also realize that some assets increase in value (our houses) whereas others fall (our car, our computer, etc). In the same way business assets either appreciate in value or depreciate. Assets that fall in value will eventually need to be replaced and by depreciating the value of the asset on an annual basis the business is, technically, building up the resources to permit this. However, it is rare that these resources are earmarked for a particular purpose.

Looking again at the fixed assets, with the exception of property, all the assets are likely to fall in value as time goes by. Therefore, it must be right and proper to reflect this reduction in the accounts. Imagine the chaos and scope for manipulation if this reduction were done on an ad hoc basis. In actual fact there are strict guidelines for the depreciation of assets which, by and large, will be done by two approved methods, explained below.

1. *Straight-line depreciation* – under this system the asset value is reduced by the same amount every year. The actual amount is determined by the lifetime of the asset. So that, if an asset cost £25,000 and has a lifetime of five years, then the depreciation charge will be 25,000/5,000 = £5,000 per annum. The value of the asset would reduce in the balance sheet as follows:

	Yr 1	Yr 2	Yr 3	Yr 4	Yr 5
Cost	25,000	25,000	25,000	25,000	25,000
Dep	5,000	10,000	15,000	20,000	25,000
1WDV	20,000	15,000	10,000	5,000	nil

At the end of the fifth year the asset would appear as of no value even if it was still being used.

2. *Reducing-balance depreciation* – some assets lose the majority of their value in the early years and, therefore, less later on. This rate of depreciation depends on the asset and a typical profile would be:

	Yr 1	Yr 2	Yr 3	Yr 4	Yr 5
Cost	25,000	25,000	25,000	25,000	25,000
Dep	12,000	18,000	21,000	23,000	25,000
WDV	13,000	7,000	4,000	2,000	nil

Every year the depreciation charge will be deducted from the profit and loss account as an expense (this reduces both the profit and the tax). However, depreciation is a notional concept and no funds leave the business. Note that in examples 1. and 2. the total depreciation is the same but in example 2. the profit shown would be £7,000 less (because the depreciation charge is 12,000–5,000 more). Once a business has started to depreciate an asset by any method then it must stick with that method (consistency).

Property is not subject to an annual change in value within the accounts. Property is normally shown at cost. On occasion it is necessary to reflect the change in value (especially after, say, ten to 15 years). This is accomplished by a revaluation by approved valuers. This has the effect of strengthening the overall balance sheet and lenders should always be wary of a large revaluation reserve in the accounts because this might be hiding real problems.

Property values do not always appreciate and several (well-known) banks in the late 1980s and early 1990s had to make large provisions for potential bad debts due to overestimations of value and subsequent overgenerous lending. Many companies do, for the sake of prudence, depreciate property in the balance sheet, albeit that this is not always necessary, particularly if a programme of ongoing repairs is being undertaken.

3.5.1.2 Intangible fixed assets

A further group of fixed assets exists, known as intangible fixed assets. These are assets that cannot be touched or seen. This makes them very difficult to value. For the sake of completeness we will, however, mention the most common – goodwill.

Goodwill is created within a business as its reputation grows, and disappears if that reputation is lost. If a business is taken over, the purchaser will have to pay an amount to reflect the benefit obtained from this goodwill. A good example would be Marks and Spencer plc. Any purchaser of the company would have to pay not only the value of the net assets of the company but also something (in the case of M&S a very big something!) for the reputation. The main consideration with goodwill is that M&S cannot include the value of the goodwill in its balance sheet. It can be included only in the accounts of the buyer. This is further complicated by the fact that this value must be written off so that the value in the buyer's balance sheet reduces to zero over a few years.

There are a few other intangible fixed figure assets such as research and development, trademarks and brands, but again these are beyond the scope of this text.

3.5.1.3 Current assets

The second group of assets recorded within the balance sheet are the current assets. These have no long-term existence within the business and are usable only once. We could consider them to be the lifeblood of the business.

3.5.1.3.1 Cash

Either in the tills and cash boxes of the business or in the current account of the business. Once you have spent the cash, you cannot reuse it. Obviously cash is very easy to value.

3.5.1.3.2 Stock

Not all businesses have stock. For example, an Internet service provider sells access to the Internet – can such access be stock? Other businesses have large amounts of stock – supermarkets are a good example. Some businesses, especially manufacturers, have three types of stock. This is when a business purchases an item (say a block of wood), carves it and sells the finished carving. This business (normally a manufacturing company) will have:

- raw materials;
- work in progress; and
- finished goods.

The danger with stock is that it can become unsaleable. In this case its value falls to nil and this in turn reduces profits. Overall the valuation of stock can be highly problematical. Assuming 200 items of identical stock are bought and only 180 are sold. What is the value of the remaining 20?

(a) Is it the value of the last 20 bought, ie you sold in the order you bought?

(b) Is it the value of the first 20 you bought?

(c) Is it the average value of all 200 which is applied to the remaining 20?

This apparently pointless scenario caused much confusion in the past. Some businesses chose method (a) this is called First In First Out (FIFO). Others chose method (b) Last In First Out (LIFO), and scenario (c) is called Average Cost (AVCO). The effect of choosing a different stock valuation method was to increase or decrease the level of profit in the business by adjusting the value of the stock. This occurs because gross profit is calculated as:

> Sales – cost of goods sold, where cost of goods sold is (opening stock plus purchases) less closing stock.

In the scenario above there would be no problem if the cost of the stock was the same throughout the accounting period. If, however, the first 100 units were purchased at £10 per unit and the last 100 at £12 per unit we would have three different final stock valuations under the three different bases:

> FIFO stock remaining is the last 20 bought at £12 each   Stock = 240

> LIFO stock remaining is the first 20 bought at £10 each   Stock = 200

> AVCO stock remaining is valued at the average of £11 each   Stock = 220

If all 180 has been sold at £20 each, the gross profit under each method would have been:

	FIFO	LIFO	AVCO
Sales	3,600	3,600	3,600
Opening stock	0	0	0
Purchases	2,200	2,200	2,200
Closing stock	240	200	230
Cost of goods sold	1,960	2,000	1,970
Gross profit	1,640	1,600	1,630

Thus, in this scenario, using the LIFO method has shown less gross profit (and thus less net profit). Is this a real difference or a difference arising from the accounting treatment of the stock? Obviously the latter. Why might a business want to show less profit? Well, taxes are based on profits and so if a lower profit is made (shown) then a lower tax charge will be levied. Similarly a business whose profits are lower than might be acceptable to shareholders or lenders could increase profits by adjusting the stock valuation method.

Eventually the Accounting Standards Board issued a SSAP which set limits on the stock valuation methods based on the concepts of prudence and consistency. This SSAP together with the restrictions imposed by the Companies Act 1985 have meant that stock should now be valued either by the FIFO method or AVCO. Both of these methods of valuation is subject to the overriding consideration that stock valuation should be "at the lower of cost (FIFO or AVCO) and net realizable value". Net realizable value is used to cover the situation of obsolescence. For example, 30,000 386 computer chips bought two years ago for 50p per chip are now worthless – their net realizable value is zero. The only prudent method of accounting for their value in the balance sheet is to record it as zero regardless of the original cost.

3.5.1.3.3 Debtors

These are those customers who owe money. That is, they have yet to pay for the goods or services received. Most businesses have debtors although some do not. Your local chip shop will have no debtors whereas your local garage may have some debtors. Obviously it would be better if everybody paid as soon as they are supplied, but many businesses extend credit to their customers to encourage those customers to stay with them. The major concern relating to debtors is whether they are going to pay. In the normal course of events the answer would be yes. However, there will be occasions when the debtor cannot (or will not) pay. This might be due to his own financial problems or because there is a dispute over the quality of the goods or over the level of the outstanding debt. Is this debt still an asset? If there is a belief that the debt will be repaid, fine, however if this is doubtful, the level of debtors should be reduced and provision made for the doubtful debt in the profit and loss account. Unfortunately there is no hard-and-fast rule about what constitutes a doubtful debt. Certainly if a debtor has been refusing to pay an amount owed for six months, the chances of payment being made are slim. But six weeks? Eight weeks? In practice a lender will consider the credit given period (see Unit 13) to try to spot any problems. Increasingly, customers are asked for an aged list of debtors. This report, compiled by management, splits the debtors into time periods.

Business A

Aged list of debtors

less than 1 month	1-3 months	3-6 months	more than 6 months	Total
100,000	50,000	30,000	10,000	190,000

this is a great deal better than:

Business B

less than 1 month	1-3 months	3-6 months	more than 6 months	Total
10,000	10,000	50,000	120,000	190,000

It is important that the client's terms of trade are always understood before assessing an aged list, for example, a high percentage of debts due in over 60 days would be of great concern if the client only gave 30 days' credit.

3.5.2 Liabilities

The liabilities are the amounts owed by the business. These are again split into current and long-term liabilities. Long-term liabilities are those due for repayment outside the current accounting period, ie repayment is more than 12 months away. They normally consist of loans used to purchase fixed assets and may or may not be secured on those assets. Generally speaking the lenders are receiving a fixed rate of interest on the debt and know the date of repayment of the loan. Liabilities due for repayment within the accounting period are called current liabilities and ordinarily consist of the following.

3.5.2.1 Overdraft

An overdraft is moneys owed to a banker on current account. It is generally used by businesses as a trading facility to allow for the mis-match in time periods between goods bought and paid for, and goods sold and paid for. It is a vital part of most businesses within the UK and provides a bedrock of income to the lender.

3.5.2.2 Trade creditors

These are the suppliers who have not yet been paid. The granting of credit is a common business tactic as, it can be argued, it encourages buying. From one point of view the longer these remain unpaid the better. But remember that one man's creditor is the other man's debtor and the creditor will be seeking repayment. If the bank increases the overdraft by £100,000 and the creditors go down by £100,000 who has benefited? Certainly not the bank. It is also becoming common also to request an aged list of creditors from borrowing customers.

3.5.2.3 Tax

This is the amount owed to the Inland Revenue and is determined by the level of profits the business has made. For sole traders the profit is taxed as income tax and for partnerships each partner's share of the profits is also treated as income and taxed accordingly. For corporate bodies the government levies corporation tax. Both income tax and corporation tax are staggered so that the greater the income the greater the tax. Tax is a preferential debt on insolvency. This means that in the event of business failure the tax due gets paid before other unsecured debts, or debts secured by a floating charge.

3.5.2.4 Hire purchase

As an alternative to purchasing an expensive asset (which could involve a large capital outlay) the business can hire the asset from a third party. In exchange for not using the asset the third party receives regular payments from the business (lessor) for a fixed period of time. The agreement also obliges the lessor to purchase the asset at the end of the hire period.

3.5.2.5 Dividends

Dividends are the share of the profits owed to, but not yet paid to, the company's shareholders. Obviously this type of liability does not exist in sole traders and partnerships.

3.5.3 Capital

This is the amount of the owner's money in the business. Remember the accounting equation.

$$Assets - Liabilities = Capital$$

This is also looked at in another way.

$$Net\ worth = Capital$$

The correct phraseology to use is:

The net worth of the business is financed by the capital.

3.6 Limitations of Financial Statements

Audited accounts have several weaknesses and limitations, which should be borne in mind when examining the figures.

(a) Audited accounts are historic and may be well out of date when received. This can make it difficult to identify problems before it is too late.

(b) They look backwards and not forwards. Recent and future charges will not appear.

(c) The balance sheet represents a single moment in time, which may not be typical, particularly if the corporate's business is seasonal.

(d) The figure shown for assets may not reflect their true value.

(e) Some "assets" may not appear on the audited accounts; for example, goodwill, brand names and staff expertise.

(f) They are usually drawn up with potential tax liability in mind. Profit may be understated by carrying on. Sales or making large provisions against stock.

(g) Conversely, a poor year's result may be hidden by provisions, or changing the year end, or by changing accounting practices such as the basis of stock or the rate of depreciation.

3.6.1 Non-financial Data

Financials are not the only part of the story as management, competitors and changing market trends will have a massive impact on a corporate. This will be discussed in the next unit. The use of non-financial data can be more meaningful in certain cases. Market share information can be used as a useful indicator of future prospects and physical rather than financial, measures of size are often found helpful.

For a car manufacturer, for example, the analyst might find the profit-per-vehicle number more interesting than the profit-margin ratio. This is more likely where products are homogenous than in a company which produces a range of products with very different specifications and prices. Once again it is up to the banker to exercise judgment in deciding which ratio will provide the most useful information for gaining insights into the particular aspects of company performance.

3.6.2 Management Accounts

Every large business, and many smaller ones, now produce (for their own benefit) an internally generated set of management accounts. This process has been made substantially easier by various software packages. It is possible to purchase off-the-shelf bookkeeping and accounting packages inexpensively or, for more complex businesses, to tailor-make a package based on the industry-standard spreadsheet packages. The essence of all these programs is that the operator inputs all the day's business – sales, purchases, wages, aged list of debtors and creditors, etc – and the program translates these details into the approved financial statement formats.

The value of management accounts computer programs is immense. A business is able to see daily how it is performing, and to take action to correct problems or take advantage of opportunities. In addition, from the lender's point of view the figures show an up-to-date picture. While this picture might not be completely accurate, it will be a far clearer picture than accounts that are six months old, unless the management is trying to pull the wool over your eyes.

In addition to producing accounts, many businesses – often at the behest of their bankers – produce forecast figures. These are a projected profit and loss account and balance sheet based on the last audited accounts and what the management of the business thinks (believes) will be achieved in the current trading year.

The best businesses not only produce forecasts of future performance, but also formulate the plans that will, they hope, assist in achieving them. Budgets are a mechanism whereby the quality of the forecasts and the efficacy of the plans can be checked.

3.6.3.1 Sales Budget

The sales budget shows the expected sales on a month-by-month basis for the business as a whole or for different sections of the business. If a business had 300 different products it would be important to know that, while sales were up overall, which particular brands were selling better. For example, Tesco management might see that sales are up 4%. This is good but what if this is based on a 150% increase in coffee sales and an 80% fall in tea sales? Can this be ignored or is some action indicated?

3.6.3.2 Cash flow

Cash flow is vital to a business. Even banks. Too much cash in tills is unproductive, as are large cash balances in bank accounts. So a business will want to plan for the most efficient level of liquid cash.

3.6.3.3 Stock

Stock is somewhat linked to the sales budget. If tea is not selling do you want to keep high levels of tea in stock? If you are overstocked this is going to adversely affect your profits because of having to discount or write off through the profit and loss account or by interest costs on higher than necessary overdraft debt used to purchase it.

3.6.3.4 Expenses

A prime area for improving profitability is in the control of expenses. In some ways expenses are far easier to forecast than sales. Telephone costs will increase by a known amount. Thus if the level of calls remains constant then the cost this year will be x% greater than last year. If the first quarter's bill is in excess of this then the number of calls must have increased.

With expenses, one important fact needs to be borne in mind – whether the expense is fixed or variable? A fixed cost will not rise as production or sales rise and so should be very easy to budget. A variable cost will increase as sales increase. This means that the link between the level of sales and the expense needs to be established. This is a specialized area of accountancy which you will encounter in a few years time. Budgeting for variable costs can prove quite complex.

3.6.3.5 Cash flow forecast

Probably the most important budget produced is the cash flow forecast. This enables a business and its banker to consider what level of cash will be in the business's current account and whether or not an overdraft will be required. A standard cash flow consists of all income and expenditure items expected within the business and is shown below.

Standard cash flow forecast

£,000	Jan	Feb	March	April	May	June
Sales	20,000	20,000	20,000	20,000	20,000	20,000
Receipts						
Cash	5,000	5,000	5,000	5,000	5,000	5,000
Credit		15,000	15,000	15,000	15,000	15,000
Total	5,000	20,000	20,000	20,000	20,000	20,000
Expenditure						
	Jan	Feb	March	April	May	June
Purchases	12,000	12,000	12,000	12,000	12,000	12000
Wages	3,000	3,000	3,000	3,000	3000	3,000
Power			1,000			1,000
Rent	500			500		
Rates		250			250	
Telephone		175			175	
Interest	−1,500			1,500		
Total	14,000	15,425	16,000	17,000	15,425	16,000
Opening bal.	−3,000	−12,000	−7,425	−3,425	−425	4,150
Net cash flow	−9,000	4,575	4,000	3,000	4,575	4,000
Close bal.	−12,000	−7,425	−3,425	−425	4,150	8,150

- All figures will be estimates.

- The forecast will normally be for a full 12-month trading period.

- In January £20m of sales are made. However, only £5m of the sales are for cash with the remaining £15m made on credit. The length of credit will be different for different customers so in our example the full £15m is received in February. In reality perhaps only £8m will be received in February with the remainder not received until March. This staggered receipt of income will continue throughout the year. At the end of the year the amount of sales made on credit which has not been paid for will form the debtors of the business and will appear as an asset in the balance sheet.

- Notice that some of the expenses are monthly and some quarterly. The list of expenses shown is by no means exhaustive.

- The opening balance for January will be taken from the last balance sheet dated 31 December.

- The cash flow forecast shows that this business will require an overdraft for the first four months.

- Just as credit is given on sales it is probable that the company will be taking credit on its purchases and there will be a stagger caused by this. Indeed if the business took credit for only one month the need for an overdraft would seem to disappear.

The most important test for all budgets, including the cash flow forecast, is how close do they match actual performance.

At the end of January (in a January to December financial year) the management will look at the actual performance and, if necessary, take corrective action. Precision is not expected in budgets; there are far too many variables. However, the actual figures should be in the ballpark of the projections. For example, an actual overdraft at the end of January of between £10.5m and £14m would be acceptable whereas an overdraft of £28m would be cause for serious concern.

Banks can also perform sensitivity analysis on the management accounts to see for example what happens if sales were only 90% of what has been forecast and then see what other figures alter. Banks will try to see what variables in the financial position of a corporate are most sensitive or whether a corporate is very sensitive to movements in interest rates (if it were say highly geared) or say inflation. Banks will perform sensitivity analysis by playing with the figures for say sales/turnover. Overheads or others like interest paid and adjusting the percentages of them up and down to see how the financial health of the corporate is affected.

3.6.3.6 Importance of monitoring actual to budgeted figures

As with any planning and control process the discipline of forecasting is pointless unless there is adequate provision for monitoring actual figures against that in a profit or cash flow forecast. Such monitoring allows early corrective action and an early warning to avoid future problems or at least minimize them. The most important use of a budget is to use it as a tool to monitor the corporate. If subsequent management accounts differ widely from the budget, an explanation should be sought together with details of any action proposed to rectify the position.

Banks use interim management accounts from corporates to seek assurances from the figures that the underlying business remains profitable and it is not suffering from any actual or potential liquidity problems. The bank may also use such figures to monitor the value of any debenture taken as security. The provision of management accounts or other financial information to banks can be incorporated as a term in any facility letter or loan agreement.

A corporate banker should always examine the assumptions behind all budgets to see that they are realistic. If the sales figures are unrealistic, the profit figure will not be achieved: if the periods of credit given and taken are incorrect, then the last forecast will bear no relation to the cash flow forecast. The actual gross margins and overhead expenses should always be compared, as well as turnover, to the budget figures in both the most recent management accounts or audited accounts.

It should be noted that cumulative figures are more important for monitoring performance than the figures for a single period as these will smooth out any monthly fluctuations.

If a bank is the sole banker to a corporate then the forecast or cash budget should reflect in broad terms the position and activity that may be seen by the bank on the bank account. Where a corporate is multi-banked this analysis is not possible.

The following is an action or check list that any corporate banker should think of when comparing actual to budgeted figures:

(a)   Are the assumptions underlying the budget realistic? If not enquire why?

(b)   Is the forecast reality or is it just a pipe dream done to satisfy the bank?

(c)   Is there evidence of consistency and co-ordination in that the figures in the profit forecast and cash flow forecast are similar?

(d)   Are there any omissions form the forecast such as planned capital expenditure or expansion?

(e)   Is the business seasonal or cyclical and has the forecast taken account of that?

The most important use of a budget is to use it as a tool to monitor the corporate. If subsequent management accounts differ widely from the budget, an explanation should be sought, together with details of any action proposed to rectify the position.

Banks use interim management accounts from corporates to seek assurances from the figures that the underlying business remains profitable and it is not suffering from any actual or potential liquidity problems. The bank may also use such figures to monitor the value of any debenture taken as security. The provision of management accounts or other financial information to banks can be incorporated as a term in any facility letter or loan agreement.

4

EVALUATION AND CREDIT ASSESSMENT OF CORPORATES

4.1 Introduction

1. **Bank Policy.** The following elements of a bank's policy in relation to the following factors should be considered as part of any evaluation of the corporate:

    Risks in banking: the risk of not being repaid or a liquidity crunch.

    Adequate balance sheet management by the bank.

    The supply and demand for both loans and deposits

    Capital adequacy: to ensure an adequate return for the bank over and above its cost of capital that is allocated to the loan.

    Policy formulation: what the bank determines should be its minimum return.

    Target marketing: what corporates the bank wants to target.

2. **Credit Assessment.** This is a fundamental banking skill which when applied to the analysis of a corporate and a banker will need to consider the following factors:

    (a) ability to repay of the corporate;

    (b) relationship to the corporate;

    (c) is there adequate return to the risk;

    (d) reputation of the corporate.

3. **Context of the corporate in question.** The following information is required before any meaningful analysis of a corporate can be compared:

    Industry

    –   Competitors (who are they?)

        Markets: what type of market(s) does the corporate operate in?

        Growth prospects of the corporate

Cyclical products or new technology, such as WAP phones?

See further 1.8–1.9.

Price Taker/Price Maker

– If the corporate has a significant market share then can it influence the market or is it a niche player? The alternative is that the corporate has to follow prices set by other competitors.

Management

– Corporate governance (Autocratic Chief Executive such as Robert Maxwell)

Non-executives: who are they? Are they considered worthy or are they merely figureheads?

Balance, what is the ownership of the corporate? Are there significant shareholdings?

Relationship

– Between the treasurer and the accounts officer or relationship of the bank.

Annual Reports

The following aspects should be scrutinized:

– Profitability

Cash Flow

Capital

Liquidity.

4.2 Balance Sheets

4.2.1 Characteristics

● Statement of fact.

● Statutory requirements.

● Provides a record of past performance.

● Trends are the most important item to analyze.

● Enables ratio analysis to be undertaken.

4.2.2 Constraints of Balance Sheets

● A balance sheet is merely a snapshot in time – they are historic and often out of date.

- Beware of the manipulation/smoothing of balance sheets – especially in the following circumstances:

  (a) preparing to launch a bid,

  (b) defence against an unwanted bid,

  (c) preparation for sale of a business,

  (d) preparation for flotation/rights issue, and

  (e) preparation for entering new markets.

4.2.3 Management

Accounts do not show the impact of management personalities. This is key since you must look at the case of Robert Maxwell and the Mirror Group or the successes of Bill Gates and also how a company can fail when a key person leaves or retires form the firm, for example, if Richard Branson were to leave Virgin. Banks have been badly caught out in the past by putting too much emphasis on the financials of a corporate and not enough on appraising the management of a corporate.

Bad management can destroy a corporate and even good management can take bad decisions. Just consider names like Marconi and BT and ask what went wrong. Other corporates can get their strategy wrong, as with Marks and Spencer a few years ago, and the financials may suffer as a result.

If a company is poorly managed, this may feed through to the financials. Banks must appraise the management of a corporate and its governance. A bank must also consider what would happen if any key individuals were to leave, die or retire from a firm. Poor management can destroy the previously good financials of a corporate.

4.2.4 Competitors

It is important for the bank to understand who the competitors of the corporate are as these will not be stated in the accounts. Competitors may have an enormous effect on a corporate and any analysis of a corporate on its own is useless unless a comparison is also made against the balance sheets and financial statements of their competitors.

To gain a correct view of the corporate's position a banker should undertake a cross-sectional analysis of the corporate's financial position that will involve the comparison of several corporates' financial accounts. Comparison is required for several reasons:

(a) to determine whether a company is correctly valued and resourced in comparison with its competitors. If a company is undervalued in relation to its competitors it can for example be subject to a takeover bid;

(b) to examine the managerial performance of a firm in comparison to its competitors;

(c)   to predict the likelihood of financial distress by comparing certain financial characteristics such as gearing with its competitors;

(d)   to examine whether a firm has made excess profits in comparison to its competitors and to enquire why that has arisen; and

(e)   to enable a banker to see whether management expectations or budget forecasts are realistic when compared to the financials of their competitors.

Financial accounts do not, however, show the future plans and strategy of the corporate or the impact of changing market trends and habits. Again, this is a crucial part of the analysis. Just look at the experience of dot.com companies. Look at the recent history of technology and telecommunication corporates who invested in new technologies/markets with short-term, but not long-term success. A banker must take great care in lending to corporates for expansion into new markets.

A banker must not base his or her analysis on the financial statements or other financials of a corporate alone. Too many bankers have done so in the past to the cost of a bank. The impact, and consequently the analysis, of management, competitors and market trends are of equal importance in the analysis of a corporate.

4.3 Financial Analysis

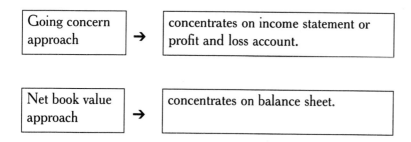

Banks are always concerned with the margin of protection that either a lending proposition gives or the security of an asset or the balance sheet strength or capacity of a corporate.

4.3.1 Cashflows

It is important for the bank to be aware of:

1.   the exact amount of cash generated by operations;

2.   the amount needed to service the debt;

3.   the amount that has to be raised in new financings to cover any shortfall.

It is also important that any depreciation is deducted.

4.3.2 Financial Ratios

Efficiency Ratios	Capital Turnover – Sales/Tangible Assets
	Sales per employee
	Cost of goods sold/inventory
Profitability Ratios	Net Profit/Sales
	Net Profit/Total Assets
Growth Ratios	Growth in sales, net profit, earnings per share
Stability Ratios	Maximum decline in times interest earned
	Percentage decline in return on capital
Liquidity Ratios	These do not pick up unused committed lines, ie current ratio, acid test
Leverage Ratios	Debt to equity ratio
	Interest cover
Market Value Ratios	Earnings, dividends, book value per share, price earnings ratio
	Dividend yield – dividends per share/market price per share

For further details on financial ratios, see 4.5.

4.3.3 Uncertainty

1. Assigning probabilities to key assumptions.

2. Presenting the financial forecasts as a range.

3. Preparing a series of forecasts under different scenarios.

4. Sensitivity analysis on key assumptions.

4.3.4 Budgeting

The bank should be aware of whether the corporate sets financial benchmarks.

4.3.5 Business Strategy

The lender should consider the strategy of the corporate, taking particular note of any strategies likely to impact upon the risk profile of the corporate or the debt levels carried and the corporate's ability to service them.

4.3.6 Cash Restraint

The bank should consider the following cash restraint questions in relation to the corporate. Does the corporate:

● prioritize and rank resources between business units;

● set limits/targets on each division's budget?

Cash requirements should include the three major elements of cash flow, ie

● net profit;

● working capital requirements; and

● capital expenditure.

4.3.7 Setting Budgets

The bank needs to know how the corporate sets budgets.

● The corporate's budget strategy should examine division/units, including sales, marketing, production, distribution, technology, personnel.

● The level of delegation needs to be considered and the capex authority should be set.

● The financial criteria could include margin, overhead, net profit/turnover, ROCE, net debt gearing.

● The budget should take account of general economic indicators, interest rates and currency rates.

● It is normal to have a preliminary budget and then a central one.

● Budgets are a vital management exercise for decision-making.

● Should budgets be targets or yardsticks – this may vary from corporate-to-corporate?

4.4 Summary

To summarize, banks will concentrate their analysis on the following variables:

1. Economic and competitive markets.

2. Management.

3. Financial, track record.

4. Repayment.

5. Security – depends on risk.

6. Remuneration to the bank in terms of margins and fees.

For examples of where financial analysis can be used by lenders, see Unit 25, Case Studies 1 and 2.

4.5 Ratio Analysis

4.5.1 Gearing

In calculating gearing, the total borrowing by the business (overdraft, bank loans, HP, etc) should be compared to the capital base. This is done by calculating the gearing ratio, which measures the financial relationship between borrowed funds and owners funds.

$$\text{Gearing ratio} = \frac{\text{Total borrowing}}{\text{Total capital}}$$

Total borrowing should include all instruments that carry a rate of interest, including for example, cumulative preference share holdings.

It is important to include within the capital figure any hidden reserves or quasi-capital, and to deduct intangibles.

Ideally, the gearing ratio should be less than 1:1, for it is not appropriate for lenders to have a larger stake in the business than the owners. The normal interest margin is insufficient to compensate for the higher level of risk.

Businesses with a ratio in excess of 1:1 are said to be highly geared, and are vulnerable when interest rates rise as profits will be substantially reduced as a result of the risk.

High gearing levels increase the risk of the corporate but can be offset where strong earnings yield high interest cover ratio's. It is also important to recognize that certain industries have inherently high gearing levels due to the capital intensive nature of them (hotels for example) and in these cases it is essential that a comparison of gearing is made to the industry norm.

4.5.2 Liquidity

Liquidity is vital to a business. It is of greater importance than profitability, for a liquidity shortfall can lead to insolvency (on the basis that the corporate is unable to meet its debts as they fall due).

Liquidity is measured by examining the working capital position of a business, ie the excess of current assets over current liabilities. A business should ensure it has sufficient liquidity to meet its current liabilities as they fall due.

The rules covering bankruptcy and corporate insolvency are included in the Insolvency Act 1986 and the Insolvency Rules 1986. While both sole traders and partners are fully liable for all their business debts, the directors and shareholders of a company are protected by the separate legal existence of the company. In the past this has provided comfort to directors, some of whom took advantage and continued to permit a company to trade to their advantage but to the detriment of the creditors. This problem was addressed by s 214 of the Insolvency Act 1986. Under this section the directors can be held personally liable for the debts of the company if the director had allowed the company to continue trading when the director: "knew or ought to have concluded that there was no reasonable prospect that the company would avoid going into insolvent liquidation".

In this scenario the director will have to prove that he had taken every step which ought to have been taken to minimize potential loss to creditors. There is an ancillary point for a lender to consider. Can the lender be considered to be acting as a director of the company? The legal term is "shadow director" and has been defined by the Insolvency Act as: "a person in accordance with whose instructions a company is accustomed to act".

The company, although a separate legal entity, interacts with the outside world via its directors. It is possible that a board of directors has such a good relationship with its lending account manager that they treat his suggestions as instructions and act accordingly. Under this scenario there is a possibility that the bank could be considered to be a shadow director and liable for losses to creditors under s 214. This principle was almost tested in litigation in 1989 but the liquidator pulled back. However, it is important for the lender to consider carefully its position in this respect.

Given the importance of the liquidity how should it be measured?

Working capital ratio (Current Ratio)	$\dfrac{\text{Current assets}}{\text{Current liabilities}}$
Acid test ratio (Quick Ratio)	$\dfrac{\text{Current assets} - \text{stock}}{\text{Current liabilities}}$

Both the working capital and acide test ratios attempt to ascertain the ease with which the company can utilize its current assets to meet current liabilities. It is important to remember that the current assets are generally cash, stock and debtors while current liabilities are those debts due for payment in less than 12 months. These include debts owed to trade creditors, overdrafts, and payments received on account. Neither of these definitions is complete.

The working capital and acid test ratios should be monitored to detect signs of deterioration and the banker asking the corporate for an explanation. An indication of cash pressure accompanied by rising turnover could be indicative of overtrading. The rationale behind the acid test ratio is that stock can be less liquid than cash or debtors and as such should be ignored. The usual caveats apply, such as the fact that a current ratio that is acceptable for one type of business will be unacceptable in another. Consider for example a supermarket chain – Its acid test ratio will reflect that fact that it has few, if any, debtors but it will have a substantial amount of its current assets in the form of stock. Alternatively a central heating provider might have a substantial debtor book but very limited stock.

4.5.3 Investment

The ratios considered above have been primarily geared towards potential lenders and the management of the business. Investment ratios, which are used for plcs listed on FTSE or AIM, are of major importance to the shareholders and potential shareholders.

The key investment ratios are:

$$\text{Earnings per share} = \frac{\text{Profit after tax and preference dividends}}{\text{Number of ordinary shares in issue}}$$

This figure can also be calculated as the fully-diluted earnings per share. In this case the calculation assumes that all convertible loan stock, convertible preference shares and warrants have been converted to ordinary shares. Obviously the denominator is increased but this is offset to a greater or lesser extent by adding back to the earnings figure the interest and preference dividend paid.

This investment ratio figure, expressed in pence per share, allows a shareholder to see exactly how much each share has theoretically earned him or her. The word theoretically is used because the company will not, as a general rule, give this to the shareholder as cash. The directors of the company will decide what proportion of the earnings needs to be kept in the business to allow the strengthening of the balance sheet, and how much needs to be paid as a dividend to meet the needs and expectations of the shareholders. In a private limited company this is a far less difficult balancing act than for a public limited company. Remember that the public limited company has its share traded on a stock exchange and these shares can be bought by anybody from the man in the street to large pension funds. Should the shareholders be consistently disappointed with the level of dividend they may react by selling their shareholding. If enough shareholders do this, the price of the share could fall (which in turn could make the company a takeover target).

Directors may believe that a company has a better future as an independent concern rather than a subsidiary of a large plc and their dividend payment policy will reflect this. In addition, the directors will probably be shareholders and therefore will have a vested interest in high dividends. The dividend eventually paid will have to be approved by the shareholders at the annual general meeting.

$$\text{Dividend per share} = \frac{\text{Total dividend paid}}{\text{Number of shares}}$$

This figure is expressed as pence per share and represents the actual payment made for every share held. Shareholders will convert this to:

$$\text{Dividend yield} = \frac{\text{Dividend per share}}{\text{Market price of share}}$$

This figure is expressed as a percentage and allows a comparison between the income received from the share and other investments.

$$\text{Dividend cover} = \frac{\text{Earnings per share}}{\text{Dividend per share}}$$

Expressed as a ratio this is a measure of the security of dividend payment. It should be remembered that there is no definitive link between earnings per share and dividend per share. The major concern would be if the cover were less than one, as this would mean that the company has paid out more in dividends than it can afford to do based on the earnings for the year. This payment will have been made out of retained profits but this situation cannot continue for any great length of time.

4.5.4 How Ratios are Useful to the Lender

As illustrated above, some ratios are more important than others and some ratios support, and are supported by, others. Conversely there will be times when some key ratios contradict each other. For example, a company may have shown a good growth in net profit margin (good sign) over the last three years but an increase in credit taken and stock turnover period accompanied by a extension in credit given (bad signs). What action, if any should the lender take in response to this? The figures need to be considered and the information behind the ratios should be identified.

There are a few points to remember in relation to ratios. Firstly consider that while the accounts purport to be highly accurate and precise they have been prepared using a number of estimations and interpretations and these need to be understood to make sense of the ratio. Second, they have been prepared to meet the needs of different users. It may very well be that the needs of a lending banker have been subordinated to the need to impress shareholders. Thirdly, the accounts are only a snapshot of the position of the business on a particular day – which will be months in the past. If there was a problem, then what is the situation now?

Ratio analysis is only going to be meaningful if the ratios are compared to the ratios of the corporate's competitors. By doing this a benchmark can be established as well as the trends that the ratios can show over time in terms of them getting better or getting worse. Ratios only provide an indication of the current financial status of the corporate which is only a snapshot in time.

The credit assessment of a corporate requires an assessment of more than just the financials of a corporate. It is crucial to appraise and understand the strategy that a corporate has or is undertaking. Also, a bank must appraise the management of the corporate as well as its market, especially its competitors within a market.

Lenders should be especially aware that ratio analysis should only be used as the basis on which to ask further questions, but as a tool, in themselves they are very limited as the information is of course historic.

Ratio analysis tends to assume proportionality in that a 20% increase in turnover will lead to a 20% increase in profits. If that is so, it should never be assumed that a 20% decrease in turnover will lead to a 20% decrease in profits. This is because of the impact of overheads, but the ratios assume proportionality, so these limitations should be borne in mind.

4.5.5 Capital Structures Ratios

Fixed assets/net worth	Fixed assets
	Share capital + reserves
Net worth/total assets	Share capital plus reserves
	Fixed and current assets
Gearing	Long-term debt
	Shareholders funds
	Long term debt
	Shareholders funds + Long-term debt
Net gearing	$\dfrac{\text{Total debt} - \text{cash}}{\text{Shareholders' funds}}$
Interest cover	$\dfrac{\text{Profit before interest and tax}}{\text{Interest payable}}$
Asset utilization ratios Sales/fixed assets	$\dfrac{\text{Sales}}{\text{Fixed assets}}$
Stock turnover period	$\dfrac{\text{Average stock}}{\text{Cost of sales}}$ x 365

Debtor collection period	$\dfrac{\text{Average trade debtors}}{\text{Credit sales}}$	x 365
Creditor payment period	$\dfrac{\text{Average trade creditors}}{\text{Credit purchases}}$	x 365
Profitability Gross profit margin	$\dfrac{\text{Gross Profit}}{\text{Sales}}$	x 100
Net profit margin	$\dfrac{\text{Net Profit before interest and tax}}{\text{Sales}}$	x 100
Operating margin	$\dfrac{\text{Overheads}}{\text{Sales}}$	x 100
Return on capital employed (ROCE)	$\dfrac{\text{Profit before interest and tax}}{\text{Capital and reserves} + \text{Long-term liabilities}}$	
	$\dfrac{\text{P Profit after tax}}{\text{Capital and reserves}}$	
Liquidity Working capital ratio	$\dfrac{\text{C Current assets}}{\text{Current liabilities}}$	
Acid test ratio	$\dfrac{\text{Current assets} - \text{stock}}{\text{Current liabilities}}$	

Please note that the investment ratios have not been summarized.

4.5.6 Current Ratio

Liquidity is usually measured by the current ratio:

$$\text{Current ratio} = \frac{\text{Current assets}}{\text{Current liabilities}}$$

There is no ideal figure for a current ratio, as this will depend on the type of business, but it will usually fall within the range 1–1:1 to 2:1. A lower ratio may be indicative of problems. The figure will be lower for businesses which sell mainly for cash, eg shops, and higher for businesses involved in a lengthy manufacturing process.

As with all ratios, the trend is more important than the figure itself and a declining ratio requires an explanation from the customer as it may indicate a potential liquidity problem. It may be appropriate to request an aged list of creditors to check if these are up-to-date.

It is important to remember that, provided the current ratio is reasonably high, the corporate is stable and there are no reasons to suspect liquidity difficulties (for example, frequent excesses of an overdraft facility suggest there may be a problem), further liquidity rates may not require calculation. If, however, the current ratio is very low or declining, as against the ratio of previous years and competition ratio, or the operation of the account gives cause for concern, the following other ratios should be investigated.

4.5.7 Acid Test Ratio

The acid test ratio demonstrates the ability of a company to meet its current liabilities without having to sell stock (which may take time to convert to cash, particularly if lengthy credit periods are given).

$$\text{Acid test ratio} = \frac{\text{Current assets} - \text{stock}}{\text{Current liabilities}}$$

There is no need to calculate this figure if the business sells mainly for cash, as the debtor figures will be insignificant.

4.5.8 Stock Turnover

This shows the length of time an item remains in stock, and the figure should be related to the type of business – a dairy will have a faster stock turnover than a furniture retailer.

$$\text{Stock turnover} = \frac{\text{Stock}}{\text{Cost of goods sold}} \times \text{Number of days}$$

4.5.9 Debtor Turnover

This shows the period of credit given by the business at its customers. Again, trends are important. If the figure is increasing or falling, an explanation should be sought from the customer. Do not jump to conclusions. A longer credit period may mean poor control or it may be deliberate policy to encourage sales. The ratio needs to include any accruals or prepayments.

$$\text{Debtor turnover} = \frac{\text{Debtors}}{\text{Sales}} \times \text{Number of days}$$

4.5.10 Credit Turnover

This shows the period of credit taken by the business:

$$\text{Credit turnover} = \frac{\text{Creditors}}{\text{Purchases}} \times \text{Number of days}$$

When calculating turnover ratios it is important to use the correct number of days, corresponding to the Profit and Loss Account period from which the figures for sales, purchases and cost of goods sold have been obtained. The ratio needs to include any accounts or prepayments.

If figures are not quoted for purchases or for cost of goods sold, ratios can be calculated using the figures for sales. The results will not be accurate, but will enable examination of the trends, which are more important than the figures themselves.

4.6 Profitability

In order to survive, any business must be profitable and continue to be profitable on a regular and frequent basis. While a business can survive a few years of low profitability or losses, if these continue for a long time the business either ends up in liquidation or as a subsidiary of another business. Often loss-making businesses are taken over because the buyer wishes to acquire some portion of the target business – perhaps its name or a product or supply/distribution channels. In these cases the buyer will keep what is wanted and sell the rest. This process is known as asset stripping.

A business where the contribution earned on sales is high in relation to the net profit eventually produced is said to be highly operationally geared. Such businesses are particularly risky because a small drop in sales produces a large drop in contribution and quickly produces a position where the business moves from profit to loss. (Conversely, of course, a small rise in sales produces a large rise in net profit.)

Banks should also be aware that there are little or no assets available and in the case of, say, media or advertising, it is the people and their ideas which are the assets. In the case of IT or Internet companies, there may be no proven financial track record. Some service industries, including tourism, may be prone to downturns due to external factors such as foot-and-mouth disease and september 11. A lender should evaluate all these risks carefully.

Highly operationally geared businesses have, potentially, very volatile cash flow as sales go up and down. For example, restaurants have a cost structure that can easily result in their being highly operationally geared, and indeed many of them are – a reason for the high failure rate. They find it hard to survive if sales drop below break-even for anything but a short period of time.

Capacity may be a significant issue. A service provider that only has the capacity to get past break-even at high levels of utilization will be particularly vulnerable as it will not be able to use its profitable period to build a cash buffer to cover any future downturn. Break-even analysis and the calculation of operational gearing is dependent on having a split between fixed and variable costs. Financial accounts split costs between direct and indirect rather than fixed and variable, and financial accounts are usually all the lender has to work with.

Some interpretation of the financial accounting information has to made. Most direct costs tend to be variable while the majority of indirect are fixed. Judgment is needed, because direct labour can effectively be fixed, while gas and electricity supply may be variable. But comparing an adjusted gross profit margin with the net margin probably gives a reasonable proxy for operational gearing. Where a large GP% produces a small NP%, there is probably high potential for cash flow volatility. Lending on the basis that a stable cash flow from profits is going to be available to pay down borrowing in such a business could be fraught with danger.

The key ratios, which are all expressed as percentages, are:

Gross profit margin	=	Gross profit/Sales
Net profit margin	=	Net profit after tax and interest/Sales
Overhead margin	=	Overheads/Sales

Note: all these margins use sales figures as a denominator. The practical effect of this is that a comparison can be made with a business with £20,000 net profit and a business with £2,000,000 net profit.

For example:

	Net profit	*Sales*	*NPM*
Company A	20,000	180,000	20000
		180,000	11.11%
Company B	2,000,000	25,000,000	2,000,000
		25,000,000	8.00%

Which of the two companies is performing best for its owners? The tendency would initially be to say that 11% is better than 8% and, all other things being equal, this could be true. However, no one ratio, looked at in isolation, can tell us a great deal about the business or its performance. None of the above profitability ratios takes into consideration the level of capital invested in the business by the owners. If both of the businesses have capital of £1,000,000 then 11% is better than 8%. But what if Company A has twice the level of capital of Company B?

An important ratio that addresses this problem is the return on capital employed. This ratio is normally expressed as:

Version one:

$$\frac{\text{Profit before interest and tax}}{\text{Capital and reserves + Long term liabilities}}$$

An acceptable variation on this, which looks at return on a company's net assets, is:

Version two:

$$\frac{\text{Profit after tax}}{\text{Capital and reserves}}$$

It should be noted that, as the net assets are now being considered, only the amount of profit available to the owners should be taken into account. Therefore, as the owners receive a return only after interest to creditors and tax has been paid, these costs need to be deducted from the profit before calculating the return on capital employed.

When considering what constitutes an acceptable ROCE we are again faced with the problem of "different strokes for different folks". Similarly consistency year-on-year is important, and is the preferred variant of various corporates.

4.6.1 Sales

Sales or turnover figures should show a steady increase, at least in line with the rate of inflation. However, a rapid increase is a warning sign, as it may be an indication of overtrading. If sales are increasing rapidly, liquidity is likely to come under pressure, so a careful analysis of liquidity ratios should be made.

4.6.2 Profit Margins

$$\text{Gross margin} = \frac{\text{Gross profit}}{\text{Turnover}} = 100\%$$

$$\text{Net margin} = \frac{\text{Net profit}}{\text{Turnover}} = 100\%$$

Again, the trend is more important than the actual margin achieved. When the ratio is increasing or decreasing the lender should seek an explanation from the borrower. A lower gross margin may be a deliberate policy to boost sales, may be a sign of strong competition, resulting in a need to cut prices, or may indicate poor management. An increasing gross margin is fine if prices have been kept within those which the market will bear, but if prices have been increased substantially to achieve a good gross, sales could fall to the extent that the actual profit earned is lower.

When a business has a high gross margin, a small increase in sales will result in a large increase in profit, but if sales fall, profits will fall proportionately further.

If the net margin is declining while the gross margin is stable, overhead costs must have risen. The total overhead should be compared with the previous year's figure and if it has risen by more than the rate of inflation, the lender should endeavour to find the reason for this. It may be a result of a wage increase or a rent review, or it may be a sign that overheads are not controlled and that economies should be made.

Caution should be exercised when variations occur in the gross margin as a result of simply reclassifying expenses as costs of goods sold or overheads, particularly when comparing management with audited accounts.

4.6.3 Retained Cash Flow

Retained cash flow is an important, and simple, calculation. It shows the funds available to the business to repay or reduce borrowings or to finance capital expenditure.

$$\text{Retained cash flow} = \text{Net Profit} + \text{Depreciation} - \text{Drawings}.$$

Depreciation is added back as it does not represent a cash flow.

The level of dividends (including directors' remuneration) provides a clue to the character of the owners/directors. There is nothing wrong with high levels of drawings when profits are high, but the owner or director may be reluctant to curtail these in poorer years and the business may suffer from inadequate capital when profits are not retained.

High levels of drawings are only of concern to the bank if it is continually being asked to lend to the business, as gearing will quickly increase.

5

EVALUATION OF CORPORATES IN DIFFERENT MARKET SECTORS

5.1 Not-for-profit organizations

Lending propositions for unincorporated clubs and associations are relatively rare, but can be awkward for a banker to deal with. The propositions are rare because a club is not an ordinary business in the sense that its activities are directed to making a profit. It is, rather, a collection of individuals who get together for some common – usually essentially social – purpose. While a club may trade: for example, it will often have a bar, trading will be ancillary to its main purpose. If individual members decide to leave, they can do so quite easily by resigning or not renewing their subscriptions; they are not shareholders who cannot easily get their capital out of a limited company, or partners or sole traders who will be personally liable for the debts of their businesses.

So a great deal of circumspection is needed when lending to an unincorporated club or association. More than in the case of an ordinary business, club members should take full responsibility for providing the capital needed to run the club. In these circumstances borrowing should be rare, and this is particularly true of borrowing for working capital purposes. Clubs ought not to have debt to be financed. Their services are predominantly sold to members, who should pay cash on delivery or in advance.

There can, for example, be no justification for borrowing in anticipation of subscription income to meet short-term debts. Clubs will have some stock, for example drink, cigarettes, and so on for a bar, but breweries are generally prepared to offer generous credit terms to clubs, and there is usually a good prospect of stock's being financed by brewery creditors. All in all, it is a poorly organized club that cannot provide funds to meet working capital needs without borrowing from outside. So as far as a bank is concerned, club bank accounts should normally run in credit and any borrowing propositions ought to be only for major capital expenditure purposes.

5.1.1 Club Management

This is the first awkward problem that arises when dealing with many clubs. The management of most clubs is in the hands of members. Few clubs have professional managers, and the equivalent of a company's board of directors is the club committee.

While individual committee members may specialize in terms of function – for example, a club treasurer will look after finance and may be functionally well qualified (the treasurer of a club is very often an accountant) the committee members are normally part-time and unpaid. They cannot, therefore, be expected to give the same priority to their club work as they would to their own employment or business activities. This is a very broad generalization, as there are many clubs that are professionally run by their "amateur" managers, and there are also many club committee members who show an unusual degree of dedication to their function.

However, as a generality, a lender must not expect club "management" to be anything other than of variable quality. Club committees will often look at things through "rose tinted spectacles", and will find it hard to be objective when dealing with people who are their friends. They can, for example, often be very naïve and unbusinesslike over the handling of cash. Any good publican knows how important it is to control tightly the activities of barmen and women to ensure that cash takings do not "leak". Defalcations by club barmen are a perennial problem. Particularly in the case of clubs where the bar is manned by the members themselves, it is hard for club "managers" to find that their trust can sometimes be misplaced. The capacity of a club to maintain a reasonable gross profit margin on its bar activities is often a very good test of the professionalism of its day-to-day management.

The fact that club management may not be professional can lead them to have over-optimistic (and at worst, unrealistic) expectations of their capacity to repay any proposed borrowing. Club committee members may well be influential individuals in a community, and may also be important personal or even business customers of a bank in their own right. The pressures on a lender to agree to what the club wants may therefore be considerable. Where influential people are concerned these pressures cannot realistically be ignored, but the lender must stick to his or her guns and insist on a full appraisal of a proposition backed by all the necessary projections. If a club committee is acting in an amateur way, it is all the more important for a banker to inject the necessary professionalism.

5.1.2 Legal Issues

Unlike limited companies, clubs and associations are not separate legal entities. They do not have powers to enter into contracts and cannot be sued for their debts. Individual members are not normally personally liable for any debts undertaken by the club officers, and despite there being legal precedent to indicate that committee members could be personally liable, the position is by no means clear.

The lender will want to ensure that someone with a legal responsibility to repay a borrowing assumes full liability. The lending should be made either on a separate account in the names of the responsible club officers or in the name of the club itself, supported by appropriate guarantees. The borrowing must conform with any formalities and restrictions laid down in the club rules, and these will need to be checked for this purpose.

The financial statements produced by many clubs are often rudimentary, and need to be treated with care. They may well be produced by an amateur at accounting, and they do not have to be audited, although they usually are. However, the auditor will usually be unpaid and will be an amateur him or herself. Very often, the auditor will be another club member, so the financial statements are open to the possibility of being inaccurate or misleading, even if this is by accident. The lender, therefore, needs to be healthily sceptical when looking at the figures.

5.1.3 Security Matters

Unincorporated clubs and associations cannot own property. If a lending is required for the acquisition of, or to be secured by a charge over, property, this will have to be held by trustees on behalf of the club. The club's rules will need to contain provision for property to be held by nominated trustees and cover their powers to charge the property as security. A trust deed must be drawn up covering the powers of the trustees. Trustees have no implied power to charge trust assets so they need to be authorized to do so under the terms of the trust. Lending to trustees has to be made on loan account when secured by trust property.

A more common security for clubs and associations is simply by taking personal guarantees from committee members. For any substantial borrowing, these guarantees need to be backed by tangible security, which will often be a second mortgage on the individual's house. The interest of spouses in the matrimonial home must be fully taken into account, and it is particularly important that they have independent legal advice before committing themselves to a charge.

5.2 Professionals

This implies someone with a professional qualification. A professional person is usually fee-earning and providing a service, rather than selling goods. He or she will usually hold a qualification from a professional body, eg accountants from the Institute of Chartered Accountants or similar body, solicitors from the Law Society. He or she may require a licence to practise from the professional body.

Professionals are usually regarded by banks as key business influencers and may handle large sums of clients' money. These can be a good source of credit balances for banks.

Although some "professionals" practise as sole traders, the more usual format is that of being a partner in a partnership. The corporate banker will not normally lend to individual professionals, however, the trend towards merging of large firms of lawyers and accountants, makes professional partnerships very attractive to the corporate bankers. Partners are jointly liable for partnership debts. Advances by banks to partners always embrace a joint and several mandate to ensure that each partner is both jointly and severally liable for partnership debts. This also means that personal assets are available for creditors.

Some partnerships, such as lawyers or accountants may be huge, such as Clifford Chance and PriceWaterhouseCoopers. These are normally described as professional partnerships, where the number of partners is unlimited. Professional partnerships such as Clifford Chance and PriceWaterhouseCoopers are huge undertakings.

Normally, the workings of a partnership are covered by a partnership agreement in writing. If there isn't one, partners share profits and losses on an equal basis and partners are remunerated by drawings from the partnership. Although professional partnerships are highly regarded as potentially wealthy bank customers, the usual canons of lending need to be observed. Drawings may be taken before financial statements for the practice are published, leading to an overdrawing of profits and deterioration in net worth of the practice over the period.

Many large professional partnerships are now setting up as limited liability partnerships (under the Limited Liability Partnerships Act 2000). A limited liability partnership is a body corporate, with legal personality separate from that of its members, which is formed by being incorporated under the Act. A limited liability partnership has unlimited capacity.

5.3 Manufacturing

Manufacturing businesses are much like any other in terms of focusing on profit, cash flow and quality of information and the same techniques used for lending to other types of business apply.

It is not uncommon in manufacturing for some or all core supplies to be sourced from overseas. In addition to quality control problems, the issue of documentary credits becomes important as does the consideration of exchange rates.

5.4 Service Industries

A service industry is one which provides a service to end users. Examples of service industries are the catering industry or the tourism and leisure industry, media companies, advertising, or even technology companies like Internet Service Providers. They have a far larger role in the UK economy than the manufacturing sector and every banker will be faced with propositions from them.

5.4.1 Business Risks

Business risk is best described as the combination of the risks that a business faces as it interfaces with its external environment, particularly its market place. It is about things that are hard for the management to control because they are effectively "givens" in the area in which it operates.

Business risk is high for some service industries because:

(a) There are low barriers to entry into the business – new service providers, eg restaurants open and close all the time, and true differentiation is difficult.

(b) Substitute products are readily available.

(c) Competition in the service industries is high.

(d) The power of suppliers may be high.

(e) The power of buyers is high – where the customer base is highly fragmented.

These above factors can be managed and risks reduced. Most service providers will try to differentiate themselves from the competition by having a specific format or by targeting a particular type of customer. Just how effective the differentiation is, or is likely to be, has to be a matter of judgment in each case. For a banker, such judgments are not easy, and the existence of a good track record by the provider is likely to be the only effective guide. In some service industries, for example, internet service providers, both the market and the client will be very new to the bank and more caution will need to be exercised.

Another way in which risk can be ameliorated in some service industries, is through franchising. With the best franchise operations there is a lot of top-class professional help available to the franchisee to get him or her through all the pitfalls. Bankers are, therefore, generally going to be more supportive of franchise operations where there is a proven format.

5.4.2 Financial Risks

Service providers are exposed to the same financial risks as other businesses, but they are particularly vulnerable to the volume of business they transact because of the nature of their cost structures.

Typically, service providers have a high fixed-cost base. Premise costs are usually a major expense; the initial capital expenditure for fitting out will be relatively high in relation to likely revenue, and often produces high finance charges. Even staff costs may include a high fixed element.

However, variable costs will form a relatively low portion of revenue received. It is not untypical to see the cost of a service to be more than treble the unit cost.

There is a technique for looking at the financial impact of different cost structures and their implications called "operational gearing". Operational gearing is associated with break-even analysis and is technically defined as the reciprocal of the margin of safety. In layman's language, it compares the contribution made from sales with fixed costs and the ultimate net profit earned.

5.5 Retail/Wholesale

Retailers are those who deal directly with end users while wholesalers supply the retailers.

The power of the large supermarket and other substantial retail groups in the UK has made many types of small retailer an endangered species. For example, on current estimates, it is thought that the three largest supermarket chains in the UK have in excess of 43% of the grocery trade. The buying power this gives them makes it virtually impossible for smaller businesses to compete on price; and the whole concept of "one stop" shopping militates against the small retailer. The disappearance of some types of small retailer from the High Street, such as the family butcher, is a reflection of this. In the future in the UK small retailers will probably have to specialize in some way to be successful. To win in the marketplace they will have to offer something extra in terms of convenience (for example, location and opening hours), quality, special types of goods, service and so on. In technical marketing terms, they will have to become niche players.

5.6 Asset Finance

5.6.1 Introduction

Asset finance is where a lender looks to the asset he is financing as both the primary source of repayment and as the security for his loan. The asset could be residential property, a ship or an aircraft.

The main consideration will naturally be the asset itself, although, with particular reference to aircraft finance, we shall highlight other areas which require careful attention to ensure that a lender is only taking the risks for which he is being paid.

To put some form of structure to our proceedings, we shall first look at the nature of asset financing and some of the key considerations, before looking at an example of a real transaction to see how it all works.

5.6.2 Risk

Although it can be argued that a conventional loan secured on the asset being financed would constitute asset finance, this is not in fact the case. Under a conventional loan, the obligation of the borrower to repay is not limited to the revenue earned from the asset, and under a conventional loan the lender can look to the borrowers' other assets as an unsecured creditor if the sale of his security is insufficient to repay the loan.

True asset finance involves recourse only to the revenues arising from the use of the asset, and to the asset itself. This is one of the main risk elements in asset financing; the lack of a secondary source of repayment for the loan. Asset finance can be conventional lending to property companies or for more specialist lending for ships or aircraft.

The essential thing that a banker must grasp is that the lending is being done against the value of the asset with limited or no recourse whatsoever to the corporate entity.

The key criteria for determining the value of an asset, both now and at any time in the future, are supply and demand. Clearly the most important from an asset financier's point of view is the demand for the asset.

5.7 Farming

Lending to agriculture is no different form any other lending except that there are some specific considerations that should be borne in mind. These specific considerations are as follows:

(a)   a visit to the farm plus periodic visits after the finance has been agreed.

(b)   look at the size of the farm.

(c)   what does the farm produce in terms of crops or livestock.

(d)   look at location and layout of the farm and assess whether the land is sufficient for the crops or livestock.

(e)   look at the buildings and assess whether they are adequate for the purpose.

(f)   assess the experience and knowledge of the farmer(s).

(g)   is the farmer aware of his business and assess his management acumen.

The financial track record is very important and also the fact whether the farmer produces any kind of budget. Banks must examine the serviceability of all loan repayments to that of the turnover and prices of either crops or livestock produce sold.

5.8 Financial institutions

Lending to financial institutions should follow the same lending criteria as any other corporate with the exception that a bank should look at the asset base of the balance sheet. In particular a lender should look to see that say another lender is not taking any undue risks in its lending. An example could be lending to the self-employed without evidence of earnings. In other words the quality of the loan book is very important. Also you should look at the deposit base or the funding base of the institution and ascertain how it raises its funds. It is also very important to assess the economic vulnerability of the funding base. The smaller the financial institution the more diligent must be the analysis such as lending to credit unions.

In the case of insurance companies the crucial thing to look at is the risk/return trade off in that are the risks the insurance company is underwriting has been fully reflected in the premiums being charged. Does the insurance company underwrite high or unusual risks. Again the smaller the institution is the greater must be the analysis.

6

RISK RATING AND RELATED PRICING

6.1 Identifying Credit Risk

In most forms of business there are elements of risk. Indeed it is the taking of these risks that leads to the possibility of profit. Any business has to decide how to manage the risks within the business.

Risk of stock obsolescence – the last thing a business needs is a stock pile which cannot be sold other than at a massive loss. A business may choose to manage this by employing a number of management techniques such as "just in time" and "economic order quantity" to minimise the levels of stock held.

Insurable risks of business interruption – eg risk of factory fire. A business does not have to insure buildings against fire but if they do not then, in the event of a fire, all the costs fall on the business. All sensible businesses will transfer the risk to a third party who will agree to bear the costs of any fire. The third party (insurance company) accepts the risk in return for a premium paid by the business. The level of this premium will depend on the insurer's estimated of risk and can be reduced if the insured offers to pay the first £X of a claim.

Risk that you might have insufficient funds to allow your business to operate and grow successfully – this risk can also be transferred to the bank who, having accepted the risk by injecting funds into a business, will want a premium for doing so. This premium is called interest.

Banks are in the business of lending and thus by implication they are in business to take on board credit risk.

Credit risk exists whenever bank funds are lent to a borrower(s) as there is always a possibility that the loan might not be repaid. In a strictly mechanistic sense, credit risk can be quantified as the amount lent + interest accrued + recovery costs:

$$CR = L + Ai + Rc$$

The above definition takes no cognisance of any security that may be in place. The availability of security does not automatically make an unacceptable risk worth taking – banks are not pawn brokers. At best the availability of quality security may lower the risk premium charged by the bank.

For example, Fairfax Hotels Ltd have produced a cash flow forecast that shows that while the business will be in credit during May to October the remaining months of the year will have varying levels of predicted overdraft.

Fairfax must persuade its bankers to grant a working capital facility in order that it can continue trading through the "winter" months. Once it does this the lender has taken on credit risk. The risk premium (interest) charged will depend on the credit worthiness of Fairfax as perceived by the lender.

For large businesses there are a number of credit rating agencies (Dun & Bradstreet is a good example) who gather information on the business and give it a credit rating. These generally follow the alphabet listing with AAA being better than (more credit worthy than) BBB.

For small-, medium-sized businesses (SME's) it is far more difficult to get such precise ratings and normally we would consider such a business in a more qualitative manner.

6.2 Measuring Credit Risk (low/medium/high)

Credit risk measurement at the SME level is, at best, an imprecise measurement, with common measurements being low, medium and high risk. These are not generally linked to probabilities of default although it is not unknown for these to be linked.

Generally. the terms relate to what the funds are required for. This can be in terms of business type, eg building or retailing, but is more commonly considered to be "what does the business want the money for".

Low risk is most commonly associated with facilities granted to a well known customer/business to permit it to continue to do what it has proven experience at doing. In the Fairfax Hotels Ltd scenario above, the loan request could be considered low risk if the business was a long established client seeking renewal of an existing overdraft.

Medium risk would be where Fairfax was a long established customer/business requesting an overdraft for the first time. The need for a first-time overdraft may well be experienced by many in the tourism industry, for example, in the wake of the World Trade Center disaster. Having not lent to this customer before the lender would obviously want assurances regarding the quality of the cash flow forecasts and management team.

Medium risk could also occur if Fairfax requested a medium-/long-term loan to facilitate the takeover of another hotel. Although Fairfax might have a good track record with the bank, there could be concerns about their ability to run the new hotel. The bank should therefore consider the client's history and the permenance of the intended target.

As a further example, a customer of another bank might approach the bank for an overdraft facility and produces statements and accounts that show that such a facility is normal and affordable by the business. Many lenders would consider this to be medium risk, as they would not know the management team. A constant concern when a customer of a competitor approaches a new bank for facilities is "why aren't they going to their own bank?".

There are several possible reasons:

1. They already have and have been refused.

2. They already have and the facilities requested approved but subject to conditions which the management will not/cannot fulfil.

3. They have had had a disagreement with the lender unrelated to credit facilities, eg poor service.

4. The bank's marketing campaign has impressed them so much they have decided to "give you a go".

It can be difficult to ascertain with any great degree of certainty which of 1 – 4 is the main driving force.

High risk lending includes start up businesses as the business has no track record. In addition, any venture/expansion outside the experience of the business/owners could be regarded as high risk. One of the reasons venture capitalists lend to MBO's is because the management have proven that they can run that particular business successfully.

Other scenarios that might be classified as high risk are:

1. Expanding into different geographical areas (think PEST), for example, exporting (or importing) for the first time (a PEST analysis may be useful here).

2. Diversifying away from main areas of expertise (the SWOT analysis may be useful). An example here would be a motorcycle manufacturer moving into farm equipment production.

6.3 Managing Credit Risk

It is not possible for any lender to restrict itself to low risk ventures. Indeed, because of the small credit premium available from such loans, any lender restricting themselves in this way would be restricting their potential profits. Therefore, banks must lend, but in doing so must be mindful to spread overall the lending risk as widely as possible to reduce exposure to any one trade or industry and thus reduce overall exposure risk and profit volatility.

Banks reduce portfolio risk by making advances to a wide variety of industries, spreading the risk among a broad client base. Being very aware of the risk of over concentration in any one sector, banks usually operate within industry thresholds limiting credit exposure to achieve the best mix of individual and portfolio safety.

Although loans concentrated in one particular industry may appear sound and profitable, external factors may substantially affect some industries. In recent years cyclical economic forces have been manifest in the property market, transportation, the defence industry and electronics, as have changes in industry life cycles.

Banks may impose internal limits on lending to restrict exposure to any one sector. Economic influences may well be caused by government fiscal policy.

Risk assessment and management are the key skills of any successful banking operation. Most banks have some sort of risk rating system in place. The risk management process usually falls into a centralised or decentralised system. Such systems allows banks to evaluate and track risks on an industry, individual, or portfolio basis.

The principles underlying a risk rating system include:

- a common framework for assessing risk;

- uniformity throughout the bank;

- compatibility with regulatory requirements; and

- the ability to identify satisfactory levels of credit risk.

The principles underlying the risk rating process are:

- common training through definition and risk rating assessment guides;

- introduction and continuity of levels of achievement on a continuing basis; and

- regular reviews by senior bank officials to test for levels of accuracy and consistency.

There is a need for banks' internal audit departments to test for accuracy, consistency and appropriateness. Such a rating system is helpful in setting fee guidelines appropriate to the degree of risk involved.

Commercial lending exposes a bank to two major types of risk:

1. *Borrower risks* which may be defined as:

    - Borrower Risks

    - Industry Economic Risk

    - Covering inflation and foreign exchange risk exposure.

2. *Operating/transactional risks* which may be further defined as follows.

Industry Structure Risk: embracing the risk inherent in a company's business environment, including entry and exit barriers, the power of suppliers or customers, the impact of technology, regulatory requirements and capital requirements.

Operating Risks: inability to repay, receivership or liquidation, error or fraud.

Transaction Risks: include the risk inherent in the lending itself. Embraces terms and conditions, tenor and maturity, the security/collateral implications.

Banks may give borrowers ratings based on some, or all of the following criteria:

1. *The industry and operating environment.*

    Does the borrower operate in a strong and growing industry?

    Does the borrower hold a significant share of the market?

    Are legal and regulatory climates favourable?

2. *Earnings and operating cash flow.*

    Are earnings of high quality and growing?

    Are margins in line with others operating in the industry?

    Is cash flow strong in relation to current and anticipated debt?

3. *Asset and liability structure.*

    Are asset values realistic?

    Are assets and liabilities matched?

    Have intangibles been discounted?

    Are the assets available as security/collateral?

    Is the bank avoiding a subordinated lending position?

4. *Debt capacity.*

    Is gearing/leverage at acceptable levels?

    What alternative sources of debt and capital exist?

5. *Management and controls.*

    How competent is the management?

    Are good reporting lines in place?

6. *Financial reporting.*

    Are the auditors reputable?

Is financial information produced on time?

Is financial information accurate and complete?

6.3.1 Risk Rating

The risk rating is an index of risk intended to reflect the collectability of a specific advance in accordance with its terms. Each advance carries its own risk rating and the risk rating is the risk of the particular advance or transaction to a particular borrower.

There can be possible positive and negative variables that may impact on an advance or credit facility. Some of the common factors include security/collateral, ownership, terms, subordinated position and country risk.

6.3.2 Industry Tier Position

A company's tier position should reflect a company's competitive position relative to its peers. The factors used to determine peer position may be qualitative or quantitative. Factors that could be included in an evaluation of a company's peer position may include:

- Market share.
- Pricing:
    - price leadership; and
    - product differentiation/premium pricing.
- Cost structure:
    - Labour cost; and
    - Material costs.
- Capital intensity.
- Economies of scale.
- Technological advantages/disadvantages.
- Operating gearing/leverage.
- Managerial skills: industry reputation, expertise.
- Marketing ability.
- Long term strategic focus.
- Financial aspects.
- Cash flow measures.

- Debt levels.

- Profitability measures.

- Comparable performance ratios.

- Miscellaneous.

- Diversification.

- Acquisitions.

- Contingent liabilities/off-balance sheet obligations.

- Diversification/concentration.

- Divestiture/acquisitions.

- Credit administration.

It is often important for a bank's credit management functions to maintain an independent viewpoint and the bank's senior management must:

- Ensure that credit policy is fully understood throughout the organisation.

- Develop the training programmes needed to ensure that lenders have appropriate skills.

- Track credit documentation and decisions.

- Review policy decisions.

- Statements on advances policies which may include such guidelines as follows.

  - Advances should have a sound funding capability and be predicted on sound lending principles.

  - Advances pricing should adequately reflect bank policy and requirements.

  - Rewards sought should be in line with risk assumed.

  - Advances must comply with laws and regulations.

  - Advances not to be of a speculative nature where the bank could be placed at risk.

  - All advances to be reviewed on an annual basis.

  - Credit decisions to be made as quickly as possible bearing in mind complexity and risk.

6.3.3 The Credit Review

Lenders involved with the review and sanctioning of advances applications have a primary goal of minimising loss.

When reviewing advances applications, amongst the most important areas will be:

- Business background, nature of business, management and control.

- Macro-economic sensitivities/company problems.

- Quality of management.

- Product/service, market and trading outlook.

- Premises, machinery /vehicles – age and suitability.

- Trading performance.

- Conduct of account.

- Requirements.

- Ability to repay and source of repayment.

- Projections for the future and assumptions underlying.

- Security/collateral available.

- Remuneration.

- Other business creative opportunities.

6.3.4 Monitoring and Control-Spotting the Warning Signs of Trouble

Accountants often tell banks that they are between six and nine months too late in identifying problem lending. Part of the difficulty may be the anxiety of bankers to support a company as far as is possible through a difficult trading period, often maintaining that support longer than it should.

What bankers can do, however, is to have regard for the warning signs of business failure that may be evident and are often ignored. Too often the monitoring of progress and the telltale signs of a downturn in the affairs of a customer are overlooked. In many cases the decline is gradual and an alert lender will see danger signals long before the situation becomes critical.

Root causes and the danger signs can be analysed under four main headings:

Weaknesses in Management and Proprietors

Technical and Commercial Problems

Financing Problems

Faulty Accounting

6.3.4.1 Weaknesses in management

Bad management is the most common cause of business failure and a proper appreciation of the capabilities of the company's management is, therefore, essential in any customer monitoring exercise.

In a privately-owned family business the management of the company is frequently handed down from one generation to the next, irrespective of whether management skills have been successfully inbred. Equally dangerous is the situation where a company's management is concentrated in the hands of a single executive. There is a limit as to what one man can do, but a dominant chief executive can be dangerous in many respects, not least when he dies. It is a common failing in such cases to find no management succession. There is also more likelihood of financial impropriety where there is a dominant chief executive.

A further situation that can give rise to problems is where the size or nature of a business is undergoing rapid change. An entrepreneur may be well suited to running a small, expanding business, but there comes a time when there is a requirement for other skills within the management team such as delegation and team building; such skills are not always inherent in the initial pioneer of a business.

A well-run company will thrive on collective decisions and collective responsibility. If middle management is poor, it is hard to see how decisions can be implemented. However, there are times when decisions have to be made quickly and decisively to protect the business's competitive position, but it is the balance between autocracy and consensus that is important. Apart from being alert to the factors described above, there are other indications of management weakness that the banker should look out for in monitoring his customers. These include:

- a high turnover rate among key employees may indicate that management is unable to motivate staff with a real sense of purpose;

- extravagant spending on travel, entertainment and office accommodation may be an indication of irresponsible management. A reluctance to inject capital into the business indicates a management team lacking confidence in the business and may lead to a lack of commitment to it; and

- perhaps most importantly, a failure to take advantage of financial information (for example, by attending to variances) may indicate insufficient attention to planning and control which are so essential to good management.

6.3.4.2 Technical and commercial problems

While weak management is still the prime cause of corporate failure; increasingly the pace of technical and political change can wrong-foot even competent management as it becomes more difficult to respond quickly to the changing environment.

The banker needs to be alert to the implications of the environment in which his customer operates and to the implications of commercial decisions. A business with volatile products or markets, susceptible to changes in cost, fashion, technology, social attitudes, overseas competition or exchange rates is clearly vulnerable. Although such changes may be near impossible to foresee, their impact can spread far beyond a particular business: they can spell doom for entire industries.

A business where sales are concentrated in a small number of customers may go into a rapid decline if one of its customers goes out of business or switches to another brand. Equally, a business whose prosperity depends on one large contract has a big question mark hanging over its future. A business with sales volumes susceptible to sharp fluctuations is necessarily insecure unless its overheads can be easily controlled and flexed. If the business has a high level of fixed costs, there is an obvious cause for concern.

A business which bases its prices on marginal costing techniques can very easily get into trouble and the effect can multiply rapidly in the struggling company that seeks to "buy" volume by paring its margins.

6.3.4.3 Financing problems

Other possible indications that a business is heading for trouble lie in its financing. If the accounting system is inadequate, proper and corrective decisions cannot be made. Progress cannot be monitored if management has no information with which to work.

Creative accounting almost invariably is associated with corporate failure. It is seen, for example, in the revaluing of assets, changes in the bases of stock valuations and in expenditure being carried forward. Creative accounting improve profits and liquidity ratios, but remember that profit is merely an opinion while cash is fact.

A detection that there are shortening creditor days being given to the corporate is an indication that creditors may no longer feel comfortable extending deferred trade terms to a corporate under pressure.

Another sign of trouble is a deteriorating debt collection record, which may be caused by customer dissatisfaction with goods supplied or by more favourable credit terms offered to revive flagging sales. A successful company will demonstrate a reasonably steady pattern with regard to paying creditors and collecting from debtors and as a company moves towards failure, this pattern will begin to deteriorate since the company will not release cash in the same regular way as before – equally, it may simply be the result of poor credit control. The easiest debts to collect will be pressed for and difficult ones may be ignored. This symptom occurs late on the failure path.

A banker should be wary of a business that is over-geared or with a capital structure weighted to short-term maturities. Other danger signs include the payment of dividends in the face of losses and the granting of increasing security interests to obtain credit. A business which decides to diversify or expand its existing operations without sufficient capital to finance the high costs associated with such plans is courting trouble.

Uncontrolled capital expenditure can give rise to serious problems in the short term, if the company's cash flow position cannot bear the cost, or in the longer term, if the return from the capital investment is inadequate. Equally, a failure to invest in the development of the production system can result in the business becoming uncompetitive. An increase in the flow of status enquiries may give the observant banker advance warning that facilities are inadequate.

6.3.4.4 Faulty accounting

No company can monitor its progress (or lack of it) effectively without accurate financial information. Other warnings might include changes in accounting policy (perhaps to mask losses) such as capitalising research and development or advertising costs. Even accurate information is of little value unless it is current and produced on a timely basis; late accounting should give as much cause for concern as faulty accounting. It is often the first telltale sign of trouble.

Without current and accurate financial information, decisions are apt to be based on wrong assumptions while both favourable and unfavourable trends can go undetected. Hence, a lack of financial information or, equally, irrelevant or even excessive financial information, should be regarded as indicative of problems and as a possible root cause. In a company which incorporates several different operations, the significance of this point is amplified: it may be possible to establish that problems exist but accurate and relevant reports are essential if the problem areas are to be isolated. Current financial information is essential to management. It is (or should be) just as important to the banker for the purpose of any effective monitoring exercise. Too often the banker monitors his customer with last year's balance sheet rather than the projection of next year's profit and loss account.

Bankers are busy people, but attention to the customer's current management accounts and future projections and an understanding of the commercial problems and assumptions, which underlie them, may save time in the long run. Perhaps the most important overall feature is profitability: it may sound obvious to say that a company with a history of continuing losses is a serious risk but, especially where large and prestigious companies are concerned, this is sometimes overlooked.

Lack of profitability soon turns into adverse cash flow and soon erodes the balance sheet. Obviously, profit alone is not enough unless it can be turned into cash flow, but in reviewing financial projections it is worth remembering that a business without prospects of profit has lost its raison d'être.

6.3.5 Establishing an Appropriate Credit Risk Environment

The board of directors should have responsibility for approving and periodically (at least annually) reviewing the credit risk strategy and significant credit risk principles of the bank. The strategy should reflect the bank's tolerance and the level of profitability the bank expects to achieve for incurring various credit risks.

Senior management should have responsibility for implementing the credit risk strategy approved by the board of directors and for developing policies and procedures for identifying, measuring, monitoring and controlling credit risk. Such policies and procedures should address credit risk in all of the bank's activities and at both the individual credit and portfolio levels.

Banks should identify and manage credit risk inherent in all products and activities new to them are subject to adequate risk management procedures and controls before being introduced and undertaken, and approved in advance by the board of directors or its appropriate committee.

6.3.6 Operating Under a Sound Credit Granting Process

Banks must operate within sound, well-defined credit granting criteria. These criteria should include a clear indication of the bank's target market and thorough understanding of the borrower or counterparty, as well as the purpose and structure of the credit and its source of repayment.

Banks should establish overall credit limits at the level of individual borrowers and counterparties, and groups of connected parties that aggregate in a comparable and meaningful manner, different types of exposure, both in the banking and trading book and on and off the balance sheet.

Banks should have a clearly established process in place for approving new credits as well as the amendment, renewal and refinancing of existing credits.

All extentions of credit must be made on an arm's-length basis. In particular, credits related to companies and individuals must be authorised on an exceptional basis, monitored with particular care and other appropriate steps taken to control or mitigate the risks of non-arm's length lending.

6.3.7 Maintaining an Appropriate Credit Administration, Measurement and Monitoring Process

1. Banks should have in place a system for the ongoing administration of their various credit risk-bearing portfolios.

2. Banks must have in place a system for monitoring the condition of individual credits, including determining the adequacy of provisions and reserves.

3.   Banks are encouraged to develop and utilise an internal risk rating system in managing credit risk. The rating system should be consistent with the nature, size and complexity of a bank's activities.

4.   Banks must have information systems and analytical techniques that enable management to measure the credit risk inherent in all on and off balance sheet activities. The management information system should provide adequate information on the composition of the credit portfolio, including identification of any concentration risks.

5.   Banks must have in place a system for monitoring the overall composition and quality of the credit portfolio.

6.   Banks should take into consideration future changes in economic conditions when assessing individual credits and their credit portfolios, and should assess their credit risk exposures under stressful conditions.

6.3.8 Ensuring Adequate Controls over Credit Risk

1.   Banks must establish a system of independent ongoing assessment of the bank's credit risk management process and the results of such reviews should be communicated directly to the board of directors and senior management.

2.   Banks must ensure that the credit granting function is being properly managed and the credit exposures are within levels consistent with prudential standards and internal limits. Banks should establish and enforce internal controls and other practices to ensure that exceptions to policies procedures and limits are reported in a timely manner to the appropriate level of management for action.

3.   Banks must have a system in place for early remedial action on deteriorating credits, managing problem credits and similar workout stations.

6.3.9 Role of Supervisors

Supervisors should require that banks have an effective system in place to identify, measure, monitor and control credit risk as part of an overall approach to risk management. Supervisors should conduct an independent evaluation of a bank's strategies, policies, procedures and practices related to the granting of credit and the on-going management of the portfolio. Supervisors should consider setting prudential limits to restrict bank exposures to single borrowers or groups of connected counterparties. Supervisors will also want to analyze the expected loss of a loan portfolio, as well as an assessment of the risk cost of the loans in question.

The Basle accord, however, makes the point that the above mentioned principles should be applied in conjunction with sound practices related to the assessment of asset quality, the adequacy of provisions and reserves and the disclosure of credit risk, all of which have been addressed in other Committee documents.

Ref: *Basle Committee on Banking Supervision, Principles for the Management of Credit Risk,* publication No 75(2000).

6.4 Capital Adequacy

6.4.1 Effect on Banks

The international minimum acceptable capital level of 8% of "risk-weighted assets" since 1992, imposed by the Bank for International Settlements (BIS), has obliged all banks to assess the composition of acceptable Tier 1 and Tier 2 capital, (in order to minimize the cost of capital, thus making them more competitive). The FSA considers 8% the absolute minimum level.

Tier 1 capital comprises:

    (i)   fully paid common stock;

    (ii) irredeemable cumulative preferred shares; and

    (iii) disclosed reserves.

Taken together these must make up at least half the minimum level and represent arguably the hardest and the most expensive capital for the banks to raise.

Tier 2 capital comprises:

    (i)   undisclosed reserves;

    (ii) revaluation of fixed assets;

    (iii) general loan provisions;

    (iv) hybrid capital instruments; and

    (v) subordinated term debt.

Tier 2 capital tends to be cheaper and generally easier to raise. The UK banks have had little difficulty to date in meeting the BIS framework, although they have taken opportunities to strengthen their capital ratios. Other than a rights issue or by increasing retained profit, the only practical method of increasing Tier 1 capital has been to issue irredeemable non-cumulative preferred shares. The Bank of Scotland for example has issued sterling preferred shares. Barclays Bank, Royal Bank of Scotland and Allied Irish have all, during the past two years issued US dollar preferred shares. With much of the UK banks' Tier 1 capital being denominated in sterling, dollar preferred stock has the added advantage of helping to reduce exchange rate move-ments on non sterling assets from affecting the bank's capital ratios.

The cheapest way of issuing Tier 2 capital is for banks to issue term subordinated debt which can be raised in the Eurobond or Yankee market at rates which, for top quality banks, would tend to range from the equivalent of LIBOR to LIBOR + 50 basis points. However, subordinated term debt, although the cheapest form of capital, must not exceed 50% of Tier 1 capital. Any subordinated debt in excess of this level does not count for capital adequacy purposes and therefore becomes very expensive funding.

If it is not possible because of market conditions for a bank to increase its Tier 1 capital, and it already has the maximum permitted Tier 2 (Tier 2 cannot be greater than 100% of Tier 1), then the only other option open is to cut back and/or ration its lending. There will obviously be limits beyond which a bank cannot lend without increasing its effective capital.

6.4.2 Effect on Corporates

The inevitable consequences are:

1. Corporate borrowers, ie those with 100% asset weightings, are required to pay higher margins. It should be remembered that lending to OECD banks only attracts a 20% weighting, and therefore much smaller margins are acceptable.

2. Corporate borrowers may well be forced to use more than one bank for large facilities (the Bank of England's paper on large exposures limits the percentage of any one bank's capital that can be exposed to an individual borrower).

3. Banks are more willing to securitize part of their lending book, particularly lending on credit cards, etc which attracts a 100% weighting.

4. When low margin business is considered, the bank will need to look at the whole of the customer relationship and may continue to lend at very fine rates if sufficient commission income is generated from other banking business.

Off-balance sheet items are included within the BIS framework, and the cost of providing capital to meet such items a swaps, FRAs etc, must be carefully calculated. Most banks now have sophisticated matrix models in order to ascertain the minimum margins required to cover capital adequacy costs for all marginal lending propositions and off-balance sheet facilities. An important element in this calculation is the return on capital required by each individual bank. Those banks with a low cost to income ratio may accept a smaller return on capital employed, whereas those with a higher cost to income ratio will seek a greater return. Banks now pay close attention to return on equity which is the income made over the degree of capital set aside for the loan as a measure of attractiveness of the pricing. For major corporates, this could mean cheaper borrowing from those banks which are well capitalised and have a relatively low cost-to-income ratio.

The G10 countries have formalised the need to keep a given amount of capital against "risk" assets and off-balance sheet products unless they are both definitely non-recourse. All bank capital (Tier 1 and Tier 2) held as an investment by another bank must be deducted from the latter's capital base. In this way there should be sufficient capital available to support all bank lending.

6.5 Pricing for Risk

As a preliminary to establishing the margin and fees that a bank will charge a corporate, the following factors will be taken into account. These have already been discussed and the points are summarized as follows:

1. Bank Policy — Risks in banking

    Adequate Balance Sheet Management

    Deposits/Lending

    Capital Adequacy

    Policy Formulation

    Target Marketing.

2. Credit Assessment — Fundamental Banking Skill

    Consider: Ability to repay of the corporate

    Relationship to the corporate

    Return is there adequate return to the risk

    Reputation.

3. Context of the Corporate

    Industry — Competitors (who are they?)

    Markets

    Growth prospects of the MNC

    Cyclical products?

    Price Taker/Price Maker – If the MNC has a significant Market share then he can influence the market or is he a niche player?

    Management — Corporate governance (Autocratic Chief Executive such as Robert Maxwell)

    Non Executives

    Balance, ownership of corporate?

    Relationship — Chemistry of individuals between the corporate treasurer/Accounts Officer.

Annual Reports   –   Profitability

Cash Flow

Capital

Liquidity

6.6 The Components of Pricing

Pricing is of course a crucial determinant in negotiating a loan with a corporate. In theory, a moderately sophisticated computer program should be able to specify a required yield for any given transaction based on the following factors.

1.   Quantity and quality of the risk(s) assumed.

2.   The opportunity cost of absorbing the bank's capital (capital adequacy costs, see 6.4).

3.   MLAs for sterling. Mandatory Liquid Assets

4.   Overheads/Administration.

5.   Bank Policy.

6.   Setting a margin over the banks cost of funds.

7.   Set a Front end fee/Arrangement fee.

8.   Set a Commitment fee or a Facility fee.

Pricing transactions in the context of the above factors is, therefore, extremely difficult; in equating a given level of risk to a price the process will be highly subjective. Banks, in general, have not undertaken the research required to produce actuarial calculations for the probability of transaction failure.

Allocating administration and overhead costs to loans or corporate facilities is also difficult but most banks will have set a margin to cover these costs.

Whatever price a bank chooses to impose, it is done against intense competition, since much pricing in the corporate market is driven by competition. Premium pricing can be achieved usually only if "added value" can be put into the transaction through an innovative structure which produces additional benefits to the corporate or a niche can be found where competition is weaker, such as specialist financing, or if the corporate is prepare for relationship reasons to pay a modest premium to its selected panel banks as a price for loyalty and service.

The actual pricing of a transaction or facility will consist of the following components:

(a) a per annum margin over the bank's cost of funds on amounts borrowed; this is often expressed as a % over three- or six-month LIBOR;

(b) a one off or "flat" "front-end" fee on the total facility;

(c) a per annum "commitment fee" on amounts committed but undrawn (sometimes also known as a "non-utilisation fee");

(d) a "facility fee" payable throughout the terms on the full amount of the loan.

All these presumptions are expressed as "basis points", a basis point is 0.01%pa. Ten basis points equate to 0.1%.

Combining is where expected loss and return on equity to come out with a risk adjusted return on equity as a means of the bank making qualitative decisions on the mix of pricing and risk to determine whether a deal is acceptable.

7

INTRODUCTION TO BANKING FACILITIES

7.1 Introduction

Before we move on to the various financial "considerations" that the corporate will make when deciding which means of finance to use, it is necessary to pose the question: why do corporates require finance? There are many reasons, most of which will fall into the following categories.

7.1.1 Return

The aim of taking finance will be to make profit. This may not be immediate, indeed long-term projects may take several years before positive cash flow is generated. Detailed analysis of the project will be required and the outcome should demonstrate that, within the given timescale, the return achievable will exceed the cost of finance.

7.1.2 Financing Capital Expenditure/Expansion

This is borrowing by a company to fund its fixed assets and long-term business needs.

7.1.3 Financing Working Capital

Short-term, daily requirements such as funding stock purposes.

7.1.4 Strategic

For example, tax benefits or hedging.

As regards planning generally, clearly finance will be a key issue. The corporate will wish to ensure that sufficient finance is in place to meet future commitments and that the optimum method is used. Future requirements must be clearly established, well in advance if possible, to avoid timing difficulties and perhaps avoiding the need to borrow when rates are high or the market unreceptive.

A key issue will be the maintenance of an appropriate maturity mix of debt finance, tailored to meet the specific needs of the company, as highlighted in future cash flow forecasts. These will be prepared in the light of the following needs:

- day-to-day (particularly overnight);

- short-term (up to 12 months);

- medium-term (in excess of one year, up to ten years);

- long-term (ten years and further ahead).

It is imperative that the finance function co-ordinates fully with all operational aspects of the organisation to ensure that all information is included for assessment. The overall plan must be drawn in line with the organisation's business objectives.

7.2 Debt versus Equity

All corporate financing methods fall within one or two categories, either debt or equity. Whilst this is a fairly basic division, it is an aspect that is paramount to the financial planning and structure of corporates.

7.2.1 Debt

Debt finance is borrowed funds, usually from an outside source, ie "Lenders". It is repayable, usually against a desired programme agreed at the outset. Interest will be payable to the lender at either a fixed or floating rate, and the interest commitment remains, irrespective of the company's performance. Security may be given to support the finance, for example, a mortgage debenture, which the lender can realise in the event of default. However, the lenders have no overall controlling interest in the company, ie the proprietors' stake is retained.

If floating rate debt is used, the company's ability to repay may be severely affected by adverse movements in interest rates. (Exposure management will be necessary to avoid this.)

Increasing debt has a detrimental affect on gearing and may, however, impact on the company's ability to raise further finance (unless compensated by proportionate increases on retained earnings). Therefore, debt can be very quick and simple to arrange, and at short notice, from a wide range of sources. A wide range of debt instruments are available, giving corporates the opportunity to select the most appropriate method for their specific needs.

Interest payable is an allowable trading expense which is chargeable to tax, ie the impact on cash flow in real terms is therefore less, as interest is deducted before calculating tax on any profits made.

7.2.2 Equity

Equity finance is a form of investment, either from existing shareholders or from a new source, for example, public issue (where a public offer of shares is made) or institutional investment. It is therefore provided by "investors". It is permanent, ie is not repayable, except in those cases where companies wish to buy back their own shares (where permissible by the Companies Acts) or where the investor retains a right to "convert" at some future date. With equity finance, there is no commitment to pay dividends (equivalent to debt interest), although in reality where profits are being made shareholders will expect a fair return in line with the risks they are taking. Unlike debt, if the company experiences trading difficulties it can help its cash flow by not paying a dividend, although this may make it difficult for the company to raise further equity finance if required. As far as the investors are concerned no specific security is available, as they are effectively acquiring a part of the company. Equity holders, therefore, acquire some control in the company, their rights depend on the type of equity holder they are.

The "cost" to the company does not vary with interest rate fluctuations.

Increased equity adds capital strength to the balance sheet. It gives protection against insolvency and comfort to lenders and other creditors as to the sound financial base of the company.

However, equity may be difficult to raise if the company is unsuccessful. In addition, existing shareholders may have no further funds to inject but do not wish to relinquish control by allowing outside investment.

It does take time to arrange public issues and market reaction may be difficult to determine. "Going Public" may be good for the company's image and the benefits may outweigh the risks. Dividends are paid from past tax profits, which may be less beneficial than interest paid on debt finance.

It is crucial to understand that debt is cheaper than equity up to a point because interest on debt is tax allowable whereas dividends that are payable to shareholders are an apportionment of post tax profits. However, the more highly geared a corporate becomes its costs of debt would rise as banks would demand a higher margin for the risk. Equally, the cost of equity to a highly geared corporate would also rise as shareholders would demand a greater return for the risk they are taking. This is the basis of the capital asset pricing model, but any further details are beyond the scope of this book.

7.3 Consumer Credit Act 1974

The Consumer Credit Act 1974 is aimed at non-corporates and requires anyone who gives or arranges credit or loans up to £25,000 for individuals (not corporate loans) to obtain a consumer credit licence and comply with a number of regulations. The term credit is used to cover the following: hire purchase, credit sale, conditional sale, trading checks, overdrafts, credit cards, mortgages, personal loans, cash loans and any other form of financial accommodation that covers any arrangement where a customer is given time to pay.

The licence is obtained from the Office of Fair Trading on payment of a fee, the amount of which will depend on the category of licence required. The licence category will be determined by the type of credit arrangement involved.

7.3.1 The Main Types of Credit Agreement

(a) Personal credit agreement – where an individual is provided with any amount of credit. If the agreement is not with an individual, eg a limited company, it is outside the control of the Act.

(b) Consumer credit agreement – where an individual is provided with credit of £25,000 or less. The £25,000 limit applies to the amount of credit advanced and does not include any charges, deposits or advance payments. For example, an agreement where goods worth £27,000 are paid for by an initial deposit of £2,500, leaving a credit arrangement for the remaining £24,500, is within the Act.

(c) Fixed-sum agreement – where an individual is given a single advance or makes one purchase on a particular occasion.

(d) Running-account credit agreement – an individual is given a credit limit and can draw money or make purchases on any number of occasions. The £25,000 limit can be applied to either the credit limit or the amount that can be withdrawn at any one time.

(e) Debtor-creditor (d-c) agreement – where there are no goods or services directly involved, eg a cash loan or personal loan, or where there are no arrangements between the supplier of any goods and the creditor.

(f) Debtor-creditor-supplier (d-c-s) agreement – where the creditor is connected in some way to the supplier of the goods or services being financed by the credit agreement. A common example is where a chain of shops provides customers with a card account which is usually operated by a separate finance company. In this instance the supplier and the creditor are not the same and so there is a debtor-creditor-supplier agreement.

7.3.2 Exempt Consumer Credit Agreements

There are six types of exempt agreements: normal trade credit; low-cost credit; finance of foreign trade; land transactions repayable in four instalments or less; certain mortgage lending; certain loans for insurance policies.

Mortgage lending that is exempt includes credit to finance the purchase of, or alterations to, homes or business premises provided by building societies authorized under the Financial Services and Markets Act 2000. The insurance policy exemption applies where an additional advance is made by a mortgage lender to cover the cost of associated insurances including buildings and contents, mortgage protection or indemnity insurance. The mortgage itself must be not less than £25,000 for the agreement to be exempt.

8

SHORT-TERM DEBT FINANCE

8.1 Introduction

In the UK, the normal view is that debt finance is cheaper than equity. Indeed, with the UK overdraft system it is usually profitable to avoid non-interest bearing current account balances even when the net liquid position is positive. It is better to invest and overdraw at the same time so as to take up any overnight "slack". It would of course be a very different matter in a country like the USA where overdrawing is contrary to the law. But, under an overdraft system, at least some short-term debt is the norm.

8.1.1 The main sources of short-term funds

The main sources of short-term finance in the UK are:

- Sterling overdraft

- Sterling money market

- Sterling acceptance credits or bills

- Sterling commercial paper

- Non-sterling eurocurrency borrowings

8.1.2 Principles for managing short-term debt

There are two main principles for managing short-term debt:

- *Liquidity*: the prime objective must be to ensure that adequate facilities are available to meet current and projected financing requirements, plus a reasonable margin of contingency. Such facilities should be available for a minimum of 12 months, depending on the nature of the business.

- *Profitability*: subject to the need for liquidity, the aim is to borrow at the lowest overall cost, normally defined after tax. Given the potential volatility of short-term interest rates, there is also an increasing emphasis on the management of interest rate exposure.

8.1.3 Management information

The effective management of short-term debt depends critically on the availability of a comprehensive and up-to-date information system. In particular, it is essential to have a reliable and flexible cashflow forecasting system which includes the prompt reporting and updating of any revision to cashflow forecasts. Comprehensive information on existing borrowings and facilities is also necessary. This will include the total amount of available facilities and, in respect of outstanding debt, maturity dates, analysis between fixed and floating rate interest, currency mix and domicile. The treasurer must also have accurate information on current and projected financing costs, including interest costs and related fees, charges and commissions.

8.1.4 Liquidity

Liquidity is, of course, critical. A financially sound company is normally in a strong bargaining position with its banks and other lenders. It can normally extend its borrowing facilities by asking its existing or other lenders for facilities as well as obtaining better rates and reduced commitment fees. A company has this strength if its debt/equity ratio, its asset strength, and its revenue cashflow are not only sound, but supported by a track record and commercial market profile which make them appear reliable.

8.1.5 Illiquidity caused by constraints in the financial market

The ability of a company to borrow is affected by external as well as internal factors. An illiquid domestic market (lack of supply from banks to lend sterling or a lack of investor sentiment to invest in sterling instruments like equities or bonds) may reduce the funds available to corporates, or limit the borrowing mechanisms available. The corporate treasurer should be aware of factors affecting those markets in which he is interested and their participants in order that he may pre-empt any liquidity problems by borrowing, say, for longer periods than his immediate requirements dictate.

8.1.6 The borrower near the limit of his debt capacity

A company which for reasons of financial weakness or credit rationing cannot count on extra facilities, must not only arrange all the facilities it can, but also take a cautious stock of its potential needs and make an "inventory of liquidity". This will include:

● existing and potential borrowing facilities – noting renewal dates of existing facilities and repayment date of term facilities; and

● a careful assessment of the extent to which stock levels can be reduced, trade debtor terms shortened or trade creditor terms extended briefly in an emergency.

Alternatively, it is sometimes possible to persuade a large supplier to substitute bills of exchange with a tenor of, say, six months for open account credit of three months – a bank might well prefer to discount these bills rather than grant more overdraft. As the bank has the combined security of other companies, it might not count it against the purchaser's credit limit. A normally interest-free source of funds (trade credit) is thus widened by offering to pay interest at commercial rates on longer credit.

It is more important here to avoid the kind of action which sends suppliers reporting "adverse" collection experience to the credit rating agencies like Dun & Bradstreet – nothing closes other sources of funds faster than this. This weapon must be used either openly by negotiation with specific large suppliers (who have a commercial interest in continuing the relationship) or with very great caution, flexibility and control.

Selling the ownership of assets which the company normally owns, for example by the use of factoring, see further Unit 12.

8.1.7 Profitability – the Problems

Borrowing at the lowest possible cost sounds simple, but raises the following complications:

● Fixed or variable?

● What maturity?

● Timing of interest payments

● Commitment fees

● Administrative costs

● Compensating balances

● Foreign currency hedging costs

8.1.7.1 Fixed or variable?

Overdrafts are at variable interest rates and most other instruments at fixed rates for various maturities. The treasurer who feels confident that rates will fall, will either use his overdraft or (if he has the resources to manage his position actively) borrow in other instruments for very short maturities only. On the other hand, the one who thinks rates will rise will borrow for long maturities at fixed rates.

When interest rates are volatile, the view taken of their trend is likely to have a more powerful effect on the overall cost of borrowing than any small difference in rates.

8.1.7.2 The choice of maturity

This dilemma does not arise with overdrafts – indeed the main convenience of the overdraft system is that a great deal of management time and concentration is saved by its sheer flexibility. However, it can pay to borrow fixed for longer maturities when interest rates are expected to rise.

Apart from the expected trends in rates, the choice of maturities can be influenced by tight liquidity, or by the requirements shown on the cash forecast. Borrowing for too long can result in overfunding and the need to invest the overspill so as to avoid interest-free current account balances, until the excess borrowing matures for repayment. This is because term borrowings cannot normally be prepaid without prohibitive penalty. The combination of overfunding and money market investment is not always unprofitable; but in the absence of favourable counterforces bid-offer spreads tend to load the dice against the treasurer.

With the advent of the sterling commercial paper market, more flexible maturities are available to a treasurer than term debt or sterling acceptance credits. With the latter, the best rates are available for one, three or six-month periods, while in the former, maturities are possible for any period between seven and 364 days. Therefore, if the corporate treasurer knows that an invoice will be settled on a particular day, say in 44 days, sterling commercial paper can be issued for that exact period, rather than making a borrowing for two months under an acceptance credit line, and investing receipts from the invoice in the money market pending maturity on the acceptance credit drawing.

8.1.7.3 Timing of interest and finance charge payments

Overdraft interest is now generally charged quarterly in arrears. Acceptance commissions and discounts are usually paid "off the front". The present value of the interest payments is therefore not directly comparable. Strictly, the comparisons should be made by calculum of the present value.

8.1.7.4 Commitment fees

Short-term dealing facilities are usually uncommitted, ie at the bank's option so, while no commitment fee is payable, a treasurer may not be able to draw under the facilities except at high margins, when liquidity is tight.

8.1.7.5 Administrative costs

It is easy to overlook administrative costs. Acceptance credits need all the stationery and clerical expense to counterdraw and sign the bills and the often considerable task of getting them into the hands of the accepting bank in the short time between the decision whether and how much to draw and the time of the drawing. In sterling commercial paper programmes, the issuing and paying agent will do most of the administration, in return for annual fee and fee per note issued.

8.1.7.6 Compensating balance

Sometimes banks waive charges if certain minimum balances are kept on current account. This used to be normal practice in the USA, but UK corporations in a passive net liquid position have never had to overdraw one account in order to keep another account in credit as a compensating balance.

8.2 Overdrafts

An overdrawn current account balance is a simple current account balance owed to the bank instead of by the bank. The bank permits overdrawing within a limit which is agreed with the customer for a period, often a year. A short facility letter usually sets out the period; the maximum amount or limit; and formula for interest – such as 1% above the bank's base rate each day on the daily cleared balance; the intervals at which interest will be debited (usually quarterly), and any provisions concerning security, default or cross-default. There may be provision for a commitment commission.

Overdrafts are contractually repayable on demand, but in practice they are regarded as available for the stated period of (say) a year. The undrawn balance of a facility therefore constitutes liquidity for the borrower. Indeed in a new issue on the London Stock Exchange, the requirement of a certificate from the directors (and checked by the auditors) that the company's facilities are adequate for its needs over the next year, implicitly assumes that the bank will not use its right to require repayment of an overdraft facility on demand before its expiry date.

Opportunities arise, from time to time, to invest funds at a higher rate than the overdraft cost. This is called "round tripping" and is unethical if carried out as a deliberate strategy. The overdraft facility is uncommitted and may be withdrawn by the bank if abused.

The great convenience and flexibility of overdrafts has been stressed throughout this lesson.

8.3 Term Loans

A term loan is simply a loan for a specific period with fixed for repayment of the amount of the loan dates (normally for a period of between three and ten years). A term loan may be made either by a single lender or by a group of lenders (if the latter, the loan is called a *syndicated loan*). A syndicated loan is normally arranged and 'managed' by one of the lenders which is called the 'agent bank'. The funds advanced under a term loan may be made available in chunks, or tranches (this is commonly known as a *facility arrangement*). Some loans may be committed to LIBOR (see 8.4), linked to a bank's base rate, or may be on a fixed rate (ie, not committed).

8.4 Short-term Libor-linked Loans

8.4.1 Definition

This is a short-term facility for larger sums in either sterling or eurocurrencies, and customers of good standing, which is linked to interbank rates, ie LIBOR (London Inter Bank Offered Rate) for UK sterling facilities. (Features may vary slightly between banks – the following is regarded as being typical.)

8.4.2 Features

8.4.2.1 Facility Type

A revolving facility which is, usually, of a committed nature, although a "repayment on demand" clause may be specified in the agreement.

8.4.2.2 Amount

The minimum facility is, usually, in the region of £250,000, with no specific restriction as to maximum. Individual drawings are, usually, permissible for amounts of £100,000 and above.

8.4.2.3 Currency

Such "market-rate linked" facilities are available in most currencies (naturally, subject to availability) and in most major financial centres around the world. Multi-currency facilities are also available. This type of facility provides the borrower with access to a nominated range of currencies. At the time of drawdown of an amount required, the borrower simply nominates the currency he requires, which must be within the nominated range agreed at the outset. (The process at drawdown is covered later.)

8.4.2.4 Purpose

We are looking here at a short-term revolving facility which is best suited to working capital purposes or as a financing means for short-term expenditure.

8.4.2.5 Term/Maturity

By its definition, this type of facility will be up to a 12-month term, usually subject to annual review. Each drawdown will be for a specified "rollover" period (sometimes called "fixture" period) – usually one or three months; in exceptional cases six, or a maximum of 12 months. Some banks may allow drawdown on an overnight or seven-day period, although this is quite unusual as part of a committed short-term LIBOR loan facility.

8.4.2.6 Repayment

As in the case of the overdraft, there is, usually, no formal repayment programme agreed; the facility "limit" will be set and the borrower will be allowed draw, repay and redraw throughout the agreed term. However, the LIBOR loans involve an element of repayment, since each is, effectively, repayable at maturity of its respective rollover period, eg a tranche of £1 million drawndown today on a one-month fixture will be repayable in one month's time. This is where the expression "rollover" comes from, since it is quite usual for "repayment" to come from a new drawdown for a further period.

8.4.2.7 Pricing

8.4.2.7.1 Fees

There will be an arrangement fee, and normally, a non-utilisation fee, in respect of undrawn balances. The former is paid up front and subsequently, on renewal; the latter is assessed retrospectively, annually or half yearly.

8.4.2.7.2 Interest

There are three elements of interest involved. First, there is LIBOR, and this will be the prevailing rate at the time of drawdown, which is fixed throughout that period. Second, a margin will be agreed at the outset, and this will apply for the term of the facility. The margin will depend on the borrower's standing and the lender's perception of the risk involved. The final element, which applies to sterling drawings, is in respect of covering the lender's reserve costs (sometimes called "MLAs" or "mandatory liquid assets"). This represents an opportunity cost to the lender, since it will be required to maintain a proportion of its liquid assets in low-yielding form, in line with Bank of England regulations. This will be assessed retrospectively and it will be added to the interest when applied, which will be at the end of the fixture period, or half-yearly if a 12-month fixture is taken. MLA's are about 0.036%.

8.4.2.8 Documentation/Security

A facility letter/loan agreement will be required, and security may be a requirement depending on the risk involved to the lender.

8.4.2.9 Sources/Availability

They are widely available to corporates of good standing from leading financial institutions.

8.4.3 Method of Operation

- Negotiation and agreement of terms, between borrower and lender.

- Completion of documentation/security formalities.

- The borrower gives drawdown instructions to the lender (often, with direct access to the bank's dealers or through its nominated point of daily contact), having obtained the rates.

- At maturity, repayment/rollover instructions are given and interest is charged.

8.4.4 User Benefits

- It is a revolving facility which is ideally suited to financing working capital or short-term expenditure needs, without involving regular negotiation with the lender.

- As in the case of overdrafts, there is no requirement for drawings to be tied to specific underlying trade transactions; nor are there any regulatory constraints.

- Documentation is of a relatively standard nature among banks, and this gives the benefit of stating quite clearly the terms of the facility and obligations of both parties.

- The committed nature of the facility gives assurance to the borrower that funds will be made available – subject, of course, to any terms/conditions contained in the facility letter.

- Flexible amounts can be catered for – especially, large sums.

- Currency finance is available at "market rates".

- Generally, rollovers are available at one, three, six and 12-month rests (in exceptional cases for shorter periods), which means that tranches can be drawn to suit the borrower's cash flow requirements.

- Interest margin is negotiable – which means that companies of strong standing will command better rates than weaker corporates.

- LIBOR is an inter-bank market rate which provides the borrower with fine-rate finance.

- Interest costs are fixed throughout the fixture period, which eliminates the risk of increases in interest rates, and it enables costs to be built into future forecasts.

- Interest is charged in arrears, which may compare favourably with alternative financing methods.

- There is no rigid repayment programme to adhere to, which gives greater flexibility, particularly at times when reduction would create cash flow difficulties (interest is charged only on amounts drawn).

- Operation is simple and speedy, with administration not at all time-consuming (telephone access).

- Early repayment may be possible but a penalty will be charged to provide any necessary compensation for the lender.

- Wide availability means that competition exists between lenders.

8.4.5 User Disadvantages/Objections

- Documentation formalities may appear restrictive and time-consuming.

- "On demand" clauses, if applicable, remove the comfort of commitment.

- The borrower is exposed to interest rate fluctuations between rollovers.

- Security may be a requirement in certain circumstances.

- Some lenders may not allow drawings for less than one month, which means that very short-term needs cannot be catered for.

- The usual minimum facility amount is £250,000, with drawings restricted to a minimum of £100,000 – thus, smaller sums are not catered for.

- A non-utilization fee will be payable on undrawn balances.

8.5 Acceptance Credits

8.5.1 Definition

"Acceptance credits", or "bankers acceptances", is a money market expression for a bill of exchange drawn in accordance with the 1882 Act, drawn by a customer on its bank and accepted by the latter. The bill can then be discounted in the market – usually, by the accepting bank – thus providing the customer with the finance required. (You will notice that the difference between acceptance credits and discounting trade bills is that the latter are drawn by one corporate on another. In the case of the acceptance credit, the bill is drawn on a bank.) Acceptance credits must relate to an underlying trading transaction.

8.5.2 Features

8.5.2.1 Eligibility

An accepted bill of exchange falls within one of two types, as follows.

(a) *Eligible* – ie it has been accepted by an "eligible" bank and it complies with the regulatory requirements of the central bank (the Bank of England, in the UK) – which means that it is available for rediscount with the latter at its prime rate (eligible bill rate, or EBR).

(b) *Ineligible* – ie it does not meet the criteria for rediscount with the central bank (for example, where the bill has not been drawn on/accepted by an eligible bank). Ineligible bills may, however, be discounted in the usual way but they will not qualify for the prime rate.

8.5.2.2 Criteria

To be "eligible" in the UK, a bill of exchange must comply with certain criteria – mainly:

- the bill must be drawn on and accepted by a bank which is designated as being "eligible" for such purposes by the Bank of England (a number of banks carry this status, including the major UK clearing banks);

- the term of the bill must not exceed 187 days (ie six months);

- the bill must be self-liquidating and it must relate to a specific, and identifiable, trading transaction; reference to the transaction must be noted on the bill – this is known as "clausing";

- the bill must be payable in the UK, preferably in London;

- the bill must not be drawn by a bank.

Such facilities can, generally, only be used by "trading" customers (normally, there are actual goods involved), and not by the "services" industry.

8.5.2.3 Facility Type

It is a revolving facility, usually agreed on a twelve-month basis, which is, generally, committed – although the documentation (see below) may contain a repayment on demand clause.

8.5.2.4 Amount

Some eligible banks will establish an acceptance credit facility for amounts down to £100,000 – most commonly, £500,000 minimum, with no specific restriction on the maximum (subject to lending criteria). Usual amounts drawn, per bill, will range between £25,000 and £1m. (Bills drawn for sums down to £10,000 may have limited acceptability.)

8.5.2.5 Currency

The London sterling and New York US$ acceptance markets are the main currencies, although other such markets are available throughout Europe.

8.5.2.6 Purpose

Acceptance credits are an effective means for trading customers to raise short-term working capital finance, tied to specific underlying transactions.

8.5.2.7 Term/Maturity

As already mentioned, the facility will, usually, be agreed on an annual basis, with individual bills being drawn for terms up to a maximum of 187 days. Bills may be drawn for varying periods – usually, 30, 60, 90 and 187 days. Some eligible banks may be prepared to discount bills drawn for shorter or broken periods.

8.5.2.8 Repayment

As in the case of a simple discounting facility for trade bills, the facility does not involve any formalised structured repayments, since the bills are self-liquidating – ie as the trade transaction progresses, cash inflows arise as settlement is due.

8.5.2.9 Pricing

8.5.2.9.1 Fees

An acceptance commission will be charged on an agreed annual percentage, based on the face value of each bill. In addition, where the facility is on a committed basis, a commitment fee may be taken.

8.5.2.9.2 Interest

Interest is represented by the discount rate – again, expressed as an annual percentage.

The acceptance commission will vary depending on the customer's standing. This charge is taken by the bank in recognition of it accepting and adding its name to the bill, ie accepting liability under it. The rate will be set through-out the term of the facility.

The discount rate is a market rate and, as such, it will vary depending on prevailing conditions. Other factors that affect this include the term and currency of the bill and, most important, whether it is eligible for rediscount by the central bank. It follows, therefore, that the discount rate for eligible bills will be finer than that for ineligible bills. The acceptance commission and discount will be applied when discount takes place (ie on day one – when the customer receives the net proceeds).

8.5.2.10 Documentation/Security

Security considerations will apply in the usual way. As regards documentation, it is usual for a facility letter to be obtained, and this will, clearly, establish the terms, conditions and operational aspects. The latter will include term and amounts of bills, commission details and procedure for presenting bills.

8.5.2.11 Sources/Availability

They are available from a relatively wide range of eligible banks.

8.5.3 Modus Operandi

- Negotiation of facility and completion of documentation/security formalities.

- When the customer requires finance (say, £500,000), it draws a bill in that sum and for the term required (say, three months) – remember that the finance has to relate to a trade-related purpose. The bill will be drawn on the bank.

- On the same day, the bill is presented to the bank for acceptance. The bill must, normally, be in the bank's hands by around 11.00 am on the day acceptance is required.

- The customer may take the bill elsewhere to have it discounted but, usually, acceptance and discount is by the same bank (under the provisions of the facility letter).

- Once acceptance/discount have taken place, the proceeds are applied to the customer's account.

- The bank will either hold the bill until maturity or rediscount in the market. The customer will have to settle the face value of the bill at maturity.

In our example, if we assume that an acceptance commission of 1% per annum has been agreed and EBR is 8%, the following applies.

DAY –   the bill is drawn, and accepted/discounted by bank.

The customer's account is credited:

Bill amount	£500,000
Less commission	1,250
Less discount	10,000
Proceeds	£488,750

IN THREE MONTHS TIME – the customer pays the bank £500,000.

8.5.4 User Benefits

- It provides a usual alternative method of short-term funding for trading customers.

- The revolving nature of the facility makes it easy and flexible to use, with no need for regular negotiation.

- The facility may be on a committed basis, which gives the customer assured funds when required.

- Eligible bills will be cheaper than trade/ineligible bills.

- EBR is, often, very favourable, as compared with other market indices – thus, acceptance credits can, often, provide access to cheap-rate finance.

- The finance is self-liquidating, and the facility does not require the customer to adhere to any defined repayment programme.

- It is flexible in terms of amount, which means that most reasonable sums can be handled.

- Major currencies are available.

- It is flexible as to term, to a maximum of six months. This, together with the amount/currency flexibility, means that most short-term cash flow needs can be catered for with relative ease.

- Commission applies throughout the term of the facility, and it will vary on the bank's risk, ie for good credit risks, the fee will be comparatively less.

- The "interest" cost is known on day one, which helps budgeting/forecasting.

- It eliminates exposure to subsequent adverse movements in interest rates.

- Wide availability.

- It is easy to establish and operate. (Some banks will be prepared to hold bills signed by the customer but otherwise incomplete pending their telephone instruction as to requirements, ie amount and term. These bills are known as "inchoate").

- There are cash flow/balance sheet benefits, since the trade transaction will give rise to a debtor which the customer is turning into cash ahead of settlement by the latter.

8.5.5 User Disadvantages/Objections

- It is only available for trade transactions.

- It is only suitable for short-term needs (up to 187 days).

- Since the discount is deducted on day one, this needs to be considered when comparing with other options which incur interest at maturity.

- By establishing costs at the outset, there is no flexibility to gain from favourable rate movements.

- Very small sums cannot be catered for (between £10,000 and £25,000, depending on the bank's policy).

- Limited currency finance is available.

- Certain banks may not be happy for bills to be drawn in broken periods, which may not, then, tie in with cash flow.

- Facility-letter documentation may be seen as too restrictive.

- The 11.00 am deadline may be difficult to meet, and the customer may not be happy with providing inchoate bills to the bank.

- As accepted bills are negotiable, the drawer must be content with the fact that its name will be publicly seen in the market.

- The criteria for illegibility may be seen as being too restrictive, certainly when compared with other methods of obtaining short-term finance.

- Ineligible bills will not attract prime rates.

8.6 Commercial Paper

8.6.1 Definition

Commercial paper is a method available to corporates to raise short-term finance by issuing unsecured bearer promissory notes direct to investors, ie bypassing the traditional channels of borrowing (banks). This process of cutting out the middleman is known as "disintermediation", and through it, corporate issuers (ie the borrowers) are able to raise finance more cheaply than through bank lines. Commercial paper is issued in specific denominations/currencies (see below), usually at a discount to the face value as shown on the note itself. The effective interest cost/return is, therefore, the difference between the discounted sum and the face value.

8.6.2 Credit Ratings

Credit ratings have been considered in another Unit but, given their importance, it is worth while making further note of them again here. Historically, investors have tended to place non-speculative funds with recognised institutions, since these provide the required level of security – in theory, at least. With the advent of increased disintermediation and corporates' needs for innovative and cost-effective financing techniques, together with the perceived relative instability of certain "institutions", investors have been attracted by alternatives available to them, such as commercial paper. However, investors will require the comfort that the issuer is financially sound and under good management, thus ensuring security of the principal sum invested plus payment of any interest sums due. This need is met by the third party credit-rating agency. In certain markets, a rating is a prerequisite – notably, in the UK – whereas, in the case of ECP and SCP, a rating is not essential, although it may, of course, enhance acceptability to the market, and command a finer rate. If the issuer is unknown, a rating may be necessary (not as a regulatory requirement) to make the issue attractive to investors.

The benefits, then, of a good rating to the issuer are two-fold:

- first, the cost of raising finance will be reduced;

- in the second place, diversification of the investor base should be achieved, which avoids the risks involved if "all one's eggs are in the same basket" and ensures a wider target audience and, thus, wider sources of funds. A bad rating, though will have the opposite effect.

8.7 Sterling Commercial Paper

8.7.1 Introduction

Because of the growing interest in the Euromarkets and increasing use of "paper" through acceptance credits as a means of raising short-term finance, the Bank of England acknowledged the need for a suitable domestic market to satisfy the needs of the UK's major corporate players.

The SCP market was introduced in April 1986 to meet this need. However, the Bank of England wished to ensure that the market operated with sufficient investor protection and hence, it stipulated a series of requirements that must be met by each issuer.

8.7.1.1 Criteria

In order to issue SCP, the following requirements must be satisfied.

- The corporate issuer must have a full listing on the London Stock Exchange and minimum surplus resources of £25 m, or be the subsidiary of a parent satisfying the foregoing, with the issue being guaranteed by the parent.

- Notes can only be issued with a maturity of between seven and 364 days.

- Minimum denomination of each note is to be £½m. (Financial institutions that qualify to issue sterling certificates of deposit are not eligible to issue SCP.)

8.7.1.2 Amount

There are two aspects to consider. First, there is the "programme" which, to be cost-effective, should not be less than £25m. (In reality, few are at this level, with £50m being the usual minimum seen, and most programmes at the £100/£200m level.) The programme is like a limit on a revolving facility, as it sets the maximum level of paper the issuer can have outstanding at any one time. Once the programme is in place, issues can be made as finance is required. As already mentioned, individual notes must be for at least £500,000. This sum and £1m are the usual denominations seen.

8.7.1.3 Term/Maturities

The individual notes may be drawn for any periods between seven and 364 days (inclusive). Most activity is seen in the one-to two-month range.

8.7.1.4 Parties Involved

The two key parties involved, once the programme is established, are the issuer and the investor. The investor purchases the paper from the issuer in return for the payment at interest and return of the principal sum on a future date. However, there are three other parties involved and these are:

- the arranger
- the dealer(s)
- the issuing and paying agent (IPA)

The *arranger* is responsible for co-ordinating and advising on all aspects of the programme, eg:

- the size of the programme
- appointment of dealers (to obtain best spread of investors)
- appointment of IPA
- preparation of information memorandum (see below)

(Quite often, the arranger is the principal dealer, and sometimes also the IPA.)

The dealers will bid for the issuer's paper with a view to placing it with investors, making a turn on the differential between the bid and offer prices. There is no guarantee that the dealer(s) will bid for the paper when it is issued; therefore, the issuer has no assurance of funds, nor at which price the paper will be acceptable to the market. (A group of dealers bidding competitively for the issuer's paper is known as a "tender panel".)

The IPA carries out the administrative aspects of the programme.

- He maintains safe custody of the notes.
- He issues the notes and delivers against payment.
- He authenticates the notes on issue.
- He provides the issuer with the issue proceeds.
- At maturity, he receives proceeds from the issue to settle any notes due for payment.
- He pays out on maturity against surrender of the appropriate note(s).

8.7.1.5 Back-up Lines

A supporting back-up line of finance is not a pre-requisite, although, as we have seen above, the issuer has no guarantee that his notes will be taken by the market, at the price he wants, at any given time. Therefore, it is common for supporting committed lines to be available for drawing in case of need.

8.7.1.6 Documentation

There are a number of documents involved.

8.7.1.6.1 The Notes

These must show the following.

- Issuer's name

- The amount

- Date of issue

- Maturity date

- The IPA's certificate of authentication

- Authorised signatory(ies) of the issuer

- A statement to the effect that the note has been issued in compliance with Regulation 15 of the Banking Act 1979 (Exempt Transactions) Regulations 1986

- A statement whether the issue does or does not carry a guarantee

8.7.1.6.2 The Information Memorandum

This is prepared by the arranger to "sell" the issue. It outlines all operational aspects of the programme as follows.

- Issuer's name

- Programme/denomination amounts

- Purpose of the programme

- Method of delivery/settlement

- IPA dealer details

- Date of issue

- Background details of the issuer

- Financial summary of the issuer

- A brief analysis of the issuer's business activities

- Any other information relevant to the programme

8.7.1.6.3 The Dealership Agreement

This sets out the terms of the relationship between the dealer(s) and the issuer.

8.7.1.6.4 The IPA Agreement

This sets out the terms of the relationship between the IPA and the issuer.

8.7.1.7 Secondary Market

While there is no physical constraint applied in connection with secondary activity, very little exists with SCP. This is owing to the short-term nature of the maturities which is leading investors to hold the paper for its full term.

8.7.1.8 Pricing/Fees

As already mentioned, the interest element is the discount at which the paper is sold below face value. For example, a note denominated (face value) at £½m would be issued at a lower price (say, £490,000). That is the amount (ie £490,000) the investor pays now to the issuer. At maturity, the issuer has to settle the full face value of £500,000.

This effective interest cost is competitive compared with other rates; often, finance at around LIBID can be achieved.

As far as fees are concerned, these can be quite high to set up the programme, especially if the programme is only for a small sum. The fees, usually, involve the following.

- Stationery/printing (notes and other documentation, including optional publication of Tombstone in the Financial Press).

- Legal/accountancy advisers.

- IPA (usually an annual fee plus a nominal sum for each note).

- Arranger's fee (this may not be necessary, if the arranger is also IPA and/or dealer).

Depending on the size of the issue, the total fees payable could amount to £10,000 or £15,000 during the first year. Dealers, usually, do not charge a fee as such, owing to competition for this role in the market. Their money is made on placing the paper to the investors, ie the bid/offer spread.

8.7.1.9 The Investors

The investors are dominated by corporates themselves (about 70% of the market) which shows that the market's introduction was, perhaps, driven as much by the investors as the issuing companies – so, what attracts investors to SCP?

- The market provides an alternative to the more traditional options available for surplus funds.

- The issuing requirements are such that only "known" names have programmes, ie their credit standing is good.

- Amounts and maturities can be geared to suit cash flow.

- Large sums can be invested.

- Rates are attractive.

- Access is simple (through a dealer).

- Normally, there are no dealing costs.

- While secondary market activity is minimal, there is always the comfort that, if necessary, the note may be onsold prior to maturity.

- Interest income is known at the outset.

- Anyone can invest, provided he has £½m!

8.7.2 Modus Operandi

The programme will be established through the arranger and in line with the guide-lines laid down by the British Bankers Association. Timing consent is not required from the Bank of England, although the latter is to be advised of proposed programme amounts, and it must be advised of outstanding paper.

Once the programme is established, the utilisation procedure is quite straightforward. When the issuer requires finance, he contacts the principal dealer to discuss his requirements. The nominated panel of dealers will be invited to bid for the paper and the issuer will accept those which are most favourable. The usual cut-off time for same-day value is 12.00 noon or 12.30 pm.

When the deal is struck, the issuer advises the IPA of the details, and the dealer, in turn, also confirms these with the IPA. The IPA then prepares the notes for collection, or holds in safe custody, as appropriate. Arrangements are made for funds to be remitted to the IPA and, in turn, on to the issuer's account.

At maturity, the issuer makes arrangements to have funds with the IPA by 12.00 noon, to cover any paper maturing. The IPA will settle with same-day value for the investor, provided delivery of the note takes place by 2.30 to 3.00 pm.

8.7.3 Issuer Benefits

- It is a further alternative method of raising short-term finance.

- Maturities (seven to 364 days) can be used to suit specific cash flow requirements.

- It is not tied to specific transactions, which means that it can be used for a range of short-term needs.

- Once the programme is established, issues can be made to suit needs and when market conditions are favourable.

- By cutting out the middleman (banks), it is possible to achieve very cheap-rate finance.

- The interest is known and fixed at the outset, which aids budgeting and avoids risk of adverse movements.

- Large sums can be raised, to suit needs.

- Publicity will increase the profile of the company in the market-place.

- Annual fees are relatively low.

- Credit rating is not a requirement, although a highly-rated company will command finer rates and wider acceptability.

- It is easy to obtain finance, once the programme is in place.

- It is unsecured; therefore, it does not tie up any of the issuer's assets.

8.7.4 Issuer Disadvantages/Objections

- It is unsuitable for requirements of less than seven days (or more than 364).

- It is unsuitable for sums less than £500,000 (per note).

- There are stringent criteria to enable issue, which prevents many corporates from using the market.

- Initial set-up fees may be considered high, if the programme amount is small.

- Lesser-known names may require a credit rating to obtain investor confidence; the cost of this may be seen as high.

- There is no guarantee of funds, and the establishment of a back-up line of finance is an additional cost.

- It is not suitable if funds are required "privately", eg to finance an acquisition bid.

- Secondary-market activity may undermine the price of future issues.

- Documentation requirements are fairly onerous.

- Regular issues must be made, irrespective of requirements, to keep the issuer's name "in the market" and retain investor interest.

8.8 Sterling Acceptances versus SCP

In terms of sterling short-term finance, the cheapest alternatives are, usually, the above, and the borrower will need to consider the differences between each in deciding on the most appropriate method.

The following is a brief comparison.

	Sterling Acceptances	*SCP*
Company qualification:	Trading company	Stock Exchange listing £25m surplus resources
Purpose:	Trade related (clausing required)	Any
Dealing time:	Usually by noon	Usually by noon
Finance source:	Discount of bill by Bank/ Discount House	Investors
Maturities:	30-187 days (usual)	7 to 364 days
Amounts:	Min. £10,000/25,000 per Max. £1m bill	£½m/£1m per note
Type of facility:	May be committed	No guarantee of funds
Interest:	Payable up front	Paid at maturity
Benchmark	EBR	LIBID/LIBOR

It is not available for very large sums or currency finance.

8.9 Sterling Money Market Lines

This is the domestic sterling inter-bank market in which corporate customers can often obtain competitive borrowing (and deposit) rates. Each transaction is at a fixed rate for one transaction period, which can be anything from overnight to 12 months. The corporate treasurer can shop around for the best rates, either by telephoning around the banks with whom his company has credit limits (after using his screen to identify the banks most likely to be competitive at the time), or he can operate through money brokers. This costs a small commission, but may obtain keener rates. Banking relationships may be enhanced by direct dealing. It is not good policy to take funds through a broker from a bank providing committed facilities.

Where a company's credit quality gives it access to the money markets, they will almost always be cheaper than overdrafts, provided the transaction size is large enough to cover the wire transfer costs.

9

MEDIUM- TO LONG-TERM DEBT FINANCE

9.1 The Corporate Treasurer's Considerations for medium- and long-term funding

The corporate treasurer needs to have knowledge of the company's funding objectives and future financial plans such as acquisition, capex and reducing translation exposure. The treasurer will always look at the parameters of risk/reward and cost versus benefit in putting together any medium-long-term funding plans. To a treasurer bank finance provides flexibility, particularly in maturity and repayment profiles.

Most bank finance for medium or long-term funding committed or not, is provided at short-term rates. Fixed rates may be available for up to five to seven years. Repayment schedules are suited to the borrower, ie bullet repayments. Multi-currency facilities are ideal for standby/backup in case of need by a corporate.

The maturity of loan finance: the long-, medium- and short-term maturity will be dictated by the nature of company. The type of company dealing in debt finance is very important since manufactures tend to require a medium-long-term debt maturing profile whereas retailers tend to require a short-medium-term debt maturing profile.

The corporate can choose between fixed or variable rates. The bank must consider that the credit risk increases with the life of the loan, and that the rate of interest and the margin tends to increase as the maturity increases.

A bank should also be aware that some corporate treasurers take the view that there is an inherent value in obtaining the longest possible maturity almost regardless of cost, however this is no longer considered a rational argument as the medium-term bank market offers suitable compromise.

Banks will charge a corporate for the *certainty* of providing committed funds by charging a corporate a commitment fee for undrawn amounts. The corporate must fit funding to its overall plan/strategy and the bank will do its best to meet the needs of its corporate customers by providing the flexibility they need.

The treasurer's plans must take into account the maturity mix of loans and loan facilities.

The maturity profile should graph the facilities available, taking into account any evergreen (an option given to the corporate to renew the facility for a further two- or three-year period) and bullet maturities. The treasurer must avoid bunching at all times. Bunching is where a number of repayments of facilities are scheduled at or near the same time.

9.2 Types of Facilities

Medium-term loans will be discussed at 9.6 but these can be on a bilateral basis (direct lending between one bank and a corporate) or if a large amount is required it can be on a syndicated basis (where a group of banks lend to a corporate).

Long-term facilities in excess of seven years are usually on a case-by-case basis. The basis will vary in response to market conditions.

Multi-currency advances. There are occasions when borrowing can be done more cheaply in foreign currency, although this should be done on fully covered basis, by the use of hedging instruments.

A straight loan may also incorporate a number of options such as:

- Acceptance credits – bills drawn the by company on the bank.

- Commercial paper – a company's issue paper that is bought by an investor – not necessarily committed.

- Eurobonds – principally the source of fixed-rate bonds.

Interest rate/currency swaps – companies can structure their medium-term interest rate so that it caps term debt portfolios in line with specific objectives and policies. Interest rate/currency swaps and interest rate caps may also feature.

9.3 Bank Medium-term Lending Criteria

Much will depend on the bank's perceived creditworthiness of the corporate. The bank will look at the relative size of the loan in relation to amounts, maturities, and the currencies required.

The objectives of the bank in lending medium to long-term finance to a corporate are as follows:

(a) *Adequate return.* This means not just the return on the margin but that arrangement fees and commitment and/or facility fees will give a bank a return commensurate with the risk.

(b) *Assurance of repayment.* The bank's risk assessment to the customer's future cash flows to service the facility will be critical to the deal with longer-term facilities being seen as riskier propositions by virtue of the increased uncertainty in projecting cashflows in later years.

9.4 Structuring of Facilities

The corporate can combine a fee and pricing structure and this will be subject to negotiation between the bank and the corporate. The corporate could also want variations of facilities of which, say, 50% is on a committed basis – the rest being on an uncommitted basis. Banking facilities can also incorporate options to include issuing Sterling and EuroCommercial Paper back up lines in case of a sudden need for capital injection by the corporate. The construction of interest payment dates, documentation, and tax must be considered by corporate treasurer who will negotiate these terms with the bank.

Security on assets is something that very large corporates will not want to give to banks but they may give security if the bank were to significantly reduce the interest margin. This is a matter for negotiation between the bank and the corporate. Facilities provided to smaller and non-corporate borrowers on the other hand are ordinarily subject to the provision of security.

9.5 Medium-term Debt Management

When companies are formed, an initial investment of equity is made. Subsequently, a company's operations can be financed by retained profit, debt or further issues of equity.

Debt does not provide permanent financing, as equity and profit can do. Debt must be repaid and interest costs must be met within an agreed period. Debt providers have the right to repayment independent of the company's profitability. They do not, however, have any proprietorial rights.

There are a number of aspects that corporate treasurers should consider in formulating policies and strategies in relation to medium-term debt. All corporate bankers should also understand them in relation to the negotiations or the relationship that the bank has with a given corporate. The treasurer will consider:

- the company's objective (why debt rather than equity?);

- the company's debt capacity (the optimum level of debt for the company, and the maximum level of debt it can support);

- methods of control (is debt to be centralised, or do subsidiaries, especially overseas subsidiaries, have power to raise debt locally?);

- retaining the balance between fixed and floating rate debt;

- the currency of debt (what if desired currencies are not available?);

- the maturity profile (can a smooth run-off of debt be achieved?). Whether the debt has long enough maturities to enable long-term planning to take place;

- whether debt facilities should be obtained from a variety of sources (to ensure that funding is not concentrated);

- whether committed medium-term standby facilities considered necessary/available;

- what is required by way of security, covenants and documentation by the providers of funds;

- what is required/desired by way of maintaining relationships with banks and investors.

9.6 Medium-term Libor Loans (Variable Rate)

9.6.1 Definition

This is a medium-term facility linked to inter-bank rates, providing committed finance over a specified period, which is tailored to suit the individual borrowers' needs. (There are obvious similarities in this and the short-term LIBOR loans.)

9.6.2 Features: Facility Type

A medium-term LIBOR loan (variable rate) is a facility which may be on a loan or a revolving basis. It is provided by the lender on a fully-committed basis which gives the borrower the assurance of funds and availability at drawdown, plus the comfort that repayment will not be demanded throughout the agreed term (provided breaches in conditions as specified in documentation do not occur).

9.6.3 Benefits to the Borrower

Medium-term commitment by the lender means that the borrower has certainty of funds when required. This may be an essential consideration to the borrower, depending on his needs, eg property developers need the assurance of funds to see the project through to its conclusion, and therefore the point where cash will be generated.

This facility may be available either in revolving or straight loan form, to suit the borrower's need and the purpose of the facility. It is therefore flexible as to the purpose, and particularly useful simply as a "standby" facility in the event that other, perhaps cheaper, alternatives are unavailable to the borrower at the time funds are required.

When drawings are made, the rate of repayment interest on the fixture (usually one-, three- or six-month periods) is based on short-term inter-bank rates which are generally lower than medium-term rates.

The facilities are "committed" by the bank, which guarantees to provide funds in the currency in which the facility is denominated, usually for fixture periods of up to 12 months.

There is flexibility in the facility, in that rollovers for other than the "standard" inter-bank periods of one, three and six months can be arranged.

There are a number of other benefits, including the following:

- drawings can be made in a wide range of currencies;

- other lending centres (usually overseas) can be incorporated into the facility;

- the facilities can be tailor-made to the funding requirements of the borrower;

- the option to draw by means of (sterling) banker's acceptances can be written into the facility;

- the facility can be used as a "standby facility" in support of borrowing from other sources or to meet unforeseen contingencies.

9.6.4 Limitations

Short-term interest rates may have increased significantly at the time a company is obliged to borrow. Currencies and fixture periods beyond 12 months are subject to availability. However, banks will usually commit to provide a specified range of currencies and can indicate the current availability of longer-term fixtures. The bank may also wish to restrict the number of currencies drawn at any one time. Where the full amount of the loan is drawn in currency, and the sterling (or base currency) equivalent at the time of rollover, is higher than the amount of the facility the excess will have to be repaid – usually only if it is more than 5% of the facility amount. Finally, financial and other covenants may be required by the lender.

Care needs to be taken with:

- value dates (same day for domestic sterling, spot, ie two business days ahead for eurocurrencies);

- whether interest is calculated on a 360-day year (as is usual for the euro and other eurocurrencies) or a 365-day year;

- the frequency of interest payments, the likelihood of producing higher costs on an annual basis; and

- any other fees and expenses payable which increase the overall/true cost of borrowing.

10

MANAGEMENT BUY OUTS

10.1 Definition of a Management Buy Out

'Management Buy Out' (MBO) is the term applied when a business is sold to the existing management team. Often this occurs when large companies seek to dispose of parts of the business or when the existing owner-manager is looking to retire. The existing management are often the people in the best position to take the business forward as they have expert knowledge of the company and its workforce. Strategically, they also present a more favourable option to the existing owner than selling to a competitor or closing down the business. The main problems for the MBO team will be securing the necessary finance. MBOs generally require more capital than a start up/expansion scheme. This should be contrasted with that of a Management Buy In (MBI), which is where a group of managers from outside the business join together and make an offer for the company to its owners. This approach may of course be rejected by the owners but it is likely that the buy in-team will have selected the target company carefully. MBIs are more risky than MBOs and a good example was Lowndes Queensway which collapsed in 1992. A Leveraged Buy Out (LBO), is where very high gearing is employed in excess of a ratio of 5:1 and were popular in the 1980s but many such ventures collapsed under an unserviceable degree of debt. In general, after an MBO the management's aim will be to reduce the gearing as rapidly as possible through operating cash flow and disposal of under-utilised assets.

For an example of an MBO, see Unit 25, Case Study 7.

	SFLGS	SLAS
Per cent of guarantee		
New businesses	70%	70%
Established business	85%	85%
Amount of guarantee		
New	5000-100000	5000-30000
Established	5000-250000	5000-30000
DTI premium		
Fixed interest rate	0.5 %	0.5 %
Variable rate	1.5 %	1.5%
Capital repayment holiday	Max 24 months	6, 12 or 24 months
Drawdown	Instalments	Lump sum

Thus, a new business seeking a loan to purchase a retail outlet could receive a loan guarantee of up to 70% of the purchase price (up to £100,000) and make no capital repayments for two years. This obviously helps the venture to bed down. From a lender's point of view it has been able to lend to a viable project which would otherwise have been rejected for lack of security.

10.1.1 Principal Features of an MBO

Usually, an MBO is an acquisition involving existing management but recently there have been instances where the management team of a publicly quoted company buys the shares held by the public. Management will obtain a meaningful equity stake and there will generally be other investors such as venture capitalists. Funding involves a high degree of leverage and for the MBO to be succesful the underlying business must be capable of generating sufficient cash flow and profits to service the finance raised for the acquisition.

10.1.2 Key Criteria for an MBO

There are certain key criteria for the MBO to be succesful and also these criteria will also determine the price to be paid in an MBO. Firstly, there must be a strong and highly motivated management team who are prepared to invest their own money. Secondly, there must be strong cash flow and hence capable of supporting a high degree of leverage. This in turn must determine a realistic buy-out price to ensure a satisfactory investment return. Finally, there must be exit potential through flotation or trade sale within three to five years

10.1.3 The MBO Structure

Once a price has been established the structure of the MBO must be determined as to how much should be raised by way of equity capital and what amount by way of debt. Again what will be crucial is the ability of the underlying business to generate cash flow to service and repay debt. There are certain legal restrictions to be overcome concerning the prohibition of a subsidiary giving financial assistance to a parent company for the purchase of the subsidiary's shares. It is therefore usual that an MBO will involve the formation of a new company which is used as the vehicle to purchase both the shares and assets of the business that is being sold.

Senior debt is so called because it ranks ahead of all other types of finance in the structure in terms of safety. It carries the lowest risk and as a result has the lowest reward. Mezzanine debt is subordinated debt in terms of repayment, as it ranks behind that or senior debt, but there is a higher reward for the lender in terms of the interest rate charged.

Assumptions

(1) Pre-tax earnings of £10 million

(2) 10% per annum earnings growth over three years

(3) Mezzanine providers receive a warrant of 10% (yielding aggregate return of 24%)

(4) 50% of senior debt repaid from cash flow over three years

10.1.4 The Ideal MBO Target

An ideal MBO target would have the following characteristics:

— Proven and adequate management resource

— Stable, positive cash flow

— High asset backing

— No major investment needs

— Low-tech

— High market share

— Mature market

— Little dependency on customers and suppliers

— Low level of vulnerability to other economic factors

10.1.5 Exit Routes

A key component of any MBO is in how the equity investors are going to realise their investment. This can arise as a result of any of the following exit routes:

1. Redemption of the shares by the MBO company itself.

2. A trade sale or takeover of the MBO company by another company.

3. Going public by obtaining a quotation on the Stock Exchange or the Alternative Investment Market.

10.2 Management Buy Ins (MBI)

'Management Buy In' (MBI) is the term applied when an outside management team buys a stake in an existing business. Typically, this happens where the business is under-performing due to weak management or lack of suitable expertise or where the business growth demands a more knowledgeable and experienced management team. The MBI enables the business to inject the depth of experience it requires and the new managers share in the future profits they generate. The emergence of the MBI has occurred over the last decade or so. In this situation, a group of managers within a sector identifies a business which they believe has growth potential in their hands. They persuade a venture capital fund (a fund set up by venture capitalists or fund managers to which investors subscribe in anticipation of making gains if the venture is a success) of the merit of their strategy and the two parties then make an approach to the existing owners of the business to acquire it. Again a majority of debt is used in the financing structure to leverage (or increase) the potential equity returns when the growth is achieved.

Many small and medium-sized enterprises find themselves hampered by a lack of security to offer a lender – especially early in their existence, and this can often cause problems when they want to expand. One way in which the Department of Trade and Industry has addressed this problem (as growing SME's are a major economic driving force) and will provide security to the lender is by way of either the Small Firms Loan Guarantee Scheme (SFLGS) or the Small Loans Arrangement Scheme (SLAS). These loans (and the guarantees) are typically for between two and seven years and are only made available for new borrowing. The major restriction is in relation to buying into a company or partnership. As a further assistance the facilities can be made available via capital repayment holidays. The loan will be with a lender and interest needs to be negotiated as normal. It is important to note that the SFLGS and SLAS are only available for small loan amounts, nor are they available to fund share purchases.

For a sample MBI, see Unit 25, Case Study 6.

11

PERFORMANCE BONDS AND SIMILAR CONTRACT GUARANTEES

11.1 Introduction

The purpose of contract guarantees (or standby letters of credit as they are also known), is to place a bank or insurance company between the parties to a contract so that one party of the contract may claim payment directly from the bank without any need to rely on the other party's willingness or ability to pay. Contract guarantees are common in international supply and construction contracts, usually to be provided by the supplier/contractor when he makes his bid and to be converted into a performance bond if his bid is successful. In the event then of the supplier failing to complete satisfactorily the contract the buyer may claim on the bond.

11.2 What are Bonds and Guarantees?

There are occasions when a corporation finds that its own willingness to enter into a contractual (or otherwise legally binding) obligation to make a payment in certain circumstances to one of its customers or to some other organisation is not enough. The other party is looking for the corporation to provide it with absolute assurance, through the introduction of a third party of undoubted financial strength – normally a bank or an insurance company – which will substitute its promise for that of the company and which can be trusted to make the payment if the circumstances arise. To that extent, bonds and guarantees are very similar to the letters of credit used as a payment mechanism in the course of international trade. Indeed, the letter of credit form – which clearly describes the circumstances in which the paying bank is to make payment and which has the benefit of a set of standard conditions of practice which are recognized throughout the world (the International Chamber of Commerce's Uniform Customs and Practice for Documentary Credits) – is often used where bonds and guarantees are called for. This is particularly the case where there is a requirement for issuance by a US bank, such banks being constitutionally unable to issue guarantees.

11.3 When are Bonds and Guarantees Needed?

Most commonly, a corporation will find itself involved with bonds and guarantees if its business involves it entering into large, long-term contracts. For this reason, bonds and guarantees are frequently referred to as "contract bonds". Similar arrangements may, however, arise in any number of areas which may involve corporations other than those involved in contracting. The following are just two examples.

Carnet bonds. Where goods have been imported temporarily into a country on which duty would be payable if the importation were permanent, the customs department may require a bank guarantee under which the import duty can be claimed if the goods are not re-exported within a certain time limit.

Guarantees in lieu of payments into court. In some jurisdictions, where a payment into court is required or desirable in the course of litigation, it may be possible to substitute a bank guarantee for the actual payment.

These demonstrate an important principle which will be easily recognised by corporates. It is better to keep one's hands on the money for as long as possible, even if one has to pay it over later. In all normal circumstances the interest saved through possession of the money will outweigh the cost of providing the bond or guarantee.

11.4 Types of Contract Bonds

11.4.1 Tender (bid) Bonds

Tender bonds are intended to ensure that the customer's time is not wasted during the tender process by considering bids frivolously submitted by bidders who have no intention or capability of carrying out the work. Each contractor responding to a tender request will be invited to submit a tender bond for a small percentage of the bid value (usually 1–5%). If the bidder does not do so, the bid will be invalid and will be ignored. When the customer has selected the winning bid, unsuccessful bidders will have their bonds returned. The bid winner will be expected to proceed to sign the contract and undertake the work. If he does not, however, the customer will be entitled to claim the amount of his bond.

Since one of the contract conditions which has to be fulfilled will be the provision of other contract bonds, the bidder will be well advised to line up the issuers of those bonds before submitting his tender.

11.4.2 Advance Payment Bonds

On large contracts, significant advance payments are often made on the contract becoming effective. These payments, which can be for as much as 15% of the contract value, may be intended to help with the contractor's mobilisation costs. In exchange, the contractor provides advance payment guarantees under which the customer can reclaim the advance payments if the contractor fails to proceed with the contracts.

11.4.3 Performance Bonds

Performance bonds are given at the start of contracts, normally for 10% of the contract value if the "bank" bond (see below) is being given. These bonds remain in force unreduced through the construction period and sometimes to the end of the maintenance period. The purpose of performance bonds is to give the customer an instrument for obtaining quick and clear redress for damage suffered if the contractor's performance has been poor.

11.4.4 Retention Bonds

As an additional protection for the customer, contract terms normally allow for retentions, whereby 5% or so of all contract payments are held back by the customer and are paid to the contractor only at the end of a maintenance period, when any defects have been identified and corrected. The contractor will normally press for contracts to allow retention bonds to be provided instead. Ideally, such bonds will be issued at the time that the first retention would have been made, and automatically increase in value as each subsequent payment is received. Some clients, however, may decline to accept the bond and to release the retention until the maintenance period starts to run.

11.5 The Structure of Bonding Arrangements

There are two basic forms in which contract bonds may be issued. These must be carefully distinguished since they have very different effects.

11.5.1 "Bank" Bonds

Bank bonds simply lay down that, in certain clearly-defined circumstances, the provider of the bond will pay a sum of a defined maximum amount to the beneficiary of the bond. All tender bonds, advance payment guarantees and retention bonds will take this form, as will many performance bonds. They are called, generically, bank bonds but, in practice, this type of bond may be issued by an insurance company. The key feature is that the bond is purely a financial arrangement. If the laid-down conditions for payment are met, the bond provider will have no choice but to make the payment. In deciding whether to provide a bond for a contractor, the provider of the bond will be concerned primarily with the contractor's financial standing, ie his ability to reimburse the bond provider for the amount of any money paid out under the bond.

11.5.2 Surety (Default) Bonds

Surety bonds are a traditional form for the provision of performance bonds by surety or insurance companies. They are particularly common in North America. The bond may have no set financial value (though it usually will have a limit), since the surety is guaranteeing to the customer that, should the main contractor fall down on his performance under the contract, he will complete the contract himself (by employing another contractor) or will pay whatever expense the customer is forced to incur in putting the faulty work right. Before deciding to issue this type of bond, the surety company has a wider range of concerns than the provider of a bank bond. The surety company will want to examine the contract to see whether it is likely to go wrong, and to look at the contractor's expertise in performing that type of contract, as well as his financial resources.

Most of the problems concerned with contract bonds arise under the "bank" bond form of arrangement.

11.5.3 Legal Structures

The provision of contract bonds creates a legal structure which is separate from, but parallel to, the underlying contract which lays down the necessity for the bonds. Figure 1 shows how the provider of the bond enters a relationship with the contractor's customer. This relationship, if the bond is later called, involves the bond provider in making a payment to the customer. There is also an agreement – the counter-indemnity – between the bond provider and the contractor under which the contractor undertakes to reimburse the bond provider should the payment be made under the bond when effectively the client must reimburse the bank. There are essentially two categories of bonds namely "First demand" or "on-demand bonds" which are called by simple request or breach and conditional bonds.

Figure 11.1 The relationship between the bond provider, contractor and customer

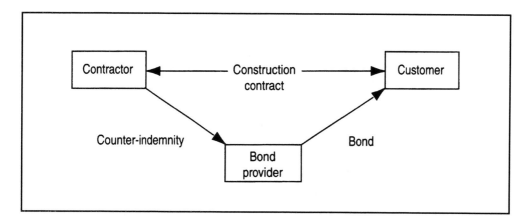

The structure may, in practice, be considerably more complicated for any of several reasons.

11.5.4 Requirement for a Local Bank Issuer

On overseas contracts, the contract conditions may lay down that the bonds have to be issued through one of a strictly limited number of local banks. The contractor probably has no previous relationship with this bank which might have neither the skill nor the inclination to assess the credit implications of its taking a counter-indemnity direct from the contractor. The contractor is then forced into using a double-bank structure whereby he makes arrangements, with an international bank, for that bank to instruct the local bank to issue the bond against the international bank's counter-indemnity. This latter document is in a standard format requiring automatic reimbursement of the local bank if it makes payment.

Figure 11.2 Double bank structure

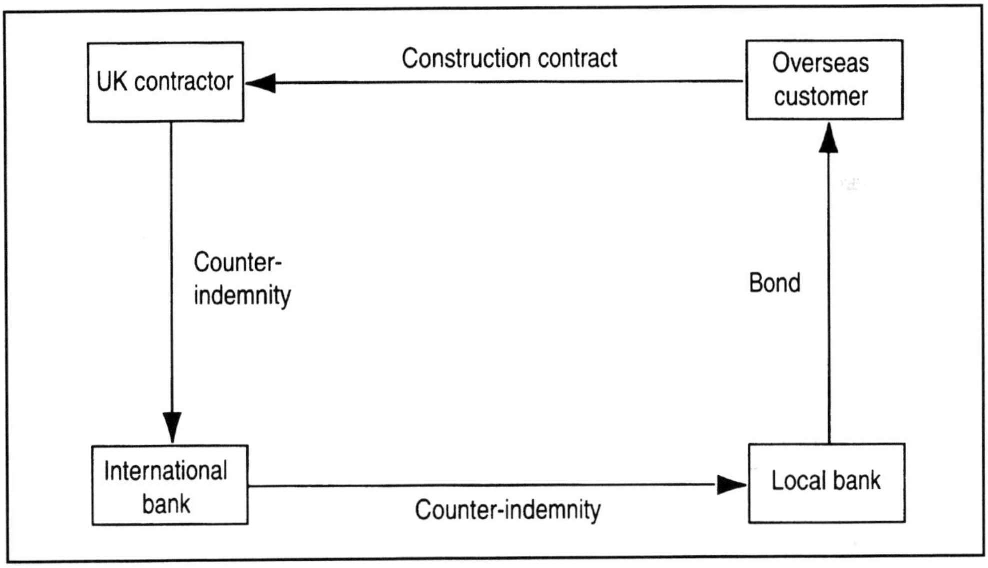

The structure is inevitable but it has disadvantages:

- *It is more expensive.* Unfortunately the local bank being isolated from the pressures of the market place tends to charge heavily for its services (often over 1% pa) even though it has the benefit of an undoubted counter-indemnity.

- *It is difficult to control the form of bond being issued.* It is not unknown for a contractor, having carefully negotiated a bond wording in a special form and having instructed his international bank to instruct the local bank to issue the bond in that form, to find that the local bank has issued a standard form.

- *It is difficult to control the situation if the customer calls the bond.* Where the bond has been issued by a friendly international bank it will always, in practice, discuss the situation with the contractor before making any payment. Where the bond has been issued by local bank, payment may well have been made to the customer before the contractor hears about it.

11.5.5 Requirement for "Several" Counter-indemnifiers

Joint ventures between a number of contractors are common. In such circumstances, the contractors often want to split the responsibility for the counter-indemnity down into their separate shares so as to control their total bond exposure. In this case they ask the bond provider to accept one "several" counter-indemnity from each joint venture member each for its joint venture share. As long as the bond provider considers each joint venture member to be equally creditworthy there is no problem. If, however, one member is weaker than the others, the bond provider will probably insist on a single counter-indemnity under which the joint ventures take "joint and several" liability.

Figure 11.3 A single counter-indemnity with joint and several liability

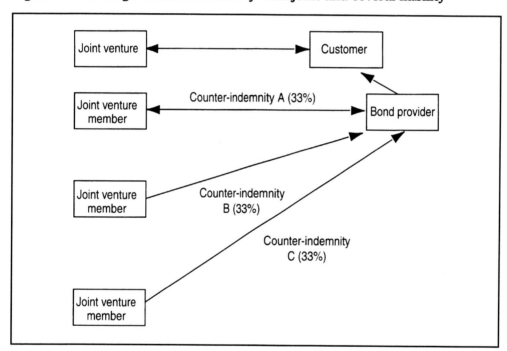

11.5.6 Building-in the Requirement for Sub-contractor Bonding

On a large contract, a contractor always employs a number of sub-contractors who undertake particular parts of the work on the contract. Plainly the bonds provided by the main contractor cover the work undertaken by the sub-contractors as well as his own work. He will, therefore, seek to obtain bonds from the sub-contractors framed in precisely the same terms as those he has to give. Then, if the sub-contractor's failure to perform leads to a call on the main bond, the main contractor can claim in turn on the sub-contractor's bond.

Figure 11.4 Sub-contractor bonds

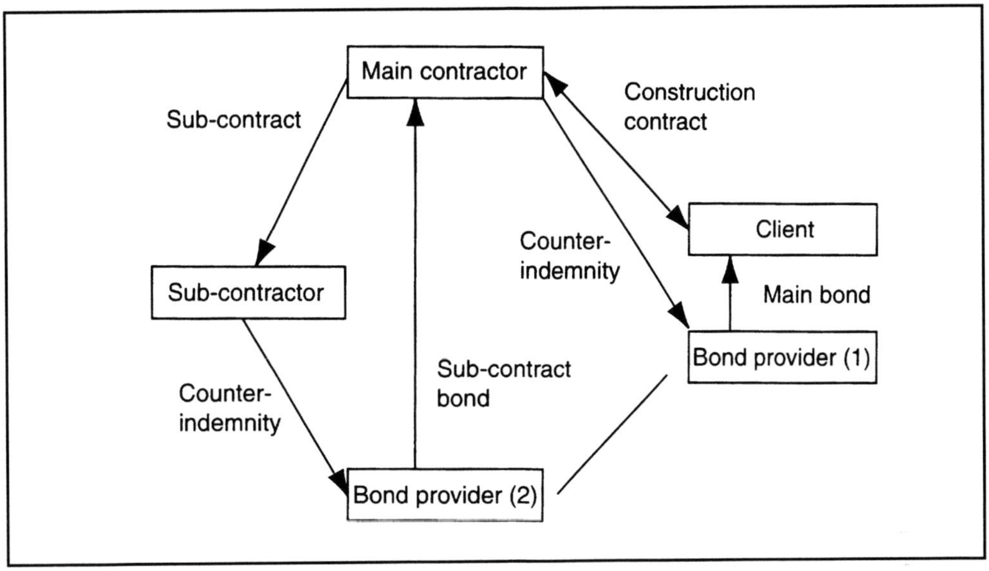

11.5.7 The Relationship Between the Bonds and the Underlying Contract

The bond arrangements provide a set of legal agreements which can survive independently of the main contract. Even if the contract is terminated by the contractor in accordance with its terms, the bond and the counter-indemnity may survive and the bond may be called if the conditions for call which are laid down within the bond are capable of being satisfied.

However, this does not mean that the main contract does not cover the provision and calling of the bonds. Indeed, ideally, the contract will lay down: what bonds are to be provided; their precise format; and the circumstances under which the customer is able to make a call under the bond. It is very important that the contract is clear on these points – not because the contract is brought into consideration when a call for payment is made by the customer on the bond, but because the contractor may retain rights under the contract if the customer can be shown to have departed from the procedure laid down by contract.

11.6 On-demand Bonds

On-demand bonds are bonds whose wording states that the bond amount is payable to the beneficiary of the bond on his first demand without the need for any evidence of a breach of the underlying contract. The corporate will readily appreciate that providing such a bond is the same as providing his customer with a bankers draft, which he may cash whenever he chooses.

11.7 Conditional Bonds

These are bonds which provide that the beneficiary must meet some condition before being able to claim payment under the bond. The introduction of this condition is plainly designed to protect the contractor against calls when he has not in fact breached his contract. It should be noted, however, that an attempt to make direct reference to a breach of the underlying contract will probably fail. The bank issuing the bond will want the circumstances in which it is to make payment under the bond to be clearly defined. Wording which says that the bond is payable "only if there has been a failure by the contractor to perform under the contract" will not be acceptable to the bank. It will not want to have to go deeply into the situation on the contract to make a subjective judgment as to the state of play between the parties.

Plainly the contractor will try and negotiate bond wordings in a conditional form. In the UK it is generally accepted as unreasonable for the customer to expect on-demand bonds. Overseas the position is different. In some countries, where contracts for public sector customers are involved, on-demand bonds in a set format are a non-negotiable requirement of doing business. It is for the contractor to consider his attitude to on-demand wording of bonds on a country by country, customer by customer basis. He may choose to set himself stronger rules against providing on-demand bonds to private sector than to public sector clients. Even here, however, he may find himself limited in his ability to negotiate by the fact that on-demand bonds are laid down in the documents provided at the time of tender. At such time he will have limited negotiating ability being only one of several tenderers. If he qualifies his tender on the subject of the form of the bonds, he may be disqualified from the tender, if he does not, he will be considered to have accepted the bonds.

12

ALTERNATIVE FORMS OF FINANCE

12.1 Factoring and Invoice Discounting

12.1.1 Factoring

Factoring involves the purchase from a company of some or all of its trade receivables with or without recourse to the company itself in the event that the receivables are unpaid. The factoring service may also involve the sales ledger administration for the company. Designed to aid a company's cash flow, factoring is mainly used by small companies where the ability to sell receivables immediately for cash can be vital.

12.1.1.1 Features of Factoring

- The customer gets immediate access to a cash injection which may otherwise not be received for some months. The factoring company can make available up to 80% of the invoice value to the seller. The balance will be paid over as soon as the factor receives payment from the buyer/debtor.

- Cash flow can be easily predicted.

- Finance available grows with turnover and, therefore, is available to fund rapid sales growth.

- The administrative burden of collecting debts can be lifted if the factor is running the sales ledger and chasing up payments.

- Even if advances are not drawn from the factor by the seller, debtors will usually pay promptly on invoice dates if they know they are dealing with a factoring company, thus speeding up cash flow.

- The customer enjoys the benefits of the factor's credit assessment techniques. The factor reserves the right to handle certain business. However, in general, the factor will wish to cover all a company's sales to get a good spread of risk because it guarantees the seller against buyer insolvency up to an agreed limit providing that it is on a non-recourse basis. Non-recourse is where the factor cannot seek to recover any losses from the corporate in the even of a debtor default. The factor's customer can therefore trade safely in the knowledge that he will be free from bad debt losses.

Factors normally expect to cover a minimum turnover of £100,000 per annum. Each debtor will be given a credit limit, which must be respected.

- As the factor purchases the debtor upon payment of the 80% of the invoice to the seller's customer it will become clear that the money is now due to the factor directly. For this reason, historically, some sellers have been reluctant to go down a factoring route as it can be seen by their customers as a sign of financial pressure in having to utilize a factoring, rather thank an overdraft, facility.

- Factors (and invoice discounters) are unlikely to factor a receivable where this has arisen as part of a larger contract (for example a stage payment due on a larger contract or a monthly payment for an annual servicing contract). The reason being that be payment could be subject to dispute after the factor has advanced the 80%, should the seller fail to meet their future obligations under the contract.

- Particularly when exporting, factoring enables the seller to offer open-account terms which increases his competitiveness in the local market and protects him against exchange risk if invoicing in foreign currency. Factoring can also aid the exporter by providing a service that allows credit checking and collection of overseas receivables, possibly in locations in which the exporter has no previous experience and few contacts.

- UK factors are also able to provide factoring services to overseas companies exporting to the UK. These services are usually provided through a correspondent factor based in the exporter's country. While UK factors can provide services directly to exporters selling into the UK market, it is normal that such factoring arrangements would relate to the "service" element only, the financial facility not normally being available to overseas companies.

- UK importers also gain considerable benefit from overseas suppliers factoring their exports to the UK because they will receive open-account terms which save them the time and expense of arranging letters of credit or making payment on delivery. All accounting communication is taken care of within the UK, making payment for imports virtually as simple and straightforward as purchasing from a UK source. See 12.3.1.1 for further details on open account terms.

- Charges for factoring:

  (a) interest on finance provided (although they do tend to be higher than conventional overdraft facilities, which has, historically, made customers reluctant to go down this route); and

  (b) management fees for sales ledger administration, credit management and collection of payments. This will vary depending on the number of accounts, the number of invoices processed and the type of customers. The management fee, typically between 1–3% of turnover, has to be weighed against the time, resource and financial savings offered

In *Re Brumark* (2001) it was held that a company's freedom to deal with any charged assets without the consent of the holder of the charge, was characteristic of a floating charge, under which the company is free to deal with the proceeds of the uncollected book debts, and therefore factor debts, for its own benefit. However, the company's freedom to deal with charged assets under a fixed charge would be subject to the approval of the charge-holder and therefore the company could not factor debts subject to a fixed charge.

12.1.2 Invoice Discounting

Invoice discounting involves the discounter advancing the seller a proportion (usually 75% maximum) of a debt, upon receipt of a copy invoice. The seller issues his own invoices and receives the debtor's payments directly, thus not revealing to his customers that he is using a discounter/factor. The buyer pays the seller as per the invoice, and the seller then repays the advance to the factor. The administration fee for this service is much smaller than for factoring because sales ledger administration is not included in the fee, but bad debt insurance can be provided if necessary. The factor will wish to vet all debtors and the minimum turnover for an invoice discounting agreement is normally £500,000. The service is particularly popular with exporters.

Note: In normal circumstances factoring or invoice discounting facilities should replace the need for an overdraft as funds will be held ahead of the need to pay suppliers. As cheques are received from the factor, the overdraft limit should be reduced. If the bank holds security, it will be asked to postpone its charge over debts to the factor/invoice discounter. It is the current view of some banks that they would not lend behind invoice discounting.

12.2 Asset finance

12.2.1 Hire Purchase (or Lease Purchase)

- Utilized when a company does not wish to use cash to purchase new assets.

- Available from bank subsidiaries, or independent HP (hire purchase) companies.

- Repayments normally set at a fixed figure over periods up to ten years.

- Interest rates fixed at the time the loan is agreed.

- Balance sheet treatment – hire purchase appears on the balance sheet of the lessee. The equipment appears as an asset and the amount owed appears as a liability.

The customer is usually expected to make a payment of 10-20% of the cost of the asset. The remaining sum (plus interest) is budgeted for via fixed monthly, quarterly, half-yearly or annual repayments. With regard to tax, the interest part of the repayments is chargeable against profits and a writing-down allowance (WDA) on the capital sum is available as soon as the initial deposit or first repayment is made. See further 12.2.3.

12.2.2 Leasing (or Contract Hire)

Leasing is the rental of an asset for a specified period of time during which the party having the benefit of the use of the asset pays a rental to the owner of the asset. The lessor is the owner of the asset, who receives a lease rental payment for the lease of the asset. The lessee is the user of the asset. A broker may act as an intermediary who may match the lessor and lessee. The two basic forms of leasing contract are operating lease and financial lease (or finance lease).

12.2.2.1 Operating Lease

Length of an asset's proposed usage may be uncertain (it may be less than the life of the asset) or the expected use of the asset may be limited. A lease is normally, therefore, more cost-effective than purchasing. The lessee normally has the additional safeguard that should the equipment fail to function correctly during the agreed period, the lessor will replace or repair it at his own expense, or alternatively that the contract may be terminated. Documentation may also state that operating leases may be terminated by either party upon giving the required notice.

Two common examples of an operating lease are for computers and construction plant equipment. Computer equipment leasing helps to protect the lessee from the effects of equipment obsolescence, because the contract may be easily terminated. With industrial plant equipment, the lessor will often hire out the plant to a construction firm, for example, for use on a specific project.

Operating leases and the assets they relate to are not shown on the lessee's balance sheet. Hence operating leases do not affect gearing and are "off balance sheet".

12.2.2.2 Financial Lease

A financial lease covers the whole life of the asset and cannot usually be cancelled by either party. The two parties to the lease agree on an estimated lifespan for the asset, and the rental is fixed on this time period. If the lifespan of the asset exceeds the agreed period, the rental payments after that time will be reduced to a nominal sum. This sum remains in force until the asset eventually ceases to function, or until the asset is sold with the agreement of both parties.

It is a long-term source of finance because, to all intents and purposes, the lessee assumes all the benefits of ownership and thus uses the financial lease as an alternative to outright purchases.

Balance sheet treatment – a financial lease appears on the balance sheet of the lessee. The equipment appears as an asset and the amount owed appears as a liability. Finance leases may include a nominal final payment, upon which equipment is transferred to the direct ownership of the customer on the lease expiry (when resale value is negligible).

12.2.2.3 Pricing

The price of a lease is normally included as an amalgam of the interest, overheads, expected tax benefits and profit. Pricing is also linked to interest-rate expectations and the risk of the lessee. An operating lease gives potential for further profit because the asset may be re leased. The lessor does, by contrast, face the risk that the resale value of the equipment is lower than the original estimate.

12.2.3 Taxation, Capital Allowances and Leasing

A writing-down allowance (WDA) may be claimed, when an asset is purchased which can then be charged as depreciation to the company's profit and loss account, whether the asset is directly purchased or held under a finance lease. The WDA effectively reduces the amount of tax paid by the owner of the asset. Clearly this is an important factor in the lease/buy decision, depending upon whether the company making the investment decision expects to pay corporation tax over the period for which the asset is required. WDAs, of course, change depending upon the latest government's budget directives.

If the company is liable for corporation tax, and it purchases the asset outright, it will claim the WDA, thereby reducing the amount of corporation tax actually paid. However, if there is little likelihood of the company paying corporation tax (the tax paid by a cororate on its taxable profits) over the relevant future period, then the WDA would be of no use, and would not feature in its investment appraisal. Here it may be better for the company to lease the asset, and it may be presumed that the leasing company (the lessor) will claim the WDA to offset against its own corporation tax liability. This tax saving is then likely to be reflected in the lease payments agreed upon.

It may still, however, be cheaper for a company to lease equipment, rather than purchase outright, even if the company pays corporation tax. The decision to purchase or lease will be taken after a full investment appraisal, probably using discounted cash flow techniques. In the case of operating leases, there are no writing down allowances for the corporate, but the costs of operating leasing are an expense item in the profit and loss account.

12.2.3.1 Leasing Applicability Check List

- Tax position – if your customer does not pay tax, leasing is probably the best method of acquiring plant and machinery.

- Type of machinery and usage – if usage is uncertain and if the machinery could soon become obsolete, operating leasing is the best method.

If neither of the above applies, ask your customer for details of expected net cash inflows to be generated by the machine over its life.

12.2.3.2 Finance Terms and Conditions for Leasing

- The minimum amount must be £5,000. If the equipment costs less than this, it is not worthwhile or profitable for the deal to be arranged.

- The client must be capable of meeting the rental payments. The leasing subsidiary will evaluate the proposition in a similar way to a bank's evaluation, but the leasing company can be more "flexible" because:

  (a) the lessor can repossess the leased asset in the event of default; and

  (b) lessors have more expertise than banks in estimating the forced-sale value of machinery and finding buyers for repossessed machinery. In a "marginal" case when a bank may not grant a medium term loan, a leasing company may grant a leasing facility.

12.3 International Trade Finance

12.3.1 Finance for Exporters

There will generally be higher risks for businesses engaged in overseas trading. For example, it will be more difficult to sue overseas debtors or suppliers (due to jurisdictional differences in law) should things go wrong and there are potential political and exchange-rate risks. Although the bulk of the finance for importing and exporting is still by means of bank overdrafts, there are several other ways of financing international trade.

The terms and method of payment in international trade are agreed between the exporter and importer in their contract. The terms required by the exporter will depend very much on previous experience, if any, of the market (including the degree of competition between other exporters for the business), the customer and the customer's financial standing. Due to the extra risks involved in international trade, the exporter will be even more concerned about the degree of security in the payment, the speed of its transmission and the costs involved in receiving it.

The main methods of obtaining payment, in increasing order of security from the exporter's viewpoint, are:

(a) open account;

(b) bills of exchange and documents for collection;

(c) payment under a letter of credit; and

(d) payment in advance.

Obviously, the order is reversed for importers, who will prefer open account and would wish to avoid payment in advance.

12.3.1.1 Open Account

Where an exporter is dealing with a first-class overseas buyer, goods are often despatched on an open-account basis. The exporter will send the documents of title for each shipment direct to the buyer and request settlement by a certain date. This is similar to the way in which credit sales are made between businesses within the same country, provided that the business's credit standing is seen as satisfactory. The only difference in international trade is that the distances involved are greater, the documentation is more involved and it is more difficult to pursue payment. The disadvantage for the exporter of open-account trading is that control is lost of the goods and the title to them. Therefore, it is advisable to establish the business integrity of overseas customers. Importers, however, prefer open-account trading, because it allows them to receive and inspect the goods (and perhaps even sell them) before making settlement.

12.3.1.2 Bills of Exchange

A bill of exchange is a means of payment used by companies to finance trade transactions. It represents an unconditional payment order for a fixed amount either at sight or at a fixed or determinable future date. The drawer of the bill (the exporter) is able to obtain money in advance of payment by the drawee (the importer), through either discounting or negotiating. Discounting is where selling is done on a modest discount to a third party who will hold to maturity and receive payment from the importer.

12.3.1.2.1 Exporting with settlement by bills of exchange

An exporter can transact his business in several ways.

1. He can export the goods and send all documents to the importer, together with a bill of exchange. The importer than accepts the bill of exchange and returns it to the exporter, who may then ask his bankers to collect the proceeds, or to discount or negotiate the bill of exchange.

2. He can export the goods, but send all documents to his banker with instructions for the documents to be released against payment, or to be released against acceptance of a bill of exchange payable after a certain term. If the documents are complete and give a good title, the goods would provide additional security so long as the documents are to be released only against payment. If the documents are released against acceptance of a bill of exchange, the goods will then be obtained by the importer.

3. He can ask the importer to arrange for a letter of credit to be established in this country whereby he can obtain payment or have a bill of exchange accepted by a banker upon presentation of stated documents.

Sometimes exporters consider that there is little risk to a banker in discounting bills of exchange, if the exporter holds a credit agency policy (issued by the Exports Credits

Guarantee Department or an investor such as Trade Indemnity) that is assigned to the bank. This can certainly strengthen the position, if the exporter is reliable and experienced, but if any of the conditions of the policy have not been observed, there will be no valid claim. This type of security falls far short of a bank guarantee.

12.3.1.2.2 Discounting and negotiating bills of exchange

There are differences between discounting and negotiating. If a bill of exchange in sterling is discounted, the resultant amount is also in sterling. If a bill of exchange in foreign currency is converted to sterling and then the sterling is discounted, the resultant amount will also be in sterling. However, an additional transaction will have taken place – ie the conversion into a different currency.

If in the second instance the bill of exchange is dishonoured, and recourse to a customer is invariably obtained by a banker, who will charge the customer with the sterling equivalent of the bill at the rate of exchange then ruling and not the rate ruling at the time the bill was negotiated. Except under the credit agency shorter-term schemes for bills and notes, bankers do not normally discount or negotiate bills of exchange of longer than six months' tenure.

A banker can discount or negotiate an unaccepted bill of exchange with recourse to the drawer. Once the bill of exchange has been accepted by a third party, a banker would have a claim on both the drawer and the acceptor. This could give the bill more substance, but a banker would prefer to rely upon his own customer of whom he has knowledge.

Bills of exchange can be drawn to be payable at sight or at a number of days after sight or date. It must always be kept in mind that bankers take the precaution of retaining recourse against their customers. This is the starting point when considering the liabilities that may have to be faced by a customer.

12.3.1.2.3 Advances against bills of exchange

An exporter with a bill of exchange, instead of asking his banker to discount or negotiate it, can ask for an advance to be made, prior to maturity, of less than the face value of the bill. The bill of exchange can be accepted or unaccepted, have documents attached or be clean. Similar considerations will apply as for discounting and negotiating. In the case of an advance, however, the liability of the customer on recourse would be less than when the full value is discounted or negotiated. The bills will be assigned to the bank as security. In addition, the bank will also take status reports on the drawees. Also it will make sure, if possible, that the goods involved are re-saleable, together with assignment of any credit insurance.

12.3.1.3 Documentary Credits

Bankers can lend to valued export customers, who are utilizing documentary credits. The bank must be certain that the customer can meet all the document criteria and will maintain full recourse to the customer. For further detail, see 12.3.2.1.

12.3.1.3.1 Smaller exports scheme

Banks can provide "non-recourse" finance, under an umbrella policy held by the bank, for customers with a low export turnover. The bank will, in effect, negotiate bills drawn by customers for exporters. If the customer has fully carried out the export transaction, the bank's policy will pay out if the bill is not paid. However, if the customer has not complied with the commercial contract or the policy rules, the bank will reserve the right of recourse to the customer. The main issuer of short-term exporter policies (up to two years), is NCM Ltd, which took over from the Export Credit Agency (ECGD) in this field.

12.3.1.3.2 Medium-term supplier credit

For longer terms of supplier credit (usually for capital exports), of between two and five years, the ECGD will guarantee to refund the bank up to 85% of the transaction if it provides finance. A 15% deposit from the buyer is taken in advance.

12.3.1.4 Payment in Advance

For the exporter, payment in advance is undoubtedly the safest way to receive payment for goods. However, from an importer's viewpoint, it is the least acceptable. Buyers are seldom prepared to pay in full for goods in advance of shipment, unless for small consignments, eg spare parts, since the buyer is not only extending credit to the supplier, but relying on the integrity of the exporter to deliver the goods in a satisfactory condition on the agreed date. It is more common to find that the buyer is prepared to pay a cash deposit in advance, with the balance being settled by another method.

12.3.1.5 General risk considerations when lending to exporters

(a) What is the credit status of your customer?

(b) What is the status of the exporter's customer?

(c) Are there political risk implications?

(d) Are any credit insurances available?

(e) What is the spread of buyers?

(f) Are transit risks insured?

(g) Can security of goods be taken as fall-back position?

(h) Have exchange-rate risk management techniques been considered?

12.3.2 Finance for Importers

12.3.2.1 Documentary Credits

An importer can arrange for his banker to establish with an overseas bank a credit in favour of a third party upon which payment is to be made, when certain specified documents are presented. If a complete set of documents is insisted upon, a good title to the goods can be obtained and the bank will therefore have the goods as security.

If an importer is unable to get the goods shipped to him on open account, he may have to establish documentary credits, and these involve him in a liability to his banker. The importer has some protection, because the money is not paid away until documents showing shipment are produced. However, the documents purport to represent certain goods, and the goods have not been examined. An importer will, for his own protection, have to assure himself of the integrity of the exporter. Also, if a banker is relying upon the goods in any way as security, he will have to satisfy himself that the importer has ability and experience of the trade. If other security is not available, a banker would have to decide to what extent he would rely upon the goods and ask for any shortfall to be deposited in cash on a margin account, before the documentary credit is opened. By issuing an irrevocable letter of credit, therefore, a bank is conditionally guaranteeing a customer's trade debt.

12.3.2.2 Acceptances

Just as an importer can arrange for his bank to tell a correspondent bank overseas to pay an overseas exporter, against the production of specified documents, so too can arrangements be made for a bill of exchange to be accepted when specified documents are produced.

As far as the importer's banker is concerned, he would be in the same position as with a documentary credit up to the time he released the goods to the importer. At that time, however, he would have given up the security of the goods, but would still be liable to the bank abroad on the bill of exchange, which would be presented for payment at the end of its tenor.

If other security was not available and a banker wished to retain the security in the goods he could either:

1. warehouse the goods after having them pledged to him and release them against payment (or part of the goods against part payment); or

2. in suitable cases, after the goods had been pledged to him, release them to the importer on a trust facility. The importer would then have to keep the goods separately, and account to the bank for all sales made. The proceeds of the sales would be credited to a separate banking account to meet the liability on the bill of exchange at maturity.

This type of facility should not be confused with the acceptance credits that are provided for exporters by merchant bankers. The exporter draws a bill of exchange on the merchant banker and produces the export documents. The merchant banker accepts the bill of exchange, which can be discounted immediately, and then collects payment against delivery of the documents.

12.3.2.3 Indemnities and guarantees

Indemnities and guarantees are often encountered in importing and exporting. In order to assess the liability involved every indemnity or guarantee has to be examined for amount, circumstances under which payment is to be made, and the period of time for which it is intended to last. Where importing is concerned, bankers are often asked to give indemnities because of missing bills of lading. A banker's liability will be the amount of the value of the goods, although this will be difficult to establish because the shipping documents are missing and he can only accept the importer's word. It is necessary, therefore, for the importer to have built a good relationship with its banker and to have audited accounts sufficient to justify the banker accepting these liabilities on his behalf.

12.3.2.4 Avalizing

Avalizing involves adding the lender's name to a bill or promissory note on behalf of the drawee, giving the effect of "guaranteeing" payment. An importer is therefore able to get his bank to guarantee a debt unconditionally to an overseas (or domestic) supplier.

As with finance for exporters, banks lending to importers must be fully aware of the risks involved. Again, currency risks should not be overlooked and should be covered if appropriate.

12.3.2.5 Bonds and guarantees issued on behalf of customers

UK exporting customers, usually those dealing with large or capital goods, are often asked to provide various forms of bonds or guarantees to the purchasers of their goods or services. The bonds will be either conditional (requiring proof before calling) or unconditional (payable on call without proof being required). The bonds will be for varying percentages of the overall contract. As contingent liabilities, they need to be assessed against the customer's lending capacity. In all cases counter-indemnities will be taken from the customer to enable the bank to debit the account immediately if a bond is called upon. A counter-indemnity should always be taken from the customer if the bank is to enter into any bonds or guarantees.

The recommended gradings of the various types of bonds and the associated risk are:

	Risk %
Tender or bid bond	20-100
Performance bond	100
Advance payment bond	100
Progress/retention bond	100
Maintenance/warranty bond	100
Stand-by credit	100

Before joining in a bond or issuing a guarantee, you must ensure that the customer is creditworthy and has a covering limit for the facility and that the document is in an acceptable format. If in doubt refer to the bank's legal department.

12.5 Forfaiting

12.5.1 Forfaiting

Forfaiting is a facility available to exporters (although also being increasingly used for domestic transactions) who want to provide non-recourse credit to their overseas buyers. It is mainly used for capital goods transactions, but can also be used by exporters of raw materials and commodities.

Forfaiting works by the forfaiter purchasing, without recourse to the exporter, bills of exchange or promissory notes that represent the payment for the goods. The credit period is generally between one and five years, with the bills being drawn usually at six-month intervals. The forfaiter buys the bills at a discount and then relies totally on the overseas importer to obtain repayment. Because there is no recourse to the exporter the forfaiter will wish to be absolutely sure that the overseas buyer will pay. Thus, the ideal transaction is where the buyer is a "blue chip" company or a government agency. Where this is not the case, the forfaiter will normally look for the bills to be unconditionally guaranteed (avalized) by the buyer's bank.

12.5.2 Countertrade/barter

Countertrade is the sale of goods or services to a country, where part or all of the settlement for the goods is in the form of an agreement to buy goods/services from that country. It is most commonly seen where exporters are dealing with countries that are short of foreign exchange, for example, Eastern Europe. There is no generally accepted code of practice in respect of countertrade contracts, and there can be significant variations between one country and another.

12.6 Equity Finance

One of the cheapest forms of finance for any incorporated business is to borrow funds from its shareholders. When buying extra shares, the shareholder is effectively lending to the company in perpetuity. Equity financing is cheap for the following reasons:

(a) the cost of this finance is the dividend paid by the company. This depends on the level of profits made by the company, the level of reserves and the dividend policy of the directors. The directors are under no obligation to pay any dividends, although the share price will not respond positively to non-payment of dividends; and

(b) the company is under no obligation to buy back the shares – effectively repaying the loan.

In a private limited company, the extra investment might never be repaid but in a public limited company the shareholder has the option to sell their shares on the stock market on which the shares are listed. Such a sale may be at a profit or a loss. Under current tax legislation (as at 2002/03) the returns in these cases can be tax efficient.

12.6.1 Types of Equity

This section will focus specifically on UK equities, taking a look at the various forms that shares can take. Remember that an equity investor is actually purchas-ing a share of the company and as such the holder will be entitled to certain rights which can vary depending on the type of share in question.

12.6.1.1 Ordinary Shares

Ordinary shares usually form the core of a company's share capital and the holders are commonly given the following rights:

- to appoint/remove directors;

- to receive dividends, provided such have been declared and any higher ranking holders have received theirs;

- to exercise one vote per share at company general meetings;

- a holder's liability is restricted to the fully-paid value of shares held, therefore in the case of partly-paid shares the holder's liability is the payment outstanding;

- in the event of the company being wound up, once all other prior claims have been settled, any assets remaining are distributed to ordinary shareholders on a *pro rata* basis in line with respective shareholdings.

The ordinary shareholders carry most of the financial risk since there is no guaranteed return, and in the event of financial disaster they may be unlikely to receive anything by way of distribution. However, the main attraction to the investor is the possibility of potentially very high rewards, subject to the financial prosperity of the company, and that a degree of control, at least, is available through voting rights.

It is typical of the various classes of shares available that the rights and obligations of holders may vary to some degree depending on the requirements of the company. Such rights and obligations will be stipulated in the company's Memorandum and Articles of Association. A common practice, in this respect, is conferring different voting rights on different holders, for example by issuing "classes" of ordinary shares ("A" Ordinary, "B" Ordinary). While the existing shareholders may thus be able to retain a greater level of control over the company's affairs. By issuing shares with either low, or even no voting rights, we must remember that this type of share is less likely to attract the equity investor.

12.6.1.2 Preference Shares

As the name implies, a preference share affords at least some differential treatment on its holder, compared to the ordinary shareholders. The "preference" refers to the priority such holders have over others in connection with the right to dividends and to obtain distribution of any assets to the value of the amount paid up, if the company is wound up. Normal voting rights are not usually associated with preference shares, although such holders will be entitled to vote in certain specified instances. For example, where dividend arrears occur or where the company is being wound-up.

Preference share dividends are at a fixed rate and may be *cumulative*, ie any arrears have to be settled in full before dividends are paid to ordinary shareholders. In the case of *non-cumulative* preference shares no such right is available to holders and therefore unpaid previous dividends need not be met in future years.

Another variation is the *participating* preference share which provides the holder with a fixed dividend element plus the opportunity to benefit further from sharing any additional surplus profit remaining in excess of the preferential amount agreed, with the ordinary shareholders.

Ordinary shares are almost issued as permanent equity, however, it is possible, although not very common, for preference shares to be *redeemable*. In this instance the nominal value will be repaid by the company either on a predetermined future date or within a specified future period.

Cumulative preference shares, in particular where these are redeemable and subject to a planned profile of repayment, are more akin to debt than equity and should be treated as such when determining the gearing of a company and its ability to service its debt liabilities.

12.6.1.3 Convertibles

There are essentially two types of "convertible" share. First, and least common, are convertible preference shares which may be converted to ordinary shares in certain circumstances. More often, though the term "convertible" relates to a debt instrume. gives the lender/ investor the right to convert to ordinary shares (or possibly prefe shares) in the future, for example convertible bonds. Conversion will be at the hole option, with the option period running between specified future dates. During the per leading up to conversion the holder will be entitled to interest (dividend) at a specif fixed rate.

12.6.1.4 Warrants

Warrants are usually associated with debt issues and are "attached" in a similar way to the conversion option, as outlined above. The warrant is effectively the right for the holder to purchase a specified number of shares at a predetermined price, either on a stipulated future date or between two future dates. The warrants themselves clearly have value and hence may be traded as separate instruments to the underlying loan stock.

12.6.1.5 What Type to Choose?

Think about the various characteristics of all the above and identify the main benefits/ disadvantages of each to the issuer.

12.6.1.5.1 Ordinary Shares

(i) *Benefits*

- Readily acceptable to investors as to the most common form of equity.

- No commitment to pay dividends.

- May retain voting control by restricting holders' rights (although this may prove unattractive to investors).

(ii) *Disadvantages*

- Loss of control follows when voting rights are given (which is most common).

- Investors regard such a high risk and will expect return to reflect this, particularly if the company is making good profits.

12.6.1.5.2 Preference Shares

(i) *Benefits*

- No loss of control, given the usual absence of voting rights, except in certain circumstances.

- May be more attractive to the investor as there is a known level of return, assuming profits are sufficient.

- May be redeemable/cumulative/non-cumulative to suit the company's needs.

he rate fixed may prove exceptionally good value in the future, if market rates
se and profits are high.

antages

Commitment to pay dividends at a pre-determined level.

Cumulative preference shares give the right to holders to have arrears met in full
from future profits.

It may prove expensive to set the rate of return at an acceptable level to attract
investors.

1.5.3 Convertibles

Benefits

- By giving an option to convert, the investor may be more likely to accept a lower
  initial return on the loan stock, in anticipation of making a gain on conversion.

- May prove attractive to overseas investors, being an alternative source of
  financing for the issuer.

(ii) *Disadvantages*

- May be expensive if the investor is able to convert at a price well below the
  market rate (ie it may well be more beneficial to obtain straight debt finance, but
  at a higher cost, and raise equity to repay, also at the higher market price
  prevailing – assuming the market moves that way).

- Some investors may have a preference for either straight debt or straight equity.

- Uncertainty as to timing of conversion, if the "between two dates" exercise
  period is allowed.

12.6.1.5.4 Warrants

(I) *Benefits*

- May be useful in keeping down the cost of the underlying stock.

- A means of combining debt and equity, ie the debt remains and new equity is
  raised (whereas with convertibles actual conversion from debt to equity takes
  place).

- The warrants themselves have trade value.

(ii) *Disadvantages*

- Uncertainty as to take up and timing.

— Overall true cost may prove more expensive, in the same way as for convertibles.

These various forms of equity are available from two broad sources. First, there is the *"private"* injection either from the proprietors or a third party such as a bank. The second source of equity are the *"public"* markets, such as flotation on the stock market.

12.7 Franchising

Franchising occurs where the owner of a successful business expands, not by the traditional means of opening more outlets and employing more staff, but by selling the right to use the business name and idea in a specific area to a third party. In return for a franchise fee, the third party gets a proven idea, product or brand together with the expertise of the franchisor in running the business. In addition, he or she may well benefit from national advertising and promotions. Probably the most successful franchise in the world is McDonalds. The advantages should be obvious. The purchaser of the franchise has all the existing marketing and brand loyalty behind him or her from day one. He or she has the in-built supplier chains. In return for providing these advantages and ongoing support and marketing, the franchisor will receive either a percentage of the profits or a fixed annual fee – or both.

Lending to buy into a franchise can be good business for a lender. The basic idea will be tried and tested. The normal pitfalls and dangers are often avoided – having already been overcome by the franchisor. Statistics suggest that franchise businesses are far more likely to succeed than stand alone start-up situations. This does not, however, mean that the normal lending considerations are ignored. Consideration of the standard criteria still needs to be undertaken, and passed.

The other side of the coin is when a customer is seeking to franchise his existing business. Although the business is successful, it is probable that the customer will require specialized assistance both in terms of finance and experience to launch a successful franchise. There are numerous magazines with details of established franchise availability. It would be beneficial to buy one and see how many household names are, in fact, franchisees. There are also advertisements from a wide variety of financial institutions offering support.

12.8 Stocking Loans

Here, as the term suggests, the bank is lending to enable a business to purchase stock. This is certainly a difficult situation, although often seen in relation to international trade,, Generally speaking, a business should be able to generate sufficient cash flow to restock as necessary. A possible scenario could be to enable a builder to purchase land which it will subsequently develop and sell. Another possible scenario would be an antiques dealer who wishes to buy a particular piece for which he already has a buyer. Here a short-term increase in an overdraft facility might be granted.

The lender may well agree to the stocking facility to generate cash to reduce an unsatisfactory position.

12.9 The Small Firms Loan Guarantee Scheme

The Small Firms Loan Guarantee Scheme guarantees loans from the banks and other financial institutions for small firms that have viable business proposals but who have tried and failed to get a conventional loan because of a lack of security.

Loans are available for periods between two and ten years on sums from £5,000 to £100,000 (£250,000 if a business has been trading for more than two years). SBS guarantees 70% of the loan (85% if a business has been trading for more than two years). In return for the guarantee the borrower pays SBS (Small Business Service, operated by the Department of Trade and Industry) a premium of 1.5% per year on the outstanding amount of the loan. The premium is reduced to 0.5% if the loan is taken at a fixed rate of interest. The commercial aspects of the loan are matters between the borrower and the lender.

The scheme is available to UK companies with an annual turnover no more than £1.5m (£5m if you are a manufacturer). Many business activities are eligible but there are a number of exclusions. Loans are available for most business purposes although there are some restrictions.

13

MONITORING AND CONTROL OF LENDING

13.1 Monitoring Facilities

Having granted the requested facility (of whatever nature) the bank cannot be complacent. Efficient and effective monitoring of lending is the best way to reduce bad debts because it reduces the number and value of loans and other facilities a lender must write off against profits. Essentially, monitoring account conduct is an easy procedure. With loan accounts a simple check that the monthly payment has been received will suffice. Overdrafts are more difficult to monitor. It might well be that the overdraft is within its limit but the limit might easily be hiding problems. How these be identified?

13.1.1 Compare With The Cash Flow Forecasts

A current account balance is not expected to agree exactly with the forecasted closing bank balance. The very nature of forecasting and business makes that an impossibility. However, a discrepancy of more than 10% may require further consideration.

13.1.2 Is a Hard-core Position Developing?

A reduction in fluctuation on a current account is always a clear sign that problems are beginning to surface. 'Hard-core' is described as any account which has been continually showing monthly average debtor balances which have been increasing over recent months, and where debt levels are at high levels and are rising to levels which may not be capable of being services by ongoing income levels. This may need to be corrected by a capital injection or consolidating borrowings on a loan account. Certainly the lender will want to speak to the customer and look at the current trading position. This usually involves looking at the management accounts of the business concerned. Lack of such accounts would be a real warning sign because this would suggest weak management.

13.1.3 Breaching of the Overdraft Limit

Most financial institutions have some form of out-of-order report. This report provides a list of accounts that will be overdrawn in excess of agreed limits at the close of business. The corporate lending officer needs to ascertain what items will cause the breach (some reports incorporate this information) and make a judgment as to what action to take.

Once the out-of-order position has been identified then consideration must be given as to how this might be regularized. This can be achieved by either returning (bouncing) a debit or having funds paid in to bring the account within the limit.

Before returning a cheque or standing order the following steps should be considered.

● Has the company contacted you or a colleague advising of the breach and making an agreement to restore the out-of-order position?

● What damage will bouncing do to the company's creditworthiness and reputation in the world at large?

● What is the debit for? It does no good to return a payment to a loan account the company has with you.

● Is the corporate part of a larger group of companies and the overdraft limit is only a nominal control limit. If this is the case the overall group position and group sanctioned limits checked before taking any action.

● Does the customer have credit balances on other accounts which can be set off? For example, if a customer has £10,000 in a deposit, it would be foolhardy to bounce a cheque for £150.

● Can the company be contacted? An item should never be returned without making every effort to speak to the customer.

The advantage of contacting the company is twofold. The company may be aware of the breach and is arranging for funds to be paid in to correct it. The breach may be a simple oversight and the company will again organize funds to be paid in later in the day.

The second benefit is that if the company has no explanation for the excess and offers no plans to regularize the situation, then the bank can tell the customer that it will be returning the item. This leaves the corporate in no doubt as to the proposed action and will often change his position. Even if he does not, then at least the corporate has a chance to warn the payee and attempt to limit the damage.

If the corporate customer cannot be contacted, you will need to inspect the corporate lending record and see whether any items have been returned before.

13.1.4 Are there Signs of Cross-firing?

"Cross-firing" or "kiting" is a means by which a customer abuses the clearing system to provide funds for his normal business activities where legitimate methods cannot be found. A bank will have systems in place to identify cross firing at an early stage; however recent events have shown that we remain vulnerable to substantial loss.

The vast majority of inter-account and inter-company transactions which pass through customers' accounts are quite genuine. They will have been correctly authorized, be carried out using cleared funds and be made for legitimate business purposes.

"Cross-firing" or "kiting" on the other hand constitutes a fraudulent act. It involves the systematic transferring of uncleared funds by cheque between two or more accounts in order to create the impression of a stronger financial position than actually exists. The accounts concerned may be held at different branches or banks and one or more connected counterparties may be involved. "Cross-firing" exploits the time delay in the clearing system and to be successful requires the banks involved to honour cheques against uncleared effects on an ongoing basis. It occurs where there are insufficient funds in an account to cover cheques, which have been drawn. The customer draws a cheque on a connected account at a different bank / branch and pays this into his account with his primary bank. This returns his account to credit, albeit on an uncleared basis. When, normally two days later, this cheque is presented for payment then the customer will draw a cheque on his other account to cover the position on the connected account.

Thus a cycle of cheques is created to ensure that the funds remain permanently uncleared. The value of cheques issued can spiral upwards as more funds are required to keep the business afloat. The cycle is broken where one of the banks in the cycle recognizes the situation and thereafter adopts a policy of payment against cleared effects only, or if the customer voluntarily stops issuing the cheques. Unauthorized borrowing will emerge on one or all of the accounts involved.

The following may indicate cross-firing:

- A rapid increase in turnover through the account with a corresponding increase in the level of uncleared effects

- Excessive turnover through the account relative to the level of balances held and the type of business.

- Customers paying in daily to cover cheques presented that day.

- Cheques payable to the drawers of cheques being paid into the account.

- Cheques for large, often round, amounts passing in and out of the account on a very regular, if not daily, basis.

- Increasing uncleared balance on a daily basis.

- Cheques are returned unpaid.

13.1.5 Is there Evidence of Overtrading?

The clearest sign of overtrading is an unexplained rise in both credit and debit turnover on an account. While on the face of things the increase in sales might seem a good thing – "more sales more profit" – often the business is selling faster than it can produce or restock, or selling more because of a decrease in prices. Although the business might be within its overdraft limit, care should be exercised. Those who run before they can walk invariably fall over. If overtrading appears a possibility, ask the customer for sight of the management accounts. As previously discussed these are up-to-date, although unaudited, financial statements eg Trading and Profit and Loss accounts, Balance Sheet, SORG (discussed further in Unit 3) and reconciliation statement. Included with statements should be an aged profile of debtors (crucial) and creditors (useful). If debtor days, creditor days and stock turnover are rising and gross margins are falling then overtrading is almost certainly happening. The best cure for this is to increase the capital in the business and/or restructure the facilities offered to the business.

Overtrading results from rapid expansion and potential failures can be difficult to detect as they are not necessarily 'problem accounts' and may, on the face of it, be successful businesses. Common characteristics of overtrading businesses are:

- Inability (or unwillingness) to raise long-term capital, therefore relying on short-term solutions such as creditors and bank overdrafts

- Debtors may increase rapidly as the principals extend generous trade credit in order to win sales

- Stocks build up as manufacturing output/purchases increase in anticipation of increased demand

- Working capital becomes inadequate to fund increased turnover

- Lack of financial information provided by the customer

- Management lose control of the business and are unaware that it is running losses and/or out of cash

- Management do not accept there is a problem and will continue expanding

- Management become preoccupied with survival rather than planning and strategy

Overtrading is therefore is characterized by rising borrowing and declining liquidity position, with management failing to detect/admit that resources are becoming overstretched. The main warning signs to assist in recognizing overtrading include:

- Frequent requests for increased facilities

- Frequent short-term emergency requests to the Bank, eg excesses to help pay wages pending receipt of a cheque

- Part-paying suppliers or other creditors – look for round amount cheques

- Paying bills in cash to secure additional supplies – look for large irregular cash withdrawals

- Exceptional cash generating activities e.g. offering generous discounts for early cash

- Management lose control of cheques returned unpaid, particularly for "Effects Uncleared"

- Become preoccupied with survival rather than planning and strategy

13.2 Control Action and Returning Cheques

Unexpected events can contribute to modify the hoped-for-trend of borrowing by a corporate banker which underlines the need for any corporate banker to continue to review all facilities. This review should be ongoing through regular discussions or through monitoring the corporates financial press.

A problem can arise through many events such as a corporate suffering through a decline in market share but often a banker will know that there is a problem when a repayment is missed or an overdraft limit is exceeded. On these occasions a banker must seek an explanation from the corporate and be satisfied that the excess is not an indication of deeper problems to come.

A banker may need to open discussions with a corporate and may need to consider the renegotiation of facilities with the corporate and/or the taking of additional security. The banker though needs up to date management accounts from the corporate to enable a sound evaluation of the financial position of the corporate.

The issue of a banker consider returning cheques should never be taken lightly by a banker to a corporate as this can often exacerbate a much deeper crisis especially if the cheques are written to suppliers or trade creditors. A bank returning cheques where facilities have been exceeded without looking at the overall position of the corporate is dangerous as it could precipitate the demise of a corporate and even undermine the value of any security that a bank may hold.

It cannot be emphasised more than in situations where a bank sees either excesses or breaches that they enquire and seek information from the corporate before considering doing anything else.

13.3 Management Accounts

The management accounts will enable the lender to confirm that the covenants are being observed and will also allow us to match actual performance with projected. Projections cannot always be exact, but they should be within certain tolerances. Indeed it may be a covenant that actual out-turn is projected +/− X%.

Despite covenants, despite management information, it is sometimes necessary to return items to control the spending of those who cannot control their own − this applies to individual as well as business borrowers. If we do not then a doubtful debt and even a bad debt may eventuate. These are both failures for lenders because they represent lost money and lost profit, which reduces the returns for investors in the lender.

Management accounts are considered so important today that their production on a regular basis is often a condition within the facility letter. It is probable that every business overdraft (certainly a very large business overdraft) will be linked to the level of debtors in some shape or form:

- eg the overdraft facility shall be £500,000 subject to 120% cover by debtors; or

- the overdraft facility shall be £500,000 subject to 120% cover by debtors less than 180 days outstanding; or

- the overdraft facility shall be £500,000 subject to 120% cover by working capital stock

The three covenants (promises by the company) get stricter as you read down.

For an example of where accounts can be used to establish additional control over a company's lending, see Unit 25, Case Study 3.

13.4 Money Laundering

Money laundering is the process by which money from an illegal source is made to appear legally derived. By a variety of methods, the nature, source and ownership of those criminal proceeds are concealed. The three stages of money laundering can be broken down as follows.

(i) *Placement* − the investment of the proceeds of criminal activity.

(ii) *Layering* − the mingling of the money from an illegal source with that from a legitimate source.

(iii) *Integration* − the withdrawal and usage of the now undetectable proceeds of criminal activity.

The consequence is that the origin of and entitlement to the money are disguised and the money can again be used to benefit the criminal and/or his associates.

The EC Directive on money laundering provides that all European Union member states should ensure that all financial and credit institutions located within the national member states should implement certain internal procedures and controls. In the UK this has been implemented through the Criminal Justice Act 1993.

The aim of those internal procedures is threefold:

(1) *deterrence* – to prevent credit and financial institutions being used for money laundering purposes;

(2) *co-operation* – to ensure that there is co-operation between credit and financial institutions and law enforcement agencies; and

(3) *detection* – to establish customer identification and record-keeping procedures within all financial and credit institutions which will assist the law enforcement agencies in detecting, tracing and prosecuting money launderers.

13.4.1 Individual liability

13.4.1.1 The offence

If any person knowingly helps another person to launder the proceeds of drug trafficking or criminal conduct, or to launder terrorist funds, he will be committing an offence.

13.4.1.2 The possible defence

It is a defence to the above offences that a person *disclosed* his knowledge or belief concerning the origins of the property either to the police or to the appropriate officer in his firm.

13.4.1.3 The penalty

The maximum penalty for any offence of assisting a money launderer is *14 years' imprisonment and/or an unlimited fine.*

13.4.2 Failure to report the offence

If a person discovers information during the course of his employment which makes him *believe or suspect* money laundering is occurring, he must inform the police or the appropriate officer of the firm, designated as such by his employers, as soon as possible. If he fails to make the report as soon as is reasonably practicable, he commits a criminal offence.

13.4.2.1 The possible defence

The only defence to this charge is if a person charged can prove that he had a *reasonable excuse* for failing to disclose this information. Whether an excuse is reasonable will depend on the circumstances of the case, but it is noteworthy that the person charged has the burden of proving that he had a reasonable excuse for his failure to disclose.

The relevant legislation specifically provides that any person making a disclosure of this kind will not be in breach of any duty of confidentiality owed to a customer.

13.4.2.2 The penalty

This offence is punishable with a maximum of *five years' imprisonment and/or an unlimited fine.*

13.4.3 Tipping Off: the Offence

If a person either knows or believes that the police are or will be investigating the laundering of the proceeds of drug trafficking, criminal conduct or of terrorist funds, that person *must not disclose to any third party any* information which might prejudice such an investigation. If he does so, he will commit the offence of tipping off.

13.4.3.1 The possible defences

It is a defence to this offence if the person charged can prove that he neither knew nor suspected that the disclosure would prejudice an investigation. Once again, the burden of proving the defence rests upon the person who has been charged with an offence.

13.4.3.2 The penalty

The offence of tipping off is punishable with a maximum of *five years' imprisonment and/or an unlimited fine.*

14

FACILITY LETTERS AND COVENANTS

14.1 Clauses in Loan Agreements/Facility Letters

1. Representations and warranties as to condition of the borrower.

2. Covenants to maintain that condition.

3. Default in the event of breach of warranty or covenant.

4. Security in event of failure of the borrower.

   (a) Warranties – conditions as to a valid contact.

   (b) Covenants – monitoring of borrower's condition.

   (c) Default – matters on which a bank can accelerate the loan.

   (d) Security – larger and more reliable credits usually lend unsecured but will have pari passu and negative pledge clauses.

14.2 Conditions Precedent

The purpose of conditions precedent is to provide a "list" of certain conditions which must be satisfied by the borrower (normally in form and substance satisfactory to the lending bank) before the lending obligation can be triggered.

The various conditions normally cover the following matters:

1. appropriate legal opinions and constitutional documentation which seek to ensure that the loan and any security, is valid and binding on the borrower in accordance with its terms and that the borrower has the power and all necessary authorizations to enter into the agreement;

2. that no events of default have occurred during the period between execution and drawdown under the agreement; and

3. the representations and warranties continue to be true in all material respects.

14.3 Representations and Warranties

Representations and warranties can be broken down into various groupings. The first are very similar to the conditions precedent in that they require the borrower to represent and warrant that it has legal status and capacity, etc, to enter into the underlying loan agreement (and any security arrangements in respect thereof) and that all relevant authorizations and permissions have been obtained in order to enable the borrower and/or any guarantor to enter into a contract which is legally valid and binding.

Examples of representations and warranties are as follows.

1. Power to borrow and authorized signatories.

2. Banks arrived with long on importance it attaches to the issue in question.

3. Standard warranties, ie validly incorporated, powers to borrow, powers to charge security, no litigation pending, approvals, consents, etc.

14.3.1 Evergreen Clause

An Evergreen clause is where the representations and warranties are repeated on drawdown or on rollover. The corporate treasurer may need to exclude some that are repeated.

14.4 Covenants

Covenants provide triggers which once breached give the bank the opportunity to re-negotiate the terms of a loan or in extreme circumstances request repayment. As such they are only appropriate for committed lines where we do not have the ability to request repayment "on demand".

14.4.1 Ratio Covenants

Financial covenants are frequently included in loan documentation and are designed to protect the lender's position should the borrower's credit-worthiness be deemed to deteriorate. Such covenants which often take the form of ratios require a flow of financial information from the borrower to the lender which enable the lender to monitor the borrower's financial health. Such covenants are given "teeth" by linking them to an event of default clause in the event that the covenant is breached. The essential problem of financial ratios is to make them meaningful and not too tight where they are continuing to be breached by the corporate or too loose to be of no value. Ratio covenants, if used properly, are a valuable tool in monitoring the loan and can enable the bank to convert a term loan to an on demand loan if the financial condition of the borrower deteriorates during the life of the facility.

Examples of ratio covenants are identical to those you have studied already in Unit 3 Financial Statements. These ratios will include the gearing ratio, an interest cover ratio, a minimum tangible net worth ratio and a cash flow to debt servicing covenant. Other ratios such as minimum liquidity may well be included which rely on calculating them to the figures contained in the financial figures that are made available by the corporate.

14.4.2 Material Adverse Change Clause

An alternative to ratio covenants is a continuing material adverse change clause which typically provides that it shall be an event of default in the event that there is any material adverse change in the financial condition of the borrower which the lender reasonably determines may impair the ability of the borrower to perform its obligations. Such a clause is obviously much less precise in its application and will not provide a monitoring function in the same manner as that provided by financial covenants which require a regular flow of financial information to be given to the lending bank.

The problem is one of definition in that what is material? What is adverse? Both are nebulous. The clause is used as a catch-all substitute for a ratio covenant.

Also in whose opinion determines the definition of "material"? If it is the bank then the reasonable opinion of the bank is likely to be rebutted by the treasurer.If on the other hand there is a materiality test, then this makes it a ratio covenant.

14.4.3 Negative Pledge

The negative pledge covenant is an attempt, in the context of an unsecured loan, to prevent the borrower from creating security in favour of third-party creditors which, if created, would prejudice the position of the unsecured lending bank.

A letter of negative pledge executed in favour of the Bank by an individual, firm/partnership, limited liability partnership ('LLP') or company is an undertaking:

- not to grant security over any of its/their assets;

- not to create a lien over any of its/their assets;

- not to grant any guarantees or indemnities; and

- in favour of any party other than the bank without the bank's written consent, although the bank acknowledges that the terms of the letter are not breached where this occurs by operation of law and/or in the ordinary course of business.

14.4.4 Pari Passu Clause

The pari passu clause is allied to the negative pledge whereby the borrower undertakes not to create any debt which on liquidation would rank for payment ahead of the bank. Therfore the effect of this clause is to ensure that the lending will rank equally with all other debt of the borrower with any lender.

14.4.5 Other Ratio Covenants

1. Interest cover for liquidity, poor cash control, ie current ratio used.

2. Capital gearing ratios, ie long-term borrowings to net worth.

3. Total borrowings/liabilities.

4. Operating cashflow.

14.4.6 Cross Default

Primarily this is a cross-default between two facilities offered to the same customer by the same banker (ie if an overdraft is called up then the loan becomes due irrespective of whether it is in technical breach). This is a clause in the event of default whereby if a borrower defaults under someone else's agreement then it is a default in their agreement. Therefore banks gain comfort and protection from other banks or lenders in events of one defaults by the customer. In this way it means the bank can demand immediate repayment if another lender declares an event of default. The borrower must however be aware of what is known as the "Domino Effect" whereby one default means all loans in default with all lenders.

14.5 Issues on Loan Documentation

14.5.1 Definition Problems of Covenants Generally

The problem with setting financial covenants in a loan agreement is in defining them. When you refer to gearing what do you mean: long-term or short-term debt or both? Whatever, the definition must be clear. Different accounting practice in different jurisdictions should also be borne in mind. Finally, a bank must set the ratio parameters at realistic levels. If the parameters are too loose, then the ratio covenants are not worth having.

14.5.2 Setting Appropriate Levels for Ratio Covenants

The bank will want to be in a position to act where there is time to rescue a situation. The risk may change during the term of the loan but bank should price the risk at the outset by relating this to the interest rate.

14.5.3 Negative Pledge

The negative pledge has already been explained at 14.4.3 but a lender must be aware that in taking any security from a corporate there is the possibility that another lender or bank has a negative pledge.

14.6 Other Clauses in Loan Agreements

14.6.1 Contra-disposal Clause

This is a clause where the borrower undertakes not to sell a material portion of its assets without seeking the consent of the bank. The problem is in defining material and it is usual to have a threshold – 20% to avoid working capital disposals. The clause could however be absolute. Disposal for value is key but bank could have power to ratify all disposals. Disposals could be used for reduction/settlement of loans and in some loan documentation this may well be mandatory. In short, there is therefore the dilemna of having flexibility as against the problem of materiality.

14.6.2 Dividend Restrictions

This is a clause prohibiting or restricting the distribution of profits if ratios are breached. It is a clause that is strenuously resisted by corporates. Companies may try to maintain dividends but the bank could disagree, which may affect the corporate's relationship with its shareholders.

14.6.3 Increased Costs

These are clauses to cover erosion in the bank's margin as a result of taxes, reserve requirements or illegality.

15

Bad and Doubtful Debts

15.1 Outline of Default

The lender's right to accelerate the loan, ie to declare all sums owing due and payable immediately and to cancel the commitment to advance further loans, is normally provided for in the loan agreement as the express remedy for an event of default. In the absence of express provision, the common law remedies of rescission for misrepresentation and repudiation for breach of condition will have the same effect, if available to the lender, as acceleration. Insolvency or liquidation of the borrower will constitute an act of default. A borrower's failure to make one or more payments when due would only entitle the lender to sue for these payments. In this type of action or in one following an acceleration, the lender is suing for a debt due which would include capital and interest due. He has a right to sue for damages for breach of representation or covenant but will only receive compensation for actual loss incurred, and only then if that loss was reasonably foreseeable when the contract was entered into.

15.2 What are Bad and Doubtful Debts?

So what are doubtful debts and bad debts? Most businesses sell goods on credit with the belief that within a short period of time the buyer (now technically a debtor) will pay for the goods purchased.

- Doubtful debts are those amounts owed that in the judgment of the creditor (eg lender) may not be repaid in full.

- Bad debts are those amounts owing that will definitely not be paid.

Once a doubtful debt has been identified, action must be taken to recover all (or as much as possible) of the debt. There are a number of stages in this recovery process.

For examples of where bad and doubtful debts have an impact on the lender's return on debt, see Unit 25, Case Studies 3 and 4.

15.3 Internal Remedies

15.3.1 Acceleration/Formal Demand

This is usually by means of a formal letter to a customer requesting repayment of the debt and the cancellation further commitments to lend within a specified timescale. It will also advise the customer of the potential remedies and actions open to the lender.

15.3.2 Set-off

Set-off is potentially one of the most useful remedies available in relation to loans or overdrafts as it does not involve court action. Terms of set-off may be incorporated within the terms of an international loan agreement; they also exist at common law subject to certain conditions being fulfilled.

The right to set-off depends upon the debt in question being due and payable; if it is not the borrower should be free to withdraw his funds. The loan agreement may make the disposal of assets or the commencement of liquidation an event of default so rendering the debt due and payable. In the event of an individual insolvency, s 164 of the Insolvency Act 1986 allows set-off against unmatured debts except those incurred after the lender knew of the presentation of a bankruptcy petition, similar rules are extended to corporate insolvencies (Companies Act 1985, s 612).

A deposit cannot be set-off against a loan unless the loan is due and payable.

Set-off is a useful remedy since it requires no court action by the lender, rather it is up to the borrower to take action to recover the seized funds. The classic scenario is the setting-off of a credit account against an overdrawn account under the same name with the same bank, but there are also further variations.

There may be a problem if set-off funds are set-off in another jurisdiction or in a currency not of the loan as the courts of other jurisdictions may not recognize a banker's right of set-off in the jurisdiction. Also the Companies Act 1985, s 395 states that such a clause may constitute a registerable charge (in the case of *BCCI (No. 8)* (1998)).

15.4 External Remedies

15.4.1 Freezing Orders/Mareva Injunctions

Mareva injunctions are more generally known as pre-judgment attachments. They are sought by a plaintiff who wishes to ensure that an early stage that, should he win his legal action against a defendant, there will be sufficient assets belonging to the defendant available to meet the court's award of damages and costs. In practice, the pre-judgment attachment immediately becomes an execution attachment on judgment. In England the conditions for obtaining one are that the plaintiff is likely to win his case at trial, that the defendant has assets in England which he is likely to render unavailable by the time of judgment, and there is a real risk he will fail to satisfy the claim and there is a balance of convenience in the plaintiff's favour (Supreme Court Act 1981, s 37).

15.4.2 Specific Performance

Specific performance and injunctions are discretionary remedies available to the court. The general rule is that these remedies will only be available if damages are considered to be inadequate. Further, they are not available if their effect has to be supervised or it would be futile to award them. Specific performance of an agreement to create a charge should, however, be available and an interim injunction to prohibit a threatened act by the borrower such as granting a charge contrary to a negative pledge covenant or the selling of valuable assets.

Therefore, English courts will not normally grant an order for specific performance where damages would be an adequate remedy or where the loan agreement makes provision for a more suitable remedy, ie termination and acceleration. The general rule is that they are only available if damages would be inadequate.

15.4.3 Prohibitory Injunction

English courts look more favourably on prohibitory injunctions, particularly those which would restrain the borrower from performing acts which are in breach of its obligations such as breaching the negative pledge or by selling assets.

15.4.4 Other External Remedies

These other remedies can be summed up as having:

(1)   the right to sue for *damages*;

(2)   the right to rescind loan agreement; and

(3)   the right to sue for unpaid amounts.

The court has power to award interest on a money claim but this is at the standard court rate and from the date of the writ only. A lender would normally insert a default interest clause into the agreement whereby a premium rate is charged for sums paid late and whereby the default interest may be compounded at intervals. Some jurisdictions, eg Germany, Switzerland treat an obligation to pay interest on interest as unenforceable.

A "remedies cumulative" clause in the agreement removes a possible argument that the express remedies are exclusive of common law and court-awarded remedies.

15.4.4.1 Agreed settlement

After receipt of an agreed settlement letter the customer often makes a proposal to repay some or all of the debt immediately or by instalments. If the customer makes such a proposal it should be treated very seriously. The prime aim is to get the debt repaid not to sue the customer. Legal action is always expensive.

15.4.4.2 Legal Action: England

15.4.4.2.1 Garnishee order

A garnishee order is an order freezing money owed to the debtor by another person. If the Debtor has money in a bank or building society account in excess of the amount owed under a judgment that money can be frozen and paid into court for the benefit of the judgment creditor. If the customer refuses to respond to the formal demand, or reneges on an agreed settlement, the option of a garnishee order should be considered. This order, granted by the court, freezes all the bank accounts of the debtor in the UK and enables repayment to the creditor to be made from the debtor's accounts. This does, however, pre-suppose that such accounts exist and are in credit.

15.4.4.2.2 Charging order

A charging order is a court order to enforce a county court judgment. If a creditor obtains a county court judgment because an individual did not pay a debt and do not keep to the payments of the court order a court can order a charging order to be placed on the individual's property. A charging order gives the creditor security for the debt, in other words the debt would become "secured" like a mortgage on a property or other land. The court allows a legal charge to be placed on the assets of the debtor. This means that when the asset is sold, funds must be remitted to the lender to discharge the debt before the asset owner receives the funds.

15.4.4.2.3 Execution of assets

Here the court orders that the assets to be sold to repay the indebtedness, and thus is done through bailiffs appointed by the court.

The last resort, is to seek the insolvency of the borrower. This is bankruptcy for individuals and liquidation for companies

15.4.5 Restructuring Corporate Debt

Restructuring corporate debt is an alternative to the bank using court procedures to enforce liquidation or to appoint an administrator. The bank's first consideration must therefore be whether it is possible and appropriate to save the company by restructuring it and consider the borrowing request in addition to profit forecasts, and the willingness of the directors to continue, the possible liability of the directors for *wrongful trading* (s 15 of the Insolvency Act 1986) and even of the bank as a *"shadow director"* on the basis that it is giving directions on the running of the company, eg to sell assets.

Restructuring may take a number of different forms:

(1) if the object is to *preserve cash flow*, the current debt may be deferred, converted into long-term *debt or into equity*. Altering the nature of the debt may jeopardise the bank's existing security, taking equity for debt may be prohibited and taking preference shares may make the bank an "associated person" (a person connected to the company).

(2) A *divestment* and contraction of business may involve exchanging debt for assets, a takeover of the business, a hiving-down (scaling back or reducing the operation) into a new company or a straightforward winding down or cessation of trading and sale of assets. Restructuring into a new company may avoid these problems as the new company pays cash for the assets then transfers the assets to the bank. Some other creditors may have to be paid off to permit this process. Termination of existing contracts may lead to an action by the third party for inducing breach of contract.

(3) *Joint action* with other creditors may be taken involving perhaps a sharing of security, providing new finance, an agreement to share future losses and profits and a sharing of equity. Where some creditors are bondholders (where the company has issued a Eurobond) this hinders action as they cannot be found in order to be brought into the negotiations.

Many restructured loans themselves face restructuring a little later in time. This need not indicate a failure, rather the first restructuring may serve as a softening-up process.

The court process may be used to bring a reluctant creditor into line or to administer the entire restructuring, although this will restrict freedom of negotiation. The role of the corporation's government may be relevant in making foreign exchange available, nationalising the company, limiting rates of interest payable, providing subsidies and even to legislate to permit a desired restructuring which would otherwise offend local law.

15.4.5.1 Corporate Restructuring – the process

The corporate should always plan ahead to avoid a default at all costs by ensuring that it has the right levels of gearing, the right financial structure, the right mix between short- and long-term debt. Also is there the right mix of floating and fixed rate debt and very important are back-up facilities adequate and are they reliable.

If the corporate then faces a severe crises the corporate should compile a worst case scenario of cashflow analysis to assess the situation and also for discussion with its bankers. The corporate's officers should have kept his few selected or core banks informed of the worsening situation. Most good banks will bear with a corporate with whom they have a good relationship if there is bad news providing they are adequately and honestly informed in time.

If banks are not informed adequately and honestly of the position the corporate may face a *siege situation* of disgruntled bankers clamouring for their money back. At worst, the interest of different groups of banks may diverge to the extent that one group of banks may decide to push for receivership as nearly happened to Laura Ashley in 1990. From this the lesson for corporates is to carefully select their banks with which they wish to do business with. Corporates who have borrowed from a large number of banks have found that non-relationship banks are more reluctant to co-operate, for example, in amending covenants in times of crisis. This underlines the fact that the corporates should develop close relationships with selected banks at an early stage and not wait until there is a need to refinance or restructure.

If, however, banks are genuinely and honestly informed of situation of the company's finances they are likely on the whole to be supportive. This process is the informal remedy of a consensual support operation as outlined by the Bank of England and known as "The London Rules".

If the corporate does get together with its banks then the first object may be to put in place a *standstill agreement*, which would give the corporate time to formulate a strategy to deal with the crisis situation. A standstill agreement is where the banks agree to standstill all of their borrowings at the date of default and also agree to take not action in taking any acceleration or enforcement against the borrower until the outcome of negotiations has taken place. The negotiating phase usually takes up to three months to complete. A solution will require the involvement of all the banks and the corporate will want to know that he is negotiating with banks who have the confidence in the corporate. Equally, the banks must have the confidence that they are receiving honest and regular information from the corporate and regular updates.

An all-bank meeting is likely to be called which will have the object of setting up a steering committee to handle the restucturing negotiations with the corporate. With the committee being composed of different bank's representatives, there are, however, problems of syndicate democracy and the question as to what decisions are made by the steering committee. The steering committee will also handle the negotiation of the standstill agreement. The steering committee should insist on the borrower disclosing such information to all banks.

Despite this there may be conflicts amongst the banks and between the corporate management who will be attempting to represent the interest of the shareholders, employees and creditors as a whole, whilst the banks have their sights on getting their money back. The corporate will need to present a refinancing plan to its bankers which will need to provide an incentive to them for continued support. What is crucial is to avoid giving a plan which initiates conflict between the various groups of banks who may feel they are being treated inequitably.

The corporate will need to use its own resources in helping with the refinancing together with their merchant bank advisors and also the help of their lead bank. There may be the necessity of having investigative accountants and the corporate may be required to give security especially if the refinancing plan requires new or additional financing. The corporate will probably have an increased burden in providing regular information to its bankers concerning the cash position and compliance with its covenants. It should be stressed that such information must be accurate.

Following the refinancing plan that will be negotiated between the borrower and the banks there will be new documentation for the restructured facilities.

15.5 Insolvency Procedures

15.5.1 Bankruptcy

A bankrupt is a person who has been deemed by the court as being unable to repay his or her debts. The person owed the money, the creditor, can apply (petition) for a bankruptcy order. In addition, in England and Wales, a person who has committed a crime and been tried in Crown Court can, if found guilty, be made criminally bankrupt. As a consequence of the bankruptcy order a trustee in bankruptcy will be appointed to realize and distribute the debtor's assets to repay the creditors. In effect this trustee takes over the financial affairs of the bankrupt and all such dealings should be made via the trustee.

The undischarged bankrupt has a number of restrictions that will affect the financial institution. These are primarily the prohibition from:

1. acting as a company director;

2. engaging in business;

3. holding public office, eg becoming a Member of Parliament; or

4. obtaining credit or borrowing money.

How should these restrictions be dealt with?

With a sole account, the account must be stopped and all dealings must be with the trustee. Note that the bankruptcy order means that *all* accounts are stopped. The personal account of Joe Bloggs and Joe Bloggs trading as Bloggs Car Services are both covered because legally there is no difference between the individual and his existence as a sole trader. With a joint account, the account is again stopped but the joint instructions of the trustee and non-bankrupt customer should be followed.

A claim for any unsecured borrowing in the name of the customer must be made to the trustee who will, after realizing the assets, make a payment – normally x pence in the pound – to all the unsecured creditors. If the customer had given security for the borrowing this must be realized before this payment. Any surplus is then paid to the trustee in bankruptcy and any shortfall is claimed on an unsecured basis.

Normally, dealing with the accounts of a bankrupt is reasonably straightforward and each organization will have a well-defined process laid down on how to proceed. The main problem is where an account for an undischarged bankrupt is opened in error. The undischarged bankrupt will have lost control of financial affairs, which control will have passed to the trustee. The trustee is obviously interested in moneys received after the bankruptcy because these may be due to the creditors. Indeed the trustee has the power to claim after-acquired property for up to 42 days. This would mean that any and all moneys paid in must be held in the account for 42 days and permission sought from the trustee before payment is made. In reality, this is impossible and the only sensible course of action is not to open accounts for undischarged bankrupts.

There have been several occasions when accounts have been opened for undischarged bankrupts who have not declared their status or who have used assumed names. If this occurs then, if the situation were ever discovered, the financial institution might, in some circumstances, be liable for having paid away after-acquired property. In such a case the financial institution would have to compensate the trustee on behalf of the creditors. Once the deception is discovered the account must be stopped and the trustee in bankruptcy contacted. The trustee may declare that he or she has no interest in the account and the financial institution could, if it wanted, continue to operate the account. However, given that trust and honesty is the most important element of the banker/customer relationship, it is most likely that the account would be closed.

Generally a bankrupt (other than a criminal bankrupt) is automatically discharged after three years and regains full contractual capacity. This means he or she can open bank accounts and again borrow money. The rule of law in the UK is such that, once "time has been served", the offence is gone and should no longer be considered. Should a lender ignore the fact of a bankruptcy when considering a loan request? Or should the fact that a person was at one point made bankrupt mean that he or she will never be able to borrow again?

15.5.2 Insolvency for Companies

A company does not have a finite life. This does not mean that it cannot die. Death for a company is called liquidation and is the corporate equivalent of bankruptcy. As with bankruptcy, a company can be wound up voluntarily by the members (shareholders) or by the creditors. In place of a trustee in bankruptcy a company will have a liquidator who will fulfil the same role. A compulsory liquidation ordered by the courts is also possible.

The insolvency regime pertaining to companies extends to a number of possibilities. A company may set up a voluntary arrangement, it may go into liquidation, it may go into administration and administrative receivers may be appointed to manage its affairs.

15.5.3 Liquidation

A company going into liquidation must be wound up. The winding up process may be voluntary or compulsory. A voluntary winding-up commences with the appropriate resolution at the company's general meeting of shareholders. A voluntary winding up will only be able to take place if the company is considered able to repay fully all its credtitors. If at any stage it becomes clear that the company cannot repay its debts then the voluntary winding up will switch to a compulsory winding up. The company must immediately cease to carry on its business, except for the purpose of a beneficial winding up (instigated by the company itself). A liquidator is usually appointed at the meeting and the powers of the directors cease on this appointment.

A compulsory winding-up consists of a court order to this effect. Seven different grounds for liquidation are set out in s 122 of the Insolvency Act 1986. The ground relating to insolvency states simply "the company is unable to pay its debts". This ground is established by any one of four alternative routes:

(a)   a statutory demand is served on the company and no payment is received within three weeks;

(b)   a judgment creditor attempts to enforce his judgment by having court officers seize the company's assets and insufficient assets are found;

(c)   the company is unable to pay its debts as they fall due; or

(d)   the company's liabilities exceed its assets.

The compulsory winding up commences with the presentation of a petition to the court. Sometime later the court hears the case. If the petition is dismissed, there is no winding up. If the order is made, however, the winding up is deemed to commence on the date the petition was presented.

Under s 127 of the Insolvency Act 1986, any disposition of the company's property *after* the commencement of the winding up is void, unless the court otherwise orders. It has been held that the effect of this is that payments by a company into its overdrawn bank account constitute a void disposition of the company's property, and also that payments out of a company's bank account constitute a void disposition of property.

Petitions to wind up a company are published in the *London Gazette* and it is important for a bank to search each issue for names of its corporate customers. Once the petition has been presented, the bank should not pay any more of the company's cheques. If it does so, the liquidator may later obtain a court order requiring the bank to repay the funds to him. The court is empowered, however, to sanction a disposition under s 127. A bank is likely to obtain this sanction retrospectively in two situations:

(a)   if it paid cheques after the petition was presented but before it was published; and

(b)   if the disposition did not prejudice the position of the unsecured creditors of the company.

To wind up a solvent company the directors swear a declaration of solvency stating that they can/will pay all creditors within 12 months. Followed within five weeks by a meeting of the shareholders (members) to adopt a resolution to wind-up the company: having the effect of placing the company in members voluntary liquidation: a liquidator is appointed who realizes all assets, and distributes funds within 12 months of the start of the members voluntary liquidation.

15.5.3.1 The bank's liability as a shadow director

Section 214 of the Companies Act 1985, dealing with "wrongful trading", empowers the court to make an order requiring a director to make a contribution to the assets of the company in the following circumstances:

(a)   the company has gone into insolvent liquidation; and

(b)   at some time before the commencement of the winding up, the director knew or ought to have concluded that there was no reasonable prospect that the company would avoid going into insolvent liquidation.

A shadow director is defined as a person in accordance with whose instructions the directors of the company are accustomed to act. The risk for a bank is that it will set out a rescue package for a financially troubled corporate customer. The company unsuccessfully follows the rescue plan, leaving the bank potentially liable for wrongful trading as a shadow director.

In assessing (b) above, a director is assumed to be a reasonably diligent person with both the knowledge, skill and experience that may reasonably be expected of a person carrying out the same functions as carried out by that director in relation to the company and the knowledge, skill and experience that that director actually has. Since it is the corporate entity of the bank which could be deemed to be the shadow director, the level of skill and experience that that director has would inevitably be considered to be very high. The level of knowledge about the company's finances would depend on the degree of access to the facts that the bank actually had, bearing in mind it was not a de jure (legally appointed) director sitting at board meetings. A (shadow) director will not be liable, however, if he took every step with a view to minimizing the potential loss to the company's creditors which he ought to have taken.

15.5.3.2 Liquidation processes

The order or ranking of payments made out of a liquidation is as follows:

1.   *Creditors with security* – the asset given as security will be sold and any surplus paid to the liquidator. Any shortfall becomes an unsecured debt. Banks often take fixed charges over assets, especially if they lent the company the money to purchase the asset.

2.   *Liquidator's expenses.*

3. *Preferential creditors:*

    - wages up to £800 per employee;

    - deductions collected from employees in respect of income tax or National Insurance;

    - Value Added Tax;

    - Social Security contributions;

    - any money owing under pension scheme arrangements.

4. *Floating-charge holders.*

5. *Unsecured creditors* – generally suppliers.

6. *Shareholders* – if there is any money left at this stage – which is unlikely – the preferential shareholders will get their funds back before the ordinary shareholders.

15.5.4 Voluntary Arrangements

Certain "schemes of arrangement" and "compositions" specific to companies may be made under s 425 of the Companies Act 1985. Individuals may execute a "Deed of Arrangement" under the Deeds of Arrangement Act 1914. All of these, however, are little used in practice and are not discussed here.

A voluntary arrangement under the Insolvency Act 1986 involves either a company or an individual making a proposal to creditors, whereby the creditors may agree to accept something less than full payment on their claims. They may do so as a voluntary arrangement, which avoids the considerable expense of a full bankruptcy or liquidation, and therefore there will be more funds available to pay the creditors. Voluntary arrangements can either be members voluntary or creditors voluntary arrangements.

Under a voluntary arrangement the debtor must appoint a licensed insolvency practitioner to act as a nominee. The court will be asked to make an interim order and a creditors meeting will be convened. If the proposal is approved by at least 75% of the creditors who vote at the meeting, it is binding on all creditors. Creditors votes are calculated according to the value of their debts. Once the proposal has been approved nominee becomes known as the supervisor and is charged with overseeing the implementation of the proposal.

The creditors will meet to consider the proposal and a decision is taken on a majority vote, with the result that some minority creditors may have the scheme forced on them. However, the salient point for present purposes is that this is not true of secured and preferential creditors, who must either be paid in full or individually agree to the scheme. If the scheme is approved, it is implemented by a "nominee" who must be an insolvency practitioner.

Voluntary arrangements can be used (under s 425).

15.5.5 Administrative Receivership

"Administrative receiver" is the term used in the Insolvency Act 1986 for a receiver appointed under a floating charge (distinguishing him from receivers appointed by the court and receivers of rent appointed under the Law of Property Act 1925).

The following discussion of the law relating to receivers is from a banker's point of view, in that much law which would not always concern the appointing bank (but which would concern a receiver) is excluded. Also it is assumed that a standard form debenture has been executed.

Administrative receivers can be appointed in England and Wales under a floating charge.

15.5.5.1 Appointment of receiver

Standard debenture terms will permit a bank to appoint an administrative receiver where it has made demand on the company and payment has not been forthcoming, or following some other default by the company. Where the bank has become concerned about a company account, in practice the bank may suggest that the directors invite the bank to appoint a receiver. An appointment at the directors' invitation will avoid the receiver being a trespasser on the company's property, even if his appointment is invalid. If they decline, the bank may appoint an administrative receiver in any case, and assuming the appointment is legally valid and bona fide, the appointment cannot be challenged. The appointment must be in writing, but it need not be "under seal". The appointed administrative receiver must be an insolvency practitioner, authorised to act as such. Companies are not permitted to act as administrative receivers. It is common practice for two receivers to be appointed jointly, to minimise possible succession problems if one retires or dies.

Administrative receivers will not be displaced by a subsequent liquidation of the company, and they may be appointed even after the winding up has commenced. Under the Insolvency Act 1986, after being appointed, the receivers must publish the appointment, notify the company, notify creditors and notice of it must appear on company stationery. The bank must notify the Registrar of Companies within seven days and the appointment will appear on the company's charges register. It is important to note that the administrative receiver is only appointed to act as receiver over the assets which are subject to the floating charges.

If time is of the essence, eg because a judgment creditor is about to have the company's assets seized, the bank can move very quickly to appoint a receiver. For instance, in *R A Cripps & Son Ltd v Wickenden* (1973), demand was effectively made to the company at 10.45 am. No money having been forthcoming, the receiver was appointed at 12.30 pm on the same day. This was held to have allowed sufficient time for the company to comply with the demand, since the law only recognised the need to physically move the money to the bank, and not the need to negotiate the raising of the necessary funds from another source.

Receivers are expressed to be agents of the company in the debenture. This is a strange form of agency since the receiver, for obvious reasons, does not take instructions from the company and he is personally liable on contracts he makes for the company, unless the contrary is stated in each contract he enters. As he acts as agent of the company, however, the bank that appointed him cannot be held liable for his negligence. In practice, the receiver will demand an indemnity from the bank before accepting his appointment. Furthermore, the bank's interventions may negate the written terms of the debenture. In *Standard Chartered Bank Ltd v Walker* the bank had taken a standard debenture from JW Ltd and also had personal guarantees from Mr and Mrs W. A receiver was appointed (as agent of the company) and, responding to pressure from the bank, put the company's plant and machinery in an unsuitable auction sale. The bank also called on Mr and Mrs W to pay but the defence was that if a proper price had been obtained for the assets, there would have been a lower claim under the guarantee. The bank was unable to deny liability for the receiver's negligence, as it had chosen to instruct the receiver to make an early sale of the assets and thus make him its agent, regardless of the terms of the debenture.

The amount of a receiver's remuneration may be determined by the bank if the debenture so specifies. The default rate is 5% of gross receipts.

15.5.5.2 Obligations of the administrative receiver

After the appointment of the administrative receiver, the Companies Act 1985 and the Insolvency Act 1986 require the directors of the company to prepare a statement of affairs for the receiver who must, in turn, send a copy of it to the Registrar of Companies. Thereafter the administrative receiver must prepare annual (and final) accounts of his receipts and payments for the Registrar, and keep sufficient records for the company's accounts to be prepared.

The administrative receiver must pay off the preferential creditors before the floating chargeholder, although inasmuch as the bank has fixed charges, the proceeds of sale of these assets will go to the bank before the preferential creditors.

It has been seen that a bank may become a preferential creditor by having advanced money for the payment of the company's employee wages. Where the bank's claim against a company in liquidation is partly preferential and partly non-preferential and it holds some fixed and floating charges, it is entitled to set the proceeds of sale from the assets subject to the fixed charge against the non-preferential element, permitting the bank to claim as a preferential creditor for the balance still owing after realisation of the fixed charges.

15.5.5.3 Powers of the administrative receiver

The debenture under which the administrative receiver is appointed will grant considerable power to sell assets and manage the company's business. Schedule 1 to the Insolvency Act 1986 grants wide powers in any case. The receiver may petition the court for a winding up order if this may lead to preservation of the assets of the company. In any case where the court orders a winding up, a receiver who was appointed before the liquidator may continue to sell assets. In a voluntary winding up, the receiver may sell assets after the liquidator is appointed, even if the receiver was appointed after the liquidator.

16

INTRODUCTION TO SECURITY

16.1 Security in Assets

A lender may decide to seek security over the company's assets at the time of making the allowance, or as part of loan rescheduling where the facility is unsecured, to mitigate risk, in preference to enforcing a loan repayment default. This has implications regarding the negative pledge and pari passu clauses. However, as with other types of documentation, the rights of the parties, and the terms and conditions would need to be specified in the security document.

Assets pledged (and registered as such) could be itemized, or a floating charge of assets to the value of a specific amount could be detailed. The latter would allow the company to sell assets, or interchange assets, without seeking the lender's permission each time.

Companies such as property developers tend to borrow on a secured basis. In these instances the loan documentation will obviously also include the details of the security. The negative pledge is likely to have specific exclusions to property already charged, and some form of exclusion for future charges, such as to a monetary value, or replacement of existing charges, or in support of the purchase of the asset, such as in a financial lease.

16.2 Purposes of Security

(1) The lender can sell security in the event of default and has priority over unsecured lenders.

(2) Insulation from sovereign states by the use of external security such as bullion, investments, etc.

(3) Control especially in project finance transactions whereby the lender is able to exercise operational control over assets rather than by sale.

(4) Protection against other creditors: especially if borrower has given security already to domestic lenders.

16.3 General Considerations and Principles with Regard to Security

A bank should raise the following questions before making the loan available:

(a) does the borrower have good unencumbered title to the assets over which security is proposed to be taken? Investigating the effect of retention of title clauses;

(b) other creditors may have priority under local rules, eg preferential creditors ahead of a floating charge, liquidator's costs in an insolvency;

(c) are there restrictions on the nature of the security that can be taken, for example, many civil law jurisdictions do not recognize anything other than a fixed security interest whereas others, for example the UK, may recognize securities over future (after acquired) property? After-acquired property may escape the charge;

(d) will the granting of the security conflict with a contrary contractual agreement, for example, a negative pledge?

(e) A maintenance of value clause which provides for automatic topping up if the asset value deteriorates may be ineffective as a preference or there may be no available assets;

(f) a roll-over (eg on currency conversion) may discharge the security or lose the lender his priority eg *Clayton's Case* (1816);

(g) second or junior mortgagees may exercise rights to the disadvantage of a first or senior mortgagee, eg to realize the security, and priority for further advances will be lost unless there is an obligation to tack;

(h) some jurisdictions insist that the mortgage debt be expressed in local currency exposing the lender to adverse movements in exchange rates if you take cross-border security form a corporate;

(i) any prohibition or penalty on prepayment may constitute a clog on the equity of redemption;

(j) government consent may be required for the grant of security to an alien;

(k) there may be stamp duty to pay;

(l) the security may not be recognized in other jurisdictions such as between England or Scotland and, say, France or Spain;

(m) a trustee may not be allowed to hold the security, eg an agent bank;

(n) an external court may not have jurisdiction to enforce the security;

(o) in enforcing the security, the lender may have to follow a specific procedure in exercising a power of sale, may be liable for selling too cheaply (*Standard Chartered Bank v Walker* (1983) CA or may face restrictions on whom he may sell to;

(p) if he enters into possession, he may be liable for negligence, *White v City of London Brewery Co* (1889);

(q) the security may be void for want of registration which may be a multiple requirement;

(q) will the proposed security interest require to be registered in order to perfect the interest and if so are significant costs attached to such registration requirements? Will non-registration make the security interest void and or will it affect priorities?

(r) Should the security be held by a trustee in order that the bank will be able to bring some flexibility into the advancing of the facility in the event that the bank at some stage in the future decides to sell all or part of its loan to the borrower? Are stamp duties or other similar taxes payable in respect of the taking of security in any of the three jurisdictions and will the documentation in respect of the creation of the security required to be notarized?

(s) What is the position on enforcement of the appropriate security interest. What remedies are available on a default? Will the assets over which security is to be taken be capable of being sold and are particular restrictions applicable in the event of any sale post-enforcement?

(t) Are there restrictions on the currency of the security and if so will these present problems upon enforcement?

(u) There is also the need to obtain an appropriate opinion in each of the jurisdictions including England and Scotland if you are lending to a UK group and taking security in both countries covering many of the points raised above and any additional points which will invariably depend upon the specific security interest which is proposed to be taken by the lending bank.

Note: Many of these problems may be avoided by adopting a form of title financing, eg leasing, hire purchase, sale and leaseback.

16.4 Features of Ideal Security

So what is security? At the most basic level it is that which the borrower will give to the lender that in the event of default the lender will enforce the security to compensate him for any losses incurred. Briefly the most common assets are:

- land (including buildings);
- life policies;

- stocks and shares;

- guarantees;

- fixed and floating charges;

- goods and produce.

All the above have a value. Thus the loss would be a real cost to a borrower.

16.5 Security Values

Evidence that the asset has been given as security must be in such a form that it can be recognized by others and particularly by the legal authorities who will arbitrate on any dispute between the parties.

The best security will be that which lends (pardon the pun) itself to being registered and acknowledged by a party independent of the parties involved. For example, if land is taken as security, this fact can be registered at the District Land Registry and such registration offers extra protection to the lender. In addition, for companies there is a legal requirement that all assets owned by the company that are given as security must be registered at Companies House (in Cardiff for companies formed in England and Wales). However, it is the responsibility of the lender to register the fact that a legal interest exists.

16.6 Direct and Third-party Security

Today, lenders are still able to take direct security (that is security owned by the borrower) or third-party security (security given by another on behalf of the borrower). Direct security is the most favoured form of security for lenders as it ties the borrower in more. When considering taking security every lender will be asking "What is this security worth to the lender in monetary value?".

Good security has the following characteristics.

1. It has a financial value that is stable and simple to assess. If it has a value in use to the borrower so much the better.

2. It can be easily realized by the lender in the event of default.

3. The existence of the lender's rights over the asset should be clear to others.

It is to this third point that further consideration needs to be given. How can a lender show to the world at large that the asset has been given as security in such a way that others will acknowledge it and, importantly, that the asset holder cannot repudiate the deal?

16.7 Different Forms of Security

There are three main forms of security which will be looked at in greater depth: pledge, lien and mortgage.

16.7.1 Pledge

The pledge is the earliest form of security interest, in which the creditor takes possession of the debtor's asset as security until the debt is paid. It is not used much nowadays as the legal requirement for transfer of possession prevents the debtor from using the asset and also limits the use of the pledge to tangible goods.

It is common for fixed and floating charges (a form of security given by companies) to incorporate a negative pledge. Under a negative pledge the borrower promises not to grant a legal mortgage over an asset pledged within the fixed and floating charge. Importantly this negative pledge can be registered at Companies House, thus giving notice to others that a particular asset is not available as security without the prior consent of the fixed and floating charge holder.

16.7.2 Lien

A lien is a security interest which is created by law and not by the agreement of the parties involved. A particular lien provides security for one debt only, whereas a general lien covers all debts owed to the creditor. An example of a particular lien is a car left with a garage for repair. If the owner cannot pay the bill, the garage is entitled to hold the car until payment is made. General liens arise when there are regular transactions between two parties and the lien is recognized by the practice of the particular trade. Banks have a general right of lien under *Brandao v Barrett* (1846). It covers cheques belonging to a customer but items deposited in safe custody are exempt from the general lien. The exercise of a right of lien by a creditor results in the debtor being deprived of the use of the relevant property.

One of the main strengths of the lien is that it takes priority over a charge taken subsequent to the lien.

16.7.3 Mortgage

A mortgage is the most common form of security taken by lending bankers and is a form of written evidence that the rights to the asset have been transferred from the borrower to the lender. A mortgage is created by the signing of a charge form by the owner of the asset. Once the charge form has been signed the following terminology is used:

● Mortgagor – the person giving the security: in direct security this is the borrower.

● Mortgagee – the person holding the security: this is the lender.

Not surprisingly the wording of the charge form differs for direct and third-party security.

Many instances of invalid charges have occurred because the incorrect charge form has been signed. Often the lender takes the documents that prove ownership of the asset into possession at the same time as the charge form is signed. If we consider our list of assets we can expand it to show the documents of ownership:

1. Land (including buildings): land certificate or title deeds.

2. Life policies: policy document issued by an insurer.

3. Stocks and shares: share certificate issued by company.

4. Guarantees: not applicable.

5. Fixed and floating charges: not applicable

6. Goods and produce: trade note/invoice

Given that the above documents prove ownership, a lender would need to ask questions if duplicate or replacement documents were proffered by the potential mortgagor. A little cynical reflection should help you understand why. Does your employer have rules on duplicate documents of title?

16.8 Forms of Mortgage

There are two distinct forms of mortgage: legal and equitable mortgages.

A legal mortgage is created when:

1. the charge form is expressed to be "a legal mortgage";

2. in the case of land, when the charge form creates a lease in favour of the mortgagee for an unlimited period. The technical term is "for a term absolute in years".

Whenever a third-party legal mortgage is taken, it is essential that the mortgagor is given independent legal advice prior to completion. We shall look at examples in the following chapters but this independent advice is to ensure that the mortgagor is aware of his or her obligations, the extent of the obligations and to confirm that he or she enter into this contract free of any undue influence. This is especially important when the asset is in the name of Mr and Mrs Smith and the debt is in the name of either Mr or Mrs Smith.

An equitable mortgage is created when:

1. the charge form is not expressed to be by way of a legal mortgage; and far, far more frequently when:

2. the title documents are deposited with the lender with the intention that they are

security. The lender on most occasions will take a memorandum of deposit to confirm the intent. If land is the asset in question there must be written evidence of the intent.

In the case of third-party security there must obviously be some form of written evidence to show whose debt the asset is being deposited to secure.

Generally the mortgagee seeks a legal mortgage because this gives the greatest level of security. The legal mortgage actually gives the mortgagee the right to sell the asset to repay the debt if the borrower is in default, even if the mortgagor objects. The mortgagee does not usually sell the asset if a borrower is a few days late in making a payment or a little in excess of a revolving credit facility. The action of repossessing an asset under a legal mortgage is always the last, as opposed to the first, course of action.

The mortgagee will generally seek to explore all other possible avenues with the mortgagor before issuing a notice requiring repayment of debt. This formal notice is a legal requirement. From the date of service of this notice the borrower has three months before the asset can be sold. This time period can be a distinct disadvantage for a lender and, generally, s 103 of the Law of Property Act 1925 is excluded, making the debt repayable on demand.

A mortgagee can also sell the security if interest is two months in arrears or if the borrower has broken some other condition of the loan. These conditions are often referred to as covenants. An example of a covenant is that the borrower must forward monthly management accounts to a lender and that the overdraft is limited to an amount related to the working capital. Many facilities offered by lenders will contain one or more covenants.

An equitable mortgage does not give the mortgagee the right to sell the asset against the wishes of the mortgagor without the permission of the court. This is expensive, time consuming and it is not 100% guaranteed that the mortgage will get payment. Another major disadvantage of the equitable mortgage is that the mortgagee will rank behind any prior equitable mortgages, even if they were unaware of them at the time the mortgage was created.

In most cases where first and second mortgages have been granted the two lenders agree a deed of priorities between them in order to take interest into account. In simple terms, Alla Bank agrees that it will have priority for the original debt plus £X interest. X may be expressed as a number of months interest or a specific amount of interest.

There may even be a third and fourth mortgagee. In many cases the second mortgagee will have taken the mortgage simply to lock the borrower in. A usual scenario would be a company seeking to borrow from its bank. The company is owned by and run by the directors. As part of the security package the lender may want a guarantee from a director supported by a second mortgage over the director's domestic residence. It may very well be that the domestic property is worth £140,000 and the subject of a first mortgage to Beta Building Society for £125,000. The value in the mortgage would be zero.

	£
Value	140,000
% 90% (eg)	126,000
First mortgage	125,000
Value to second mortgagee	nil – the 1000 will be taken in charges.

16.9 Typical Clauses in Bank Charge Forms

16.9.1 Continuing Security

The effect of this clause is that the security continues and remains valid notwithstanding that the original money lent has been repaid. The easiest way to see this is in the case of a revolving credit facility. Let us assume that an overdraft of £20m has been granted and the borrower has taken (drawn down) the funds. Subsequently the corporate pays in £5m per month and withdraws £4.75m.

After five months the following has happened:

Credits	Debits	Balance
		20m dr.
5m	4.75m	19.75m dr.
5m	4.75m	19.5m dr.
5m	4.75m	19.25m dr.
5m	4.75m	19m dr.
Total in/out	20m	19,000,000

Within the four months the £20m borrowed has been paid back in. It could, therefore, be argued that the four tranches of £5m have repaid the original amount In 1816 the issue was considered in *Clayton's case* and the court held that the argument was valid. Therefore, in the above case although the balance on the current account was £19m, the security had ceased to be valid.

To overcome the rule in *Clayton's case* all charge forms now incorporate a continuing security clause in the following terms: "a continuing security and shall extend to cover the ultimate balance due from the customer to the lender notwithstanding the fact that the customer may have had, from time to time, a credit balance on an account between the customer and the lender".

If the charge form had incorporated the continuing security clause then the balance of £19m would have been covered by the charge form and the security would remain valid.

This would still be the case if the customer had gone into credit for x months and then become overdrawn again.

16.9.1.1 Prior charges

Where a charge secures future advances (as for example with an 'all moneys' debenture, see 16.9.2) new advances made by the chargee will rank in priority to a subsequent charge until he has notice of the later charge. Once he has such notice then further advances will be postponed to the later charge and the charge having priority will extend only to advances outstanding at that time. The result of this and the operation of the rule in *Clayton's case* (1816) is that the secured debt having priority will be progressively discharged by subsequent credits to the debtor's account unless the chargee rules off the debtor's account and credits such payments to a new account.

16.9.2 All Moneys Clause

Under an all moneys clause the customer promises to pay on demand "all moneys now due or hereafter due to the lender". Effectively, the customer acknowledges that this security covers all moneys owed on any account of the customer's at any time. The practical implication is that if a customer who owed £1m and had given two items of security each worth £500,000 subsequently repaid £500,000 of the debt then the lender can keep both items of security even though the debt has halved. The customer cannot demand the release of one of the items of security, although in many cases the lender will often be willing to release one of the items of security, perhaps in conjuncture with reducing the facility. The downside of such a release for the customer is that if he or she wished to increase the facility back to the £1m level there would be a delay and cost involved with retaking the security.

16.9.3 Successor Clause

A successor clause enables the lender's rights under the security to be transferred to a third-party who might take over the bank's rights. This clause would be very important if a takeover by clearing bank A of clearing bank B takes place.

16.9.4 Conclusive Evidence

This clause has the effect that if the bank sends a statement showing the debt to be £X and this statement is not disputed within 14 days then £X is the binding level of debt. This effectively prevents any dispute over the amount of the debt.

16.9.5 Additional Security

This security is in addition to and without prejudice to, any other security now, or at any time, held. This effectively means that the lender can take, or release, other security without having an effect on the security.

16.9.6 Repayment on Demand

It has already been noted that by excluding s 103 of the Law of Property Act 1925 the lender obtains the right to demand repayment immediately: s 103 must be excluded to give the repayment on demand clause validity. Similarly, s 93 of the Law of Property Act 1925 must be excluded to validate the all moneys clause. However, the power to sell under a legal mortgage is granted by s 101 of the Act. Under the Act, the term "property" means all assets owned by an individual (or company) and not just land.

16.10 Taking Security From Companies

The law relating to companies is contained chiefly in a consolidating enactment, namely the Companies Act 1985. This has been amended and supplemented by the Companies Act 1989. Matters relating to liquidation and receivership are contained in the Insolvency Act 1986.

A new s 35A in the Companies Act 1985 provides that in favour of a person dealing with a company in good faith, the power of the board of directors to bind the company shall be deemed to be free of any limitation under the company's constitution. It is expressly provides that a person shall not be regarded as acting in bad faith, by reason only of his knowing that an act is beyond the powers of the directors.

In s 35B of the Companies Act 1985 it is stated that a party entering into a transaction with a company is not bound to enquire as to whether the transaction is within the company's memorandum or whether it is within the powers of the directors acting on behalf of the company.

Under the rules of the Companies Acts, a bank lending to a company need not be concerned to look at the company's memorandum and articles of association to determine whether the company or its agents are acting properly. Nor will it be put on notice of lack of capacity by having seen these documents. In order to be free from doubt as to whether the persons representing the company have authority to do so, however, it is necessary that the bank deals with the board of directors or some other person authorized by the board.

Like individuals, companies own their own assets and these can be mortgaged/charged as security to a lender. Generally these assets will be real assets (land), personal assets (eg plant/machinery) and financial assets (eg shares) can also be charged. When such a fixed charge is taken over the assets of an individual or of a company, the chargee (lender) has the comfort of knowing that he enjoys first priority over the asset (assuming it is a first charge and is perfected) and that the chargor (borrower) is not able to dispose of the asset without his permission. Thus a first fixed charge over an asset which is unlikely to decline in value (such as some types of land and insurance policies) is a good security. Fixed charges over assets which will decline in value (such as some types of plant and machinery which will have to be replaced after a few years), are good security only in the early years.

The replacement asset will not automatically be covered by the charge, although the customer can be asked to provide a new charge when the asset's value declines.

In addition to the ability to grant charges over real assets, companies can also create a floating charge which allows the company to continue to deal with current assets such as stock.

The floating charge may, in theory, be expressed to be over certain classes of asset but in practice it is invariably expressed to be over all of the assets of the company chargor. In this case it is an equitable charge which "hovers" until some event crystallizes the charge, at which time it becomes a fixed equitable charge on the assets which the company happens to own at that time. The crystallizing events would typically be either the company going into liquidation or the chargeholder appointing administrative receivers, following a default by the company.

The company remains free to buy and sell those assets which are covered only by the floating charge until the charge crystallizes. The danger for the bank being that the company will run down the level of its assets, so that when the charge crystallizes, it fixes onto very few assets.

Holders of a first fixed charge will have first priority to the proceeds of sale of the asset they have a charge over – after sale expenses have been met. The floating charge enjoys no such first priority claim against any of the assets it covers and indeed it is subordinated to preferential creditors, as defined in s 386 of, and Schedule 6 to the Insolvency Act 1986, who must be paid in full before any payment is made under the floating charge.

One of the major dangers with a floating charge is that the stock covered by the floating charge may not belong to the company at all, due to a "retention of title" clause in the contract of sale which operates for the benefit of the supplier of the stock. If, as a result, the stock never became the property of the company in the first place, no charge holder or other creditor can receive the proceeds of its sale.

The holder of a floating charge is able to prevent the making of an administration order by the court under s 9 of the Insolvency Act 1986. A fixed charge holder does not have this ability and in practice this is a powerful reason for a bank to take a floating charge on every occasion it takes company security.

A floating charge becomes a fixed charge when it crystallizes and the new fixed charge captures the assets which the company owns at the relevant time which were subject to the floating charge. This will occur when the bank appoints a receiver or if the company commences winding up (whether or not the company is in default), or if the company completely ceases to carry on business, or upon the appointment of an administrative receiver (a term used in the Insolvency Act 1986 for a receiver appointed under a floating charge, to distinguish him from receivers appointed by the court).

As with all security taken from a company, a floating charge requires registration. This consists of supplying the prescribed particulars of the charge in the prescribed form to the Registrar of Companies, normally including the original document of charge. It is advantageous to include specific details of the term in the debenture which prohibits the company from granting subsequent charges to other lenders which would rank pari passu with, or ahead of, the debenture.

It is the company's duty to register a charge it creates and it commits an offence if the charge is not registered. However, any person interested in the charge may register it, and banks prefer to do so for obvious reasons.

The Registrar must provide a certificate stating the date on which the particulars of the charge were registered. This certificate is conclusive evidence that the statutory requirements of registration have been complied with. The requirement is to register the charge within 21 days of the creation of the charge, failing which it becomes void against:

(a)   any liquidator or administrator of the company;

(b)   any person who for value acquires an interest in the property subject to the charge (such as a purchaser of the property or a second mortgagee of it);

(c)   any creditor of the company (s 395 of the Companies Act 1985).

If the 21-day period has passed, an application to the court may be made for an order extending the period for registration. This can be granted merely on evidence of accident or inadvertence, but not if the company is in liquidation or winding up is imminent. The court order will usually safeguard the rights of other creditors acquired after the 21-day period expired.

The liquidator will be looking for several main types of flaws:

- Does the borrower have the capacity to contract?

- Has the charge form been properly completed?

- Are the signatures witnessed?

- Was independent legal advice given?

- Was notice given to prior mortgagees?

- Has the charge been registered correctly? (This is extremely important with corporate borrowing.)

This is not an exhaustive list – the list of security documentation will vary from bank-to-bank. Many of these will be in the form of a flow chart to ensure that all technicalities are correctly completed.

16.10.1 Preference

It is contrary to the company and insolvency legislation to prefer one creditor ahead of the others and were a debtor to do so the liquidator could ask the court to reverse the preference transaction. For example, if a lender was an unsecured creditor and then was given security shortly before the debtor company entered into liquidation, the liquidator would seek to claim preference and have the security brought back into the distribution, with the lender reverting to an unsecured creditor. The court will consider the time between the granting of the security and the insolvency of the mortgagor.

In the ordinary course of events, the claim of preference is avoided if six months have passed since the creation of the mortgage. If the mortgagee was an associate of the debtor (spouse, company director preferred by a company, etc), the timescale increases to two years.

16.10.2 Transactions at an Undervalue

This is where the debtor has transferred an asset to a creditor (or other third-party) for less than its market value. This effectively means that there is less value available to the creditors in insolvency.

In *Aveling Barford Ltd v Perion Ltd* (1989) the liquidator of Aveling Barford successfully petitioned the court to force Perion to repay over £1,000,000 after an asset owned by Aveling Barford had been sold substantially under value to Perion. The link between the two companies was a common major shareholder.

The timescale for transactions under value is two years for a company and five years for individuals.

Timescale for Challenging Transactions in Insolvency								
	Unfair Preference				Undervalue Transaction			
	Company		Individual		Company		Individual	
	A	N-A	A	N-A	A	N-A	A	N-A
England	2yrs	6mths	7yrs	6mths	2yrs	2yrs	5yrs	5yrs

Note: The table refers to transactions entered into by a company or individual which subsequently becomes insolvent (bankrupt). A refers to transactions with an associated person and N-A to transactions with others.

17

FIXED AND FLOATING CHARGES

17.1 General Features

The use of fixed and floating charges as security is restricted to companies and is not available to individuals or partnerships. A broad description of fixed and floating charges was given at 16.10 so please re-read it if necessary. This unit goes into more specific lending considerations when using the security of a debenture given by a company. A fixed and floating charge consist of several distinct features, outlined below:

(a) A first legal charge on freehold and leasehold property whether registered or unregistered title, together with building fixtures, including trade fixtures and fixed plant and machinery. The definition of fixed plant means machinery fixed to the floor but not items like vehicles as these are not covered.

(b) An equitable fixed first charge on all future freehold or leasehold property, together with building fixtures including trade fixtures and fixed plant and machinery.

(c) An equitable fixed first charge over all book debts and other debts now and from time to time owing, and over goodwill and uncalled capital.

(d) A first floating charge over all other assets whatsoever both present and future. The principal assets remaining to be caught under the floating charge are stock, moveable plant and machinery, intellectual capital and motor vehicles.

There can be doubt as to whether plant and machinery is covered by the fixed and floating element of the debenture. If the assets are of high value the bank could consider taking a separate chattel mortgage over such an asset which would provide a fixed charge over a particular asset.

A floating charge will not cover borrowing which was taken before the date of the debenture unless the hardening period has expired, or it can be proved that the company was solvent at the time the debenture was taken.

A hardening period is defined as:

(a) either, at worst, the 12-month period following the creation of the debenture;

(b) or, the time taken for the debit balance on the day the debenture was taken to be turned over by subsequent credits. This is the case where an overdraft is being secured and it is where *Clayton's case* works in the banks favour.

17.2 Floating Charge

A floating charge is an equitable security (available only to companies) over the assets of a company as subsisting from time to time, not attaching to any particular asset until the charge is crystallized when it becomes an equitable fixed charge. Meanwhile the company is free to deal in the assets concerned without reference to the chargee, *Re Yorkshire Woolcombers Association Ltd* (1903). Its advantages are that it can catch all the assets including after-acquired ones and allows the company to continue trading freely. Its disadvantages are lack of priority over preferential claims and liquidation expenses in an insolvency, any judgment creditor completing execution before crystallization gets priority (although an automatic crystallization clause may assist the lender), a fixed charge takes priority (although a pari passu clause assists the lender) the company can run down its assets, goods may be subject to retention of title clauses, and it may be void as a fraudulent preference.

In a cross-border context between *England and Scotland* a floating charge may fail for lack of recognition by another jurisdiction. In *Carse v Copper* (1961) a Scottish court held that a floating charge created by a Scottish domiciled company over its English assets was invalid as the proper law of the charge was the law of the chargor's domicile which did not recognize floating charges. some argue the lex situs (the law of the place where security is situated) should have governed validity. In *Re Anchor Line Ltd* (1937) an English court held that a floating charge granted by an English company over assets in Scotland to a Scottish bank was valid as the proper law was English law. the courts of the situs may invalidate the charge for lack of compliance with local formalities, eg *Re Maudslay Sons & Field* (1900) where an English court upheld an assignment of French debts (invalid under French law for want of procedure) to English creditors. The cynical view would be that in each case the court is applying its own security law, upholding devices familiar to it and knocking down those unfamiliar.

A receiver appointed under a floating charge takes precedence over an administrator appointed by a court and it is for this reason that some banks have drawn up simple forms of debenture comprising a simple floating charge incorporating the right to appoint a receiver. Such a bank is not interested at all in relying on any security value but is merely protecting the its position in the vent of insolvency. Many banks view the only benefit of a floating charge as the ability to appoint a receiver as in the event of insolvency there would be no value in any assets covered by a floating charge.

17.3 Registration of Charges and the Slavenburg Case

Section 396 of the Companies Act 1985 sets out which charges over company assets must be protected by registration on the companies register, they include charges created by an instrument which would require registration as a bill of sale if executed by an individual, charges on land, on book debts, on ships or aircraft, any floating charge and any charge to secure an issue of debentures. This applies to all UK registered companies and to all overseas companies having an established place of business in the UK and where the property being charged is also in the UK, *Re Oriel Ltd* (1985), CA and s 409 of the Companies Act 1985. If the overseas company has an established place of business it should be already registered as an overseas company.

The Registrar of Companies will not register a charge if the company is not registered but sending him particulars should preserve the lender's position following the decision in *Slavenburg's Bank NV v Intercontinental Natural Resources Ltd* (1980). Failure to register within 21 days of the creation of the charge renders it void against a liquidator and creditors who acquire rights in the property concerned. It is not void against the company and the chargee will in any case remain an unsecured creditor. Until the 21 days have expired the charge is fully valid against any charges taken later even if registered first. Since the *Slavenburg* case banks must attempt to register such security at Companies House which is over security situated in Britain which is owned or being charged by an overseas company.

If a lender does decide to take a fixed and floating charge (and most do), the lender must first search the Companies House Register to ensure that none of the assets covered by the charge have already been charged. If everything is in order, the lender registers the charge. As discussed, the company remains free to deal in the assets and any new assets created become caught under the charge. This continues until the charge is crystallized. Land not directly charged is also captured by the floating charge as are all other unmortgaged assets. Thus any assets purchased after the creation of the floating charge are captured if not directly charged.

Note: possessory pledges over goods and charges over insurance policies including an ECGD (Export Credits Guarantee Department) policy do not require registration.

A banker taking a charge should be alert to the possible need for registrations in several registers in one country and in other countries. This is particularly pertinent in any security being taken form a company who has assets in *both England and Scotland*. The countries concerned include the place of incorporation of the borrower, the borrower's established place of business, the places where he does business, the place where the asset is and places where it may go to, eg the Australian bus in *Lucking v Highway Motel (Caernarvon) Pty Ltd* (1975). Obviously there is a better chance of escaping a local registration law if action is taken in an external form.

17.4 Advantages and Disadvantages

The main advantage of the fixed and floating charge is that it establishes the lender's claim in the assets of the company. The advantage of this form of security to the company is that it can continue to trade in (and with) the assets covered without the permission of the lender.

However, this advantage for the company is also the main drawback to the lender. Given that the company is free to deal with the assets, what assets will remain when the lender crystallizes the charge? This gives rise to a very important question, "How much is the charge worth?".

Another major disadvantage is that the company can create a fixed charge over assets currently covered by the floating charge. This fixed charge would take precedence over the floating charge even if it were created later. This can be mitigated by creating a negative pledge (discussed in a previous unit), but although it does not prevent a charge being created it would be a breach of the covenant and thus an event of default.

17.5 Valuing the Debenture

The security value of a debenture is the amount which would be realised on receivership or winding-up less any priority claims.

17.5.1 Prior Claims

The three principal claims which have priority over a debenture holder are as follows.

1. Receivership costs – these are the fees of the receiver (which are negotiable depending on the complexity of the receivership). Average fees are around 5% of asset realizations but if the situation is more complex it could be 10%.

2. Preferential creditors – these have priority over a floating charge such as VAT, PAYE, wages and pension contributions. Note that rates and Corporation Tax are not preferential debts. You should also be aware that preferential debts tend to increase substantially when a business is in trouble because the company will defer payment of say VAT in order to maintain reasonable relations with trade creditors who supply the company with goods and services.

3. Retention of title clauses.

17.5.2 Retention of Title Clauses

Retention of title clauses are sometimes known as "Romalpa" clauses after one of the early cases in this rapidly developing area of law, *Aluminium Industrie Vaassen BV v Romalpa Aluminium Ltd* (1976), CA.

A clause which seeks to retain ownership of goods in the supplier until paid for will be effective inasmuch as the goods remain in an unaltered state in the buyer's possession and it is even possible to claim rights over the proceeds of sale of unaltered goods (*Romalpa*). Where the goods are converted in a manufacturing process, there can be no claim by the seller either for the produced goods or proceeds of their sale, eg the resin used in the manufacture of chipboard in *Borden (UK) Ltd v Scottish Timer Products Ltd* (1981). Any attempt to retain equitable ownership in the supplier whilst the buyer converts the goods will be void for want of registration of a floating charge, *Re Bond Worth* (1980). Severable assets may remain claimable by the supplier, eg the engines attached to generator units in *Hendy Lennox* (1984).

Retention of title clauses can come in different forms but all seek to cover both stock and debtors. It may not be easy to establish the full extent to which assets are subject to retention of title because borrowers take little notice of it. *Romalpa* clauses are now also so prevalent that it may not be practical to carry out a full stock check where a large number of suppliers are involved.

The situation over work in progress is not clear cut because for a retention of title clause to be enforced the goods supplied must be identifiable as belonging to the supplier. This is not case where they become mixed with other materials as part of the manufacturing process.

The situation on debtors has not been tested in the courts but a banker could be in danger where goods remain readily identifiable whilst passing through the borrower's hands to his debtor. Businesses like wholesaling could be at risk from this.

17.6 Valuation of a Debenture

A banker should be aware that the discount factor that should be applied to the book values of assets will vary with the industry or the nature of the business. Nevertheless the following considerations should be borne in mind.

17.6.1 Security Margin

In the case of land and buildings a lender needs to be aware that if you are lending 100% of a security valuation, the realization proceeds form the sale of the assets will not repay the full cost of the borrowing because it will not cover:

(i)   any fall in value between the date of the advance and the sale of the asset. The longer the term the greater the uncertainty of the asset realization and a bank could consider a greater lending margin;

(ii)   the costs of sale and other necessary costs relating to the need to keep the asset saleable, such as security, insurance and maintenance costs on a property; or

(iii) the roll up of interest since the last charging date.

For a bank to be fully secured, a security margin should include a reasonable estimate of the effect of these elements on the security value.

17.6.2 Land and Buildings

Most property valuations are based on an open market valuation which assumes a willing buyer and seller. The main problem with a property will lie in translating its present open market value into a future forced sale value. This is subjective and is dependent upon the type, location, age, quality and condition of the property. In the case of commercial property there is a much narrower market than residential property and can be very difficult to sell. A prudent banker should not lend any more than, say, 70% of an open market valuation. In the case of residential property a bank can lend to a wider margin of up to, say, 95% but again it depends on all of the factors listed above.

As with all property valuations these can change with market conditions and a bank should monitor valuations of property at least every three years or maybe more frequently if the bank is more dependent on the security.

In the case of commercial leasehold land will provide good security only rarely. Most banks treat leasehold property with a security value of nil.

17.6.3 Plant and Machinery

Realizations of security over plan and machinery may be well below the book value in the accounts typically only worth 20–25% of the book value. Older machinery may have no more a value than a scrap value whilst specialist machinery may be of limited value. Some items like motor vehicles will be more likely to hold their value. A bank could consider a professional valuation of plant and machinery if it is substantial otherwise most bank simply write down the book value to 25% as a rule of thumb.

17.6.4 Debtors

The realization of debtors is usually only around 65–75% of book value and individual banks often link the amount of the facility to a debtor formula. The reasons for this include:

(a) some debts will be doubtful in the normal course of business;

(b) counter claims by debtors for money owed to them;

(c) claims that the quality of goods or service supplied is sub-standard; and

(d) attempts by small debtors, to avoid payment in the hope that the receiver will regard their recovery as not being time or cost effective.

The discount of any security value that may be applied to debtors can be adjusted up or down according the above factors.

17.6.5 Stock

Stock realizations are very poor and usually only amount to between 10–20% of book value. This because finished goods being out-of-date or unsaleable, unfinished goods and raw materials being subject to retention of title. A bank may have to adjust the discount value of 10–20% further if the stock is subject to large retention of title claims or consists of work in progress.

17.6.6 Intellectual Property

Intellectual property includes trade marks, patents, brands and of course knowledge and expertise. The great difficulty of these items is in valuing them. For a start some companies do not ascribe any value to brands or other intellectual property in their financial accounts. The problem is that brands, patents and trade marks do have some value but what is the value?

Some companies do put the value of brands in their accounts but many banks ignore them and value them at nil whilst some banks may consider only a value of 20% of the book value in respect of intellectual property. Lenders have learnt form their recent experience of lending to Internet companies and are very reluctant to ascribe monetary value to intellectual property.

In the case of those companies who do not place the value of any brands or other intellectual property in their balance sheets then the corporate may of course have hidden value. In these circumstances banks will not ascribe any value as regards a debenture to such items.

The approach of valuing a debenture is largely on a "gone concern" basis but a corporate value is to be placed on a business then clearly you would wish to value intellectual property as it does have value.

Sample valuation of a debenture for Alfa Ltd.

Balance sheet of Alfa Ltd as at 5 April 2001

Captured by FFC				Usually
Fixed assets				
Freehold premises	45,000			Usually
			directly charged	
Plant and machinery	Cost	20,000		YES
Depreciation	5,000	15,000		
Motor vehicles	Cost	12,000		YES
Depreciation	2,000	10,000	70,000	
Current assets				
Stock	21,000			YES
			subject to Romalpa	
Debtors		20,000		YES
Bank	2,500		43,500	
Current liabilities				
Creditors	23,500		23,500	
NET CURRENT ASSETS		20,000		
Long term liabilities				
Loan	(15,000)		(15,000)	
TOTAL NET ASSETS			75,000	
Financed by				
50,000 £1 ordinary shares			50,000	
Retained profit			15,000	
Profit for the year			10,000	
	75,000			

Now, by extraction, we can summarize the assets covered under the charge.

Partial balance sheet of Alfa Ltd as at 5 April 2001

	Book value	
Plant and machinery cost	20000	
Depreciation	5000	15000
Motor vehicles cost	12000	
Depreciation	2000	10000
Stock		21000
Debtors		20000
Value		66000

Is £66,000 a fair (and prudent) valuation?

The answer is no, for three main reasons.

1. The accounts are out-of-date by the time they are available.

2. Even if up-to-date management accounts are used, there is still the problem of how accurate the directors' values are.

3. Even if the directors' values are accurate, will these values hold good if the business is in liquidation? Will all the debtors pay up in full? Will all the stock bring full value? Is some of the stock work-in-progress and thus requiring expenditure to make it saleable? Will the entire stock still be there? Can the plant, fixtures and fittings and vehicles be sold for their book values? How much can second-hand plant/cars be sold for?

All these questions mean that all fixed and floating charges are valued on a reduced value basis. For example:

	Book value		Reduction factor %	
Plant and machinery	Cost	20000		
Depreciation	5000	15000	60	9000
Motor vehicles	Cost	12000		
Depreciation	2000	10000	50	5000
Stock	21000	40	8400	
Debtors	20000	50	10000	
Value	66000		32400	

Even this £32,400 is at best a rough estimation and will be further reduced if:

1. there are any preferential creditors – their claim will take precedence;

2. the stock is subject to a *Romalpa* clause.

The above example shows two important points that:

(a) a floating charge is of limited or no value; and

(b) the security cover provided by a debenture is only as good as the ascribed valuation.

From the ensuing discussions above it will be clear that a bank has to set a debenture formula that will establish an adequate security margin and a reasonable security valuation.

If a bank is to rely on the security of a debenture for there to be secured lending then the valuation of the debenture must show a surplus and continue to do so in the future. Since the expectation of realizations from a floating charge is generally poor, the cover provided by the fixed charge is crucial. The problem for the bank is that the level of any security cover can change over time (both upwards and downwards) just as the value of assets can change. Just think of property prices and how they have changed over time.

A bank will be primarily looking to the fixed charge over any property and a fixed charge over book debts to provide the bulk of security. This is because a bank can look to a first charge as its security since there are preferential creditors or anyone else who can come before a fixed first legal charge. Also it is worth noting that even an equitable fixed charge would still be better than a floating charge. Any value form stock or plant and machinery will be incidental and any business where stock represents a major part of the security value a bank should take care.

The final problem that the bank must contend with is the source of figures for the basis of a debenture valuation which are the financial or management accounts of the company. This can mean that in the case of management accounts the company may attempt to put the best spin on them and present them to the bank as the figures they think the bank would like. A borrower has the greatest scope to spin the asset values in relation to stock and work in progress.

A lender should not fall into the trap of assuming that audited accounts are better than unaudited accounts. It is very questionable that after the experience of Enron, BCCI, Polly Peck and Maxwell that whilst auditors have a professional duty of care to provide accurate information, some auditors may not exercise this duty rigorously and in future may not provide significant comfort for a bank. The auditors are paid by the management of the company and this actual or conflict of interest you will study more in corporate governance. The lesson for any bank is to beware of inflated figures. A bank must also be aware that the worse a company's financial position appears to be then the less reliance should be placed on any reported figures, because as cash becomes tighter, the more quickly good assets will be realized, resulting in those of lesser quality constituting a high proportion of any reported figures.

Taking these issues into account a bank may need to truncate or haircut the figures produced in discounting the asset values further to take account of worsening market conditions or a general deterioration in the financial position of the company or of its assets. This underpins the constant need for a bank to continually monitor the financial position of the company and the security value of the ensuing debenture to ensure that any borrowing by the corporate will be secured by the debenture.

17.7 Industry Considerations

As will be clear from the above considerations the value of any debenture will vary from company-to-company and from industry-to-industry. If a banker looks at a corporate it should pay close attention to the markets and products of that company and its resources with those of competitors within the same industry.

If one were to look at different industries one would see that some industries have greater fixed assets than others due to the business infrastructure. A good example of corporates with strong infrastructure would be utility companies. Companies in other industries will have higher turnovers than others, such as retailers, whilst others will have considerably more in terms of cash flow and liquid assets, such as supermarkets. Likewise, corporates within some industries will be more dependent on trade credit whilst others will have higher amounts of trade debtors.

It is therefore clear that a lender should adjust any security margin up or down to an industry base as some industries are more risky than others in terms of their vulnerability.

Some industries are more prone to boom and bust or are cyclical like Internet companies or IT companies whilst others like oil companies or supermarkets are not prone to the same degree of economic vulnerability.

The clear motto of this is that a bank must value the security of its debenture by taking account of the risks of an industry by adjusting the level of security margins that were discussed earlier.

17.8 General Considerations in Taking Security

Much of the general consideration in taking security from companies has been covered in the previous unit and earlier units. You need to ensure that you are familiar with the sections on powers of the company and directors, the ultra vires doctrine, interested directors, benefit, preference and transactions at undervalue. If you are not familiar with them then please revise these sections accordingly.

17.9 Determination of the Debenture

Determination of a debenture could take place on any of the following events:

(a) the company enters liquidation compulsorily or voluntarily;

(b) in accordance with clauses in the debenture such as a breach of covenant;

(c) the bank appoints an administrative receiver;

(d) the company ceases business;

(e) when crystallization of another floating charge causes the company to cease trading;

(f) a distress levy by execution issued by a landlord.

17.10 Cancellation and Discharge of a Registered Charge

Once a company has repaid a debt, it may send to the Registrar of Companies a Memorandum of Charge ceasing to affect the company's property (Form 403a), executed by the company and signed by a director and the secretary.

17.11 Considerations of Priorities, Waivers and Postponements

17.11.1 Waivers

If a bank advancing money to a company, approaches a lender that already has a floating charge over the assets of the company, and requests the lender to waive its security rights in its favour, the bank can, instead of a waiver, give a certificate of non-crystallization. This states that to the best of its knowledge it is not aware of any event that has caused the charge to crystallize.

If the holder of the floating charge gives a waiver, unless it is under seal, it can be revoked by giving reasonable notice, or if the party to whom it is given has not relied on it. In case the bank later assigns the debt and security to another bank, the assignment and security to this other bank will be subject to this existing waiver.

17.11.2 Deeds of Postponement

If a bank has the security of a floating charge over a company's assets, and if the company susbsequently requires finance from another lender to purchase an asset against the security of a fixed charge on that asset, the company will need the consent of the bank which already holds the floating charge. If this is agreeable to the holder of the floating charge, then arrangement should be made with the new lender bank to enter into a deed of priority which will be executed under the seal of the company, the bank and the new lending bank. This deed of priority will give the holder of the floating charge a right to recover the amount of its priority, including interest and charges, and will include any variations and default clauses and details of assets which may be released from the floating charge.

17.11.3 Factoring

If a company does not have a fixed or floating charge over its assets, then it may enter into a factoring agreement. On the other hand if a company has already given a debenture to a bank creating a fixed and floating charge, the bank's consent may be required before it enters into a factoring agreement especially in cases where a bank's debenture form contains a pari passu clause. The bank will have to decide if it wants to enter into a deed of postponement in favour of a factoring company or to waive its charge over trade debtors. Normally, under the terms of the floating charge, a letter of waiver is issued in favour of the factoring company. Usually a bank will enter into a deed of priority because the bank will be able to rely on the security of:

(a) trade debts not factored by the factoring company;

(b) any other debts that are not trade debts;

(c) the balance available between the invoiced debt and the amount lent by the factor; and

(d) any sums which the factoring company owes to its client company because this will be a book debt under the bank's debenture.

17.11.4 Notice of Second Charge

Where a bank holds a debenture as security for any lending and then receives notice of a second charge created by a company, the account must be stopped to preserve its priority.

17.12 Charges over Book Debts

The item "current debtors" is normally an important asset on a trading company's balance sheet. If a charge is taken over the company's assets and one year later the company goes into liquidation, the "current debtors" asset is likely to be made up of entirely different debts owed to the company after this one year. Clearly a floating charge will encompass the new debts but it is also possible for a bank to take a fixed charge over these future debts, although this can only be an equitable fixed charge.

A charge over a company's book debts is one of the categories of charges which must be registered within 21 days. A number of complications arise, however, with equitable fixed charges over future book debts, such as the requirement that the charge takes the correct form and that certain details of it be registered. For instance, in *Siebe Gorman & Co Ltd v Barclays Bank*, the bank took a debenture from a company, which included a fixed charge over future book debts. Under the terms of the debenture, the company was legally obliged to pay the proceeds of the debts, when received, into its account with the bank, and was prohibited from assigning the debts to other parties. The bank registered the debenture but the above terms were not noted on the register. The company subsequently did assign the debts to the plaintiff in payment of a debt that it owed to the plaintiff, and the bank was given notice of this assignment. The bank continued to operate the company's current account. The court held that a valid fixed charge had been created over the debts as they came into existence. It further held that the registration of the debenture did not give notice to the plaintiff of the specific terms relating to the charge over the debts. At the moment the bank received notice of assignment of the debts, it enjoyed priority but that (due to the lack of notice of the terms of the debenture) further advances would rank after the plaintiff's claim. Since the bank's loan to the company was on current account and the account was not broken, *Clayton's case* operated to discharge the earlier debt which enjoyed priority, to be replaced by a later debt which did not.

In *Re Brightlife Ltd*, a non-bank creditor took a fixed charge over a company's future book debts but the company was legally entitled to pay the cheques it received from its debtors into its bank account and to withdraw the proceeds. The charge was held to be merely a floating charge because the chargee could not show that it was capable of exercising effective control over the company's debts.

On the terms of the charge used in *Re New Bullas Trading Ltd*, the debts received into the company's bank account were subject only to a floating charge (and thus lost priority to preferential creditors) up to the time that administrative receivers were appointed. Debts received into the account thereafter were subject to the fixed charge.

It follows from the above that:

- It is not enough to simply describe the charge on future book debts as fixed; the terms of the charge must legally oblige the company to pay the debts into its account with the bank, and to (effectively or specifically) entitle the bank to refuse withdrawals against these credits. It is therefore problematic for a non-bank to take an effective fixed charge over future book debts.

- The terms of the charge must also prohibit assignments of the book debts, and details of this and of the obligations above must be entered on the company's register when the charge itself is registered which must be within 21 days of its creation.

- Alternatively to the specific noting of the obligations on the company's register when the charge is registered, no further advances should be made to the company and current accounts should be ruled off, when notice of assignment is received.

- It should be noted that if the company does not comply with its obligation to pay the proceeds of the debts into its bank account, the bank may have no recourse other than to the company itself. This is because the debtors paying the debts can get a good discharge by paying the company and therefore cannot be held liable to the bank which has a charge on the debts. This may be different if the debtors have notice of the charge but they presumably cannot be deemed to know of the charge simply because it is registered.

17.13 Covenants

Covenants have been discussed in Unit 14, but the salient points in relation to debentures are as follows.

(a) Negative pledge which is an agreement not to give security to other lenders.

(b) Gearing restrictions where the bank places a limit on the amount the company can borrow in relation to its net worth.

(c) Minimum level for net tangible assets – this provides protection against losses or reductions in capital or reserves as a result of asset write-offs.

(d) Interest cover – a formula will be included under which interest will have to be covered by pre-tax, pre-interest profit on an agreed multiplier (times two is the usual minimum).

(e) Change of ownership – this covenant ensures that control of the company will not change hands, and is particularly important where the company is part of a larger group.

The nature and extent of covenants has to be realistic in relation to the company's size and circumstances. It is not unusual for a bank to accept less than the ideal level and scope of covenants, and, in those situations, it would be possible to agree a formula whereby the covenanted performance standards are increased over time.

17.14 Safe to Lend Considerations

Many of the main points have already been discussed but any prudent banker who wishes to rely on the security of a floating charge must consider the following issues before lending but also must continue to be aware of them and monitor them throughout the term of borrowing.

17.14.1 Considerations Prior to Lending

(a) A lender should be conscious of the 12-month hardening period.

(b) Examine the accounts to look at the amount of preferential creditors in respect of the floating charge element.

(c) A lender should ensure that the assets caught by a fixed charge are valued correctly and that a discount to that value for debenture purposes is fully assessed against the relative risks of the asset. For example, commercial property may need to be discounted by 70% or more to give a book value of around 70% leasehold property is likely to have a value of nil. Good residential property should be discounted at 80%.

(d) In the case of debtors, examination of the profile of debtors and check to see if any factoring is in progress. An examination of the profile will determine the discount.

(e) In the case of stock and work in progress consider the impact of retention of title but in any case stock the value will be discounted by about 80% or more.

(f) In the case of plant and machinery again the book value will be discounted by about 75%

(g) If the corporate has a large amount of intellectual property this may have to be valued at nil for the sake of prudence.

(h) Consideration of the impact of the industry and the nature of the company as to whether the debenture value should be discounted again or in some cases adjusted upwards.

17.14.2 Considerations During the Life of the Loan/Overdraft

(i) A bank needs to continually monitor the value of the assets that a debenture covers. It is important to realize that the value of assets vary both up and down.

(j) The financial/management accounts should continued to be monitored with the care that these figures may be cast in a favourable light.

(k) A bank should discount the value of its debenture where it is apparent that the company is in a weaker financial position – it must be aware of the run down in the quality of assets of the balance sheet.

(l) The bank should continue to appraise its security in line with any changes in the industry of the company or a change in the trade cycle into a recession.

18

LAND

18.1 Legal Estates

Land is defined in English law as "real property", as distinct from all other forms of asset which are "personal property". Under s 1 of the Law of Property Act 1925 the forms of ownership of land are defined as "estates" in land. There are two:

1. *Freehold.* This is more technically referred to as the "fee simple absolute in possession". Freehold ownership of land is as close as one can get to absolute title. It will last indefinitely and there is no rent to pay.

2. *Leasehold.* Or "a term of years absolute". Leases are granted by the freeholder and the leasehold ownership must expire at some date. A lease grants a right of possession for any period of time – it is common to find periodic tenancies which are as short as one week (although this will usually be repeatedly renewed) or as long as 999 years. There is invariably a rent attached to a lease which the lessee must pay to his lessor or landlord. In commercial properties it is common to find a series of leases on one building, so that the freeholder leases to a head lessee who in turn leases to a sublessee and so on. In this case each sublease must not expire after the lease above it. When a lease expires, the right of possession will revert to the freeholder (or to the superior leaseholder if it is a sublease). Thus freeholds which are subject to tenancies are referred to as "reversions". When a lease is granted at a periodic rental which is below market rents, a premium is charged. This is the price which is paid when a flat is "bought" on a long leasehold subject to a ground rent. The purchaser is buying the right to possession of a flat at a low rental which is fixed for a long period of time.

Freehold or leasehold ownership of land may be subject to a range of legal and equitable interests. These include:

(a) legal and equitable mortgages;

(b) easements, eg the right of a landowner to go on to a neighbour's land (a right of way);

(c) restrictive covenants, eg the right of a landowner to prevent his neighbour from building on his land.

Leases may also incorporate positive covenants which, for instance, will oblige a lessor and lessee to maintain the structure of a building. Positive covenants (unlike restrictive covenants) on freeholds are not effective against successors in title, and this is the reason why flats are usually sold on long leases rather than freehold.

18.2 Legal Interests in Land

Legal interests in land can include any of the following:

(a) Easements like a right of way.

(b) Rent charge such as a ground rent on freehold property.

(c) A charge by way of legal mortgage.

(d) A land tax or other charge imposed by law.

(e) Rights of entry.

Both freehold and leasehold are types of ownership of land. There are a number of other legal interests in land which are, effectively, rights to the land, but which are not ownership. The most widely known is the right of way. Under rights of way, members of the public have the right to walk across the land without the permission of the freeholder. A mortgage is a legal interest in land which is of primary importance, and both freeholders and leaseholders can create mortgages over their particular estate. Obviously any lender taking a mortgage over leasehold land would examine the head lease very closely to ascertain any potential problems. For example, if a loan is granted for 20 years and the lease expires after 15 years what happens? Is the mortgage effective against the freeholder? Once the land reverts to the freeholder his rights are unaffected by any interests created by the lessee. This is an important point. A leaseholder cannot bind the freeholder.

It is important that a lender knows who owns an asset and what his or her rights over that asset are. The type of estate defines the rights but we still need to consider the means of confirming ownership.

18.3 Equitable Interests in Land

Equitable interests in land include any other interests in:

(a) any of the above mentioned legal interests not executed by deed such as an equitable mortgage which is explained later;

(b) entailed freehold;

(c) conditional freehold; and

(d) beneficial interest in the land.

Legal or equitable interests are not enforceable against a bona fide purchaser for value unless it can be shown that he had notice of the charge. Hence a method of registration of interests was evolved which superseded the method of giving notice and replaced it with the doctrine that a registered charge was notice to any purchaser of the interest.

18.4 Joint Tenants and Tenants in Common

These ownerships can be either sole or joint. The first type of joint ownership, is joint tenancy. Under this type of ownership the land is deemed to be owned in full by both parties and on the death of either, the full title passes to the survivor. The alternative type is tenants in common, under which, each owner is deemed to own a portion of the land. On death this portion does not pass to the other tenant but to the heirs of the deceased tenant. The heir may, however, be the other tenant.

18.5 Valuation of Land

There is normally a ready market for land, and sales can normally be achieved within a reasonable timeframe. However, the experience of the late 1980s and early 1990s when land values actual fell (and in some cases substantially) has scarred lenders badly. Many lenders often ask for two values from the valuer.

1. *Open Market Valuation.* This is based on a ready market and a willing buyer and a willing seller.

2. *Forced Sale Valuation.* This basically restricts the valuer to assessing what price will be obtained within a fixed timeframe, which could be 30, 60 or 90 days. Obviously the price obtained if the land had to be sold within 30 days would be far less than if 90 days were available to find a buyer.

For further information on the sale of land, see 17.6.2.

18.6 Registered and Unregistered Land

Land can also be classified as:

Unregistered: where ownership of the land is evidenced by the title deeds and documents. These effectively start with the first granting of the freehold and subsequent transfers of ownership through the process known as conveyancing. If the owner borrows against the security of the land a a mortgage deed will be entered into by the landowner. The lender will take the title deeds and documents and the mortgage deed and retain them. Once the loan is repaid the mortgage deed will be discharged by the lender and the deeds returned to the landowner. Unregistered land has become increasingly rare.

Registered: most of England and Wales now consists of areas of "compulsory registration". This means that all freeholds and leases with more than 40 years unexpired must be placed on their District Land Register on the next occasion they are transferred, if they are not already registered. When a property is registered, it is identified by a title number and there are three parts to the Register: the Property Register, the Proprietorship Register and the Charges Register. The Registers never leave the District Land Registries. The "deeds" of registered land consist of a document known as the "Land Certificate", which is a copy of the register inside an impressive cover. If the land is subject to a legal mortgage the "deeds" will be a "Charge Certificate", similarly a copy of the register but also with the original mortgage deed. The mortgagee holds this document. Where two or more legal mortgages are registered on the same title, each mortgagee will be given his own Charge Certificate, incorporating the original of his mortgage and showing, in the copy Charges Register, details of this mortgage and all previously registered mortgages.

Land as security has many advantages – it is reasonably easy to value, rarely loses value (unlike most other forms of security) and is impossible to move elsewhere. However where a bank is offered a mortgage of land there is a danger that some person or persons other than the legal owner may have an overriding interest or the bank will later be deemed to have had constructive notice of a beneficial interest. If so, the bank will be left with an equitable mortgage of the legal owner's beneficial share of the property (if any).

Overriding interest: since occupation is a prerequisite of an overriding interest, the obvious approach is to discover who is in occupation and ask each if he has a beneficial interest, the Land Registration Act lays down that if enquiry is made of a person with an overriding interest and he fails to disclose it then the mortgagee gets good title.

Asking the legal owner whether others have an overriding interest does not provide any protection against claims from those others. The danger is that the bank will not discover some person who occupies, especially where the broadest interpretation of that word is used and a visit to the property would not reveal that person's existence. So far the main concern has centred on spouses (usually wives), but any person who satisfies the criteria will have an overriding interest. Where the property is occupied by non-legal owners the usual practice is to have them sign a deed of postponement. This procedure is not effective in the case of tenants, however, as their overriding interest cannot be postponed behind the mortgagee's interests. There is no minimum age limit for a person to hold a beneficial interest, but fortunately for lenders it appears that a child cannot have an overriding interest.

Beneficial interest: occupation is again important and whilst the bank may acquire good title where a person with a beneficial interest occupies the property, the vagaries of the suspicious circumstances test are such that it is clearly good policy to apply the same procedure as that followed in the case of registered land.

The foolproof approach for both types of interest would be to take the mortgage from all legal owners together with consent from those with equitable interests, and therefore to enjoy the protection of the overreaching principle.

Parliament has recognized the social problem of one spouse (usually the husband), who owns the matrimonial home as sole legal owner, secretly selling to an innocent third-party and disappearing with the proceeds. In this situation, the non-owning spouse now has a right to occupy the matrimonial home (whether or not he or she does in fact occupy it), but this right must be registered to have any effect on a purchaser or mortgagee. Only spouses have this right, which does not extend to non-married partners. The right to occupy is not dependent on the spouse having any beneficial interest in the property.

A defective title indemnity can be purchased from an insurance company to protect against defects in title that may appear in later years.

Under the Leasehold Reform Act 1967 a leaseholder has the right to force the freeholder to sell the freehold, and while this is reasonably common in domestic situations, it is not widely applicable commercially.

The Land Registration Act 1925 established a framework whereby title to land could be registered at one of a number of District Land Registries (DLR). These can be seen as a DVLA for property. Just as the DVLA keeps a record of the registered keepers of motor vehicles and issues a logbook showing the name and address of said keeper, so the DLR keeps records of the owners of land. Initially the DLR inspects the title deeds and documents (to prove title) and then issues a land certificate to the owner. This certificate has an alphabetic prefix and a numeric suffix, eg WA76583. This is unique to the land, which might be better known to its owners as 14 Paradise Gardens, Angeltown, HE4 3AN. The certificate includes a map showing (with red etching) the extent of the land covered and is valid in boundary disputes.

Most land is now in compulsory registration and any purchaser of the land owned by LM Williams would receive a land certificate as proof of title. The new owner would also receive the pre-registration deeds and documents, but these, while historically fascinating, are of no financial value. A land certificate is issued for freehold or leasehold land and usually the land certificate for leasehold land incorporates the head lease.

From a mortgagee's point of view a land certificate is wonderful. It guarantees ownership. If it transpires that title is/was defective, the government will recompense those suffering from the mistake of the DLR. But more importantly, once a mortgage has been created the DLR will register this (on the Charges Registry) and issue the mortgagee with a charge certificate while retaining the land certificate. Thus the mortgagor has no evidence of title (other than a receipt from the mortgagee) and is thus unable to create a further mortgage without the mortgagee's consent. However, a second mortgagee will be able to obtain the benefit of a charge certificate in his or her favour when a second mortgage is created.

When the land is sold the existing entries are ruled through and new entries made.

18.7 Advantages and Disadvantages of Land as Security

Why then do all lenders want land as security? If we think back to the features of good security, land does indeed stand up well. Generally speaking, land has the following advantages as security.

1. Ownership is generally simple to establish – the title will be evidenced by either a land certificate or by title deeds and documents.

2. A valuation is generally simple to obtain – there are two main professional bodies that carry out valuations on all types of land. These will give their independent opinion of the possible selling price of the land and, although they are not guaranteeing the value, their track record, as a profession, is very good. Most lenders will also have their own personal experience to draw upon.

3. The legal charge is easily evidenced by a mortgagee. The landowner will sign (or with a company, seal) the charge form and this will incorporate the standard clauses. The charge form then becomes part of the title deeds or is recorded by the District Land Registry.

4. There is normally a ready market for land, and sales can normally be achieved within a reasonable timeframe.

On the downside land has a few disadvantages.

1. The security procedure can be complicated and time-consuming. There a lot of "Is" to be dotted and "Ts" to be crossed. Mistakes in the technicalities can invalidate the security. There will be, within your circle of colleagues, a horror story to support this.

2. Valuers do not guarantee their valuations, and factors beyond the control of lenders – such as recession – can greatly reduce the expected returns. The term negative equity (now, thankfully, increasingly rare) refers to the state where a mortgagor owes the mortgagee more than the security is worth: thus selling the asset still leaves a residual debt.

3. Much of the value is often based on the fixtures on the land, ie the buildings. Although the land cannot be destroyed (other than by Act of God), the buildings can burn down, be blown up or simply be allowed to fall into disrepair. Although a lender cannot force a mortgagor to keep the property up to a certain level of repair, it can insist that the building is insured against fire, flood, etc. The cost of this insurance is normally borne by the customer but the lender may have to pay the insurance premiums if the customer is in difficulty.

4. Land can be difficult to sell. Even with the right to sell incorporated into the standard charge form, if nobody wants to buy, there is no sale. In addition to the potential difficulty in selling, there are always ancillary costs to be considered; legal fees, estate agent fees, etc will all reduce the amount the mortgagee will receive.

18.8 Procedure for Taking Security

Stage 1 – Obtain A Valuation On The Land

Valuation must be addressed to the bank and be carried out by a valuer on the bank's panel. The valuer needs to be professionally qualified and familiar with the geographical area concerned. A London-based valuer would experience difficulties assessing the value of a property in the highlands of Scotland. The basis of the valuation should be clearly set. Is the valuer to assess on an open market or forced-sale basis? Would both be appropriate?

Stage 2 – Obtain The Deeds Or Land Certificate

The availability of the title documents is a good indication that there are no charges on the land, but an equitable charge may still exist. Searches at the Land Charges Department (unregistered land) and the District Land Registry (registered land) should be undertaken to ensure that no such charges exist. If they did they would take precedence over the legal mortgage.

For unregistered land it is essential that the chain of title is investigated and proven. Some financial institutions do this in-house whereas others use solicitors.

Stage 3 – Execute The Mortgage Form

The mortgage form must obviously be signed. It is at this stage that a number of problems can occur.

1. Are all the owners of the property signing the document? Is the land in joint tenancy or tenants in common? Think how tenancy in common might affect the mortgagee's position.

2. Is the owner the borrower? If yes, then a direct charge form will be used. If the owner is not the borrower a third-party charge form would be needed.

3. Are there any parties with an equitable interest in the land? For example, does the person buying the property have a partner who will live in the property as well? The rights of a partner living in, and contributing to the property, were defined in *Williams and Glyn Bank Ltd v Boland* (1980). Here Mr Boland was the registered owner and mortgaged the marital home. The court held that the bank was unable to obtain possession because Mrs Boland had an overriding equitable interest.

The practical implication of *Williams and Glyn Bank Ltd. v Boland* is that all lenders will seek the consent to the mortgage of all occupants of a property whose name(s) do not appear on the title deeds. This applies only to those persons in occupation at the date of execution of the charge form.

The ruling in *Boland* has been revisited in, amongst others, *Midland Bank Ltd v Dobson* (1985); *City of London Building Society v Flegg* (1986); and *Lloyds Bank plc v Rossett* (1990) and, while clarifications have been made, the underlying principle remains valid.

Further equitable rights are given to a deserted spouse under the Matrimonial Homes Act 1983. This act gives a spouse the right to occupy the matrimonial home for as long as the marriage lasts. The deserted spouse would need to register his or her interest at either the Land Charges Department or the District Land Registry (DLR). Spouses can further protect their position by advising the mortgagee of their interest so that their equitable interest will rank ahead of future lending by the mortgagee.

Stage 4 – Search The Local Council Records

The local council search is done to ensure that there are no plans affecting the property. These might be local government plans or planning consents given to private concerns. For example, is the local authority planning to put a new road or motorway exit on derelict land adjacent to the security? Or are there plans to build a new school and leisure centre close to the land? While the mortgagee can do nothing about these plans, their existence could have a bearing on the valuation. If the security were a commercial property, a new road and motorway access may well increase the value. If the property is a residential property then the same plans could have a detrimental affect. If the local authority search reveals any such plans they should be discussed with the valuer to see if they change the valuation. It could be argued that a good valuer would be aware of these plans and will have incorporated them into the valuation already.

Stage 5 – Obtain The Insurance Policy

The policy document covering the land should be inspected to ensure that the land is properly and adequately insured and the policy document should be retained. It is normal for lenders to advise the insurer of their interest in the same. The insurance company then notes the lender's interest on the policy document. This means that in the event of non-payment of premiums the lender would be advised, enabling it to make the payments, thus keeping the security valid.

18.8.1 Summary of Procedure for Taking a Charge over Land

1. Stage One: obtain a valuation on the land.

2. Stage Two: obtain the deeds or land certificate.

3. Stage Three: execute the mortgage form.

4. Stage Four: search the local council records.

5. Stage Five: obtain the insurance policy.

Note: if land is being charged by a company, the usual considerations relating to company security have to be covered, including registration at Companies House.

18.9 Second Mortgages

If a second mortgage were to be taken, the procedure would be a little different. Obviously, the primary difference is that the title documents are not available – because the first mortgagee will have them. Thus the first step a second (or third etc) mortgagee would take would be to obtain details of the debt secured by the first mortgage. Each financial institution has a standard questionnaire which incorporates a mortgagor's authority to disclose the information requested. If the questionnaire is received without this authority the duty of confidentiality prevents disclosure.

On receipt of the completed questionnaire the second mortgagee has the following important details:

1. Confirmation of the name(s) of the landowners.

2. The amount of the outstanding debt. This will allow the second mortgagee to calculate the value of the security. This will be the value of the asset less normal reduction less amount owed to the first mortgagee.

3. Any obligation on the first mortgagee to make further advances. If such an obligation exists, these advances would take preference over the second mortgage even if the further advance were drawn down after the second mortgage. This can be overcome by a deed of priorities.

4. Details of any mortgages granted by third parties to the mortgagor. For example, there may already be a second mortgage in place. The existence of charges created subsequent to the first mortgage can also be ascertained by searching the Land Charges Department and District Land Registry.

Once the lender is satisfied as to the above points, the charge form can be signed (all the considerations detailed under stage three above will apply) and notice of the mortgage sent to the first mortgagee. The first mortgagee will confirm the level of debt outstanding and any further lending by the first mortgagee will rank after the second mortgage (barring, of course, any further advances made under the obligations discussed in point 3. above).

Because the title deeds are held by the first mortgagee, the charge of the second mortgagee needs to be registered. For unregistered land this will be by way of a Class c(1)9 at the Land Charges Department and, for registered land, the charge form will be forwarded to the relevant DLR and exchanged for a charge certificate. In the case of unregistered land, the mortgagee would search the land charges department a second time to ensure that the second mortgage has been registered.

It would be prudent to check with the local authority as in stage four above. Stage five is probably unnecessary, because the first mortgagee will have done this. It will, however, do no harm to check.

The above stages for taking first and second mortgages are generalist only and different financial institutions have specific programmes for ensuring that all the technicalities are correctly completed.

18.10 Specific Lending Considerations for Second Mortgages

Apart form the general considerations outline above, the following points should be borne in mind:

(a) ensure that the bank has sufficient equity by considering the value of the property and the amount of the advance;

(b) if the first mortgagee decides to sell, he or she will recover capital plus interest. Therefore, in calculating net value, retain a wider margin. In some cases, banks pay off the first mortgagee and take a first charge on the property so that they can control the position; and

(c) on commencement of foreclosure proceedings by the first mortgagee, the second mortgagee would be extinguished. Although the second mortgagee will be given the option of either paying off the first mortgagee or losing its security, a court can direct a sale of property instead of foreclosure at the request of the mortgagor or second mortgagee.

18.11 Realizing and Enforcing Security

We have dealt with the correct taking of security over land, so let us see what options are available to the mortgagee if the loan (which is supported by the mortgage) goes wrong.

18.11.1 Sue

A lender can sue independently of the security it holds if it so desires. This is rare and would indicate that the lender believes that there may be a fault in its security or that the security has fallen to little value.

The mortgagee will, of course, be entitled to sue the borrower for repayment under the loan agreement which is secured by the mort gage. However, if the mortgage contains a covenant to repay, the mortgagee will have the additional right to sue the mortgagor for repayment under the terms of the mortgage. Where the mortgage secures lending to someone other than the mortgagor, the covenant to repay will, in effect, be a guarantee and will give the mortgagee the right to sue two parties (the borrower and the mortgagor) for repayment.

If the mortgage is a deed, the mortgagee will be entitled to sue on the covenant to repay for up to 12 years after demand has been made under the mortgage, and this period may start running some time after demand has been made under the loan agreement. An action for repayment under the loan agreement must usually be commenced within six years of demand, since the loan agreement will usually be under hand, not executed as a deed.

In *Bank of Baroda v Dhillon*, the bank had taken a legal mortgage over the matrimonial home, the legal title to which was in the husband's sole name. The wife successfully claimed an overriding interest in the property. The bank claimed on the basis of its charge which was still valid against the husband's share of the property and the court granted an order for sale under s 30 of the Law of Property Act 1925. There was a bankruptcy order against the husband but as the bank was claiming under its charge, it was paid first from the share of the proceeds which arose from his share in the property. In *Re Zanfarid, BCCI v Zanfarid*, Mr and Mrs Z had given the bank a charge over their home to secure a loan to a company with which Mr Z was associated. Mrs Z's liability on the charge was in doubt due to the effect of the *Barclays Bank v O'Brien* case. The bank surrendered its charge over the property and petitioned for Mr Z's bankruptcy. It was then open to the trustee in bankruptcy to seek a sale order of the house. The proceeds relating to the husband's share in the house would then be paid to the husband's creditors generally but in this case there were no significant creditors apart from the bank.

Where the mortgage (legal or equitable) secures the grant of credit which is regulated by the Consumer Credit Act 1974, a court order under that Act must be obtained before any enforcement takes place.

18.11.2 Appoint a Receiver

This procedure is generally used where the property is not occupied by the borrower but by tenants. The receiver is then entitled to receive the rent instead of the borrower. An important consideration would be the level of the rent compared to the costs of the mortgage.

Under the terms of a standard mortgage, a receiver may be appointed when the debt has become due, which will be when demand is made. The appointment must be in writing and is effective from the moment the receiver accepts his appointment. The receiver is the agent of the mortgagor and the mortgagee is therefore not responsible for his acts or omissions. However, in *Standard Chartered Bank v Walker* the bank was liable for the receiver's negligence, as it had been directing him. It is common practice in any event for the receiver, when he is appointed, to seek an indemnity for any liability in negligence from the mortgagee.

The receiver is most commonly appointed when the mortgaged property is income-producing, such as the freehold of a block of flats which is let at market rents. The proceeds must then be applied according to s 109(8) of the Law of Property Act:

1.	Payment of certain expenses of the property.

2.	Paying prior mortgagees (if any).

3.   Paying his commission, insurance premiums and proper repairs.

4.   Paying interest to the mortgagee.

5.   Paying principal to the mortgagee.

18.11.3 Foreclosure

This procedure must be approved by the court. Under foreclosure, ownership of the property is transferred to the lender regardless of the amount of debt compared with the value of the property. Lenders rarely attempt this procedure because it is time-consuming, expensive and unlikely to succeed.

In its true legal meaning, foreclosure refers to a process of applying for a court order of foreclosure, the effect of which is to render the mortgagee the owner of the mortgaged property, and to discharge the debt irrespective of the value of the property and the size of the debt. This remedy is rarely obtained nowadays since the court would order a sale instead; the term has become used to describe the process of obtaining possession and exercising power of sale.

18.11.4 Enter into Possession

Basically, this involves the lender evicting the borrower from the property. Again this needs court approval incurring time and expense. If the court approves the possession which is by no means certain, the lender becomes a mortgagee in possession and, as such becomes responsible for the upkeep and insurance of the property until it is sold. The court may decline to allow the possession for a time to allow the borrowers time to find a buyer themselves. The logic here is that an occupied property is more attractive to potential buyers than an empty property which a buyer would know the lender needed to sell.

Entering into possession frequently precedes the exercising of the mortgagee's power of sale. In fact, most mortgagors would be surprised to learn that any legal mortgagee has the right to go into possession of the mortgaged property even if there is no default. The original legal concept of a mortgage being a transfer of the mortgaged property to the mortgagee means that it is the mortgagee, not the mortgagor, who is primarily entitled to possession. The mortgage will provide for the mortgagor to be entitled to possession while he complies with the terms of the mortgage. Taking possession by the mortgagee is, therefore, no more than the assertion of his common law right. In practice, possession may take place where the mortgagee wishes to let the property, and the acceptance by the mortgagee of rent will constitute taking possession. The mortgagee will be liable to the mortgagor for any damage, or for devaluing the property (eg by letting to a Rent Act tenant), or for rent received, or for rent which should have been received. He is allowed, however, to keep the property empty pending a sale without being liable for rent.

A mortgagee in possession of empty property will be liable to third parties who go onto the property, or who own land adjacent to it, and who have a claim under the Occupiers

Liability Act 1957 or in private nuisance. For these reasons, the mortgagee will prefer to appoint a receiver to act on his behalf, but as the agent of the mortgagor, thus avoiding being deemed at law to have taken possession himself.

A mortgage will usually provide that the mortgagor cannot grant leases. The mortgagee will thus be entitled to possession as against a tenant whose lease was not agreed by the mortgagee, unless the lease was granted before the mortgage was executed.

18.11.5 Sell

If the property is occupied by the borrower(s) – which is the most common situation – then the lender has the right to sell the property against the wishes of the borrower. In the event of a sale the lender has a duty to obtain a fair price and account to other mortgagees and the owner for any surplus received. Any lender selling under the power within the charge form would need to search the land charges department or District Land Registry to ascertain whether or not there are second (or third) mortgagees. This caused a number of problems during the late 1980s and early 1990s when lenders lent 95–100% (and occasionally more) of the purchase price in the expectation that the massive increase in land and property prices seen in the early 1980s would continue unabated. The outcome was that when property values peaked and then fell sharply, many lenders, especially second mortgagees, were left with debts that exceeded the value of the security. The lender would rarely lose out by selling quickly because the mortgage guarantee indemnity would meet the shortfall, but the borrower was often left with no property, none of the equity it had originally invested and a debt to the indemnifier.

An order is always necessary in the case of residential property, unless the property has been abandoned. The court has power to adjourn the proceedings or to suspend the order for possession if it appears likely that the mortgagor can pay off the arrears within a reasonable period and this can extend to the whole of the remaining term. In the case of an instalment mortgage, this means that the mortgagor must pay the normal instalments and a fixed proportion of the arrears each month until the arrears are repaid. If he misses a payment, the order will automatically become effective without the need for a further application to court. Where the mortgage is to secure an overdraft with no repayment by instalment, the court may only suspend its order if it is likely that the mortgagor can repay the whole debt. Where the order is not suspended, it will usually grant possession 28 days hence.

The court may agree to grant the mortgagor time to sell the property if thereby a full repayment can be achieved within a reasonable time. The court may also be willing to order a sale on the mortgagor's application (and against the mortgagee's wishes) where he is otherwise unable to sell because of negative equity. In deciding whether or not to order a sale, the court can take into account non-financial matters.

A spouse who has registered a right to occupy under the Matrimonial Homes Act will not be able to resist possession unless the registration of this right was in place before the bank took its charge.

The Mortgage Code applies to a bank dealing with a "personal customer" who took out a mortgage loan (other than to secure an overdraft) that is secured on a home that the customer owns and occupies. It does not apply to loans regulated by the Consumer Credit Act. It provides that lenders will consider cases of mortgage arrears sympathetically and positively and will follow the general principles of the "Statement of Practice on Handling Arrears and Possessions" issued by the Council of Mortgage Lenders, including developing a plan for dealing with the arrears which is consistent with both the lender's interests and those of the customer. It states that possession of the property will only be sought as a last resort when attempts to reach alternative arrangements with the customer have been unsuccessful.

In strictly commercial terms, the mortgagee will not have an interest in obtaining a price for the property that is any higher than the debt owed to him. The law is therefore careful to protect the interest of the mortgagor, and imposes a duty on the mortgagee to act in good faith and to take reasonable care to sell at a proper price. He is not, however, obliged to delay a sale in the expectation of a rising market.

If the courts do regard the price to be improper, the mortgagee is still liable but he has a right to pursue a claim by way of indemnity against the valuer.

The law relating to claims against valuers has recently been given a thorough airing by a substantial number of cases flowing from property price deflation in the early 1990s. This caused many secured properties to be sold at less than the value of the loan secured on them and lenders could sometimes establish that the valuer had been negligent in placing an over optimistic value on the property. The cornerstone decision is now that of the House of Lords in *South Australia Asset Management v York Montague*. It holds that where the valuer was negligent, the lender's claim against him in damages will normally amount to a figure which is the lesser of (i) the lender's total loss and (ii) the amount of the overvaluation plus interest. For example, if a property is valued at £100,000 (at a time when its true value is £80,000) and the lender lends £90,000 on it and it realizes £75,000 net of costs on a forced sale one year later, the lender's total loss will be £15,000. The amount of the overvaluation will be £20,000, to which figure a year's interest would be added. Thus in this example, the damages payable would be £15,000 (taking the lesser of the two figures).

The courts are prepared to find contributory negligence on the part of a lender who should have suspected that the valuation was too high or who lent on a very high ratio to the valuation figure.

Lenders have also made claims against solicitors who acted in the transaction, for instance on the grounds that the solicitor (acting for both mortgagor and mortgagee) knew about a mortgagor's poor past borrowing record and failed to inform the lender of this before the mortgage was taken. On these facts it was held that the solicitors were not under a duty to inform the lender if no specific instructions had been issued for them to do so.

Once the sale proceeds are received the moneys are distributed as follows (assuming the mortgagee has a first charge):

(a)   proper expenses of the sale;

(b)   his claim including costs; and

(c)   a second mortgagee (if one exists), or otherwise to the mortgagor, unless he is bankrupt, in which case to the trustee in bankruptcy.

If there are insufficient funds to repay junior mortgagees, their mortgages are discharged by the sale in any case.

In the unlikely event of a sale by a junior mortgagee, the senior mortgagee must be repaid first. If there is insufficient to repay that senior mortgagee, the purchaser acquires the property encumbered by that mortgage.

18.12 Considerations for Mortgagees of Leasehold Property

It will frequently be commercially attractive to lend against the value of leasehold property, as this may have a very high resale value. Clearly the value is likely to diminish over time as the lease shortens but this will not be a concern with long leases, and can in any case be taken into account when deciding the extent of the loan. There are several other matters, however, which are peculiar to mortgages of leaseholds.

1.   There is a possibility that the lessor may forfeit the lease, with the result that the lease vanishes and renders worthless any charge on it. Forfeiture may result from failure to pay rent or from persistent breaches of covenants in the lease. The law requires the lessor to follow a lengthy procedure in order to obtain forfeiture, and the court has power to grant relief against forfeiture, which it will give on any reasonable application by the lessee, but the mortgagee of the lease will not necessarily hear of the forfeiture proceedings until it is too late. The lessee would not normally sit idly by while a valuable lease is forfeited but he may not act if it is overmortgaged and he has no equity in it. If the mortgagee applies for relief from forfeiture, the court will commonly require him to rectify or pay the mortgagor's breach and to guarantee against future breaches, or take over the lease in the mortgagee's name as tenant. Some leases contain a clause which provides for automatic forfeiture in the event of the lessee's bankruptcy. Such a lease is obviously not suitable security for a mortgagee. In such a case the lessor would have to be approached to execute a deed of variation to the lease, in order to remove the clause.

2.   The lease may contain some restriction (absolute or conditional on the lessor's consent) on mortgaging or assigning the lease. If there is a restriction on mortgaging, a bank can decline to accept the lease as security unless the lease is varied or the

lessor's consent obtained. In the case of a restriction on assigning, a mortgage will be effective if the charge by way of legal mortgage is used, as opposed to the charge by demise. A problem may later arise if the mortgagee wishes to exercise his power of sale, which will require an assignment of the lease to a purchaser. Where the restriction is conditional, the lessor's consent may not be unreasonably refused. Where the restriction is absolute, the mortgagee would be well advised to have the lease varied before accepting it as security.

3.   The lease will commonly contain repair covenants, to deal with repair and maintenance of the building and contributions to the costs of these by the lessees. The lease may also contain easements to permit passage of services such as water, gas, drainage, etc, through parts of the building demised to other lessees. These provisions are notoriously complex to draft, and care must be taken in each case to tailor them to the precise design of the building in question. It is false economy to avoid the expense of having a lawyer scrutinise the covenants and easements in the lease. Even when this precaution is taken, it can happen that a matter has been overlooked and a purchaser refuses to buy the lease as it stands, and the lease is therefore heavily devalued unless it can be varied. If an independent lawyer was employed to examine the lease, an action should lie against him in these circumstances.

To summarize the risks of lending against land:

(a)   some defect in the mortgagor's title, which may not be clear from search of the Land Register or Land Charges Register and Local Land Charges Register. This may be an overriding interest accruing to another in the case of registered land, or a beneficial interest in the case of unregistered land;

(b)   a forged signature on the mortgage deed. The charge will then be void. If there are two co-owners and the signature of one is forged, the mortgagee has an equitable mortgage over the share of the property beneficially owned by the genuine signatory;

(c)   the various pitfalls which present themselves in the case of mortgages of leaseholds; or

(d)   a claim of undue influence or *non est factum* by one of the mortgagors.

18.13 Safe to Lend Considerations

Before a bank should advance the moneys against the security of land the following points must be addressed by the lender:

(a)   ensure that the borrower has a good unencumbered title to the property;

(b)   ensure that all searches have been carried out and that there is nothing adverse;

(c)   ensure that there is adequate insurance over the property and give notice to the insurance company of the banks interest;

(d) ensure that the valuation undertaken by a member of the bank's valuation panel and addressed to the bank is sound and reliable;

(e) in the case of second mortgages ensure that there is sufficient equity in the property for the advance;

(f) ensure that all legal charges are registered at the land registry or the land charges department as appropriate; and

(g) in the case of any security taken form a company that the Companies House registry is searched. Also any charge given by a company must be registered at Companies House.

However a banker must turn his attention to other risks in connection with security as follows.

18.13.1 Overriding Interests

Overriding interests are unregisterable but are binding on a person who acquires an interest in land such as a mortgagee/rights of persons in actual occupation of the property, or those contributing money or moneys worth to a property and providing they are in actual occupation can have overriding interests.

A wife or cohabitee or adult children who are not registered as legal owners can have overriding interests that render a mortgage valueless as the bank will not have a power of sale. A bank must make adequate enquiry and ascertain all persons who are in actual occupation of the property at the time of the mortgage. A bank must obtain a letter of consent from all such persons otherwise the lending will be effectively unsecured.

18.13.2 Undue Influence and Misrepresentation

Undue influence and misrepresentation only occur where an individual – not a corporate – is giving security. It can occur with the giving of any security, be it, inter alia, land, guarantees, stocks and shares.

When taking any form of security a bank must take cognisance of the possibility of undue influence and misrepresentation where the security is being taken from an individual.

It is a general principle of law that where one party to an agreement has been subject to the strong influence of the other party, so that he does not form an independent judgment as to whether to enter into the agreement, then the transaction becomes voidable for undue influence, ie the influenced party may choose to void it if he wishes. This defence is to be distinguished from that of duress, whereby physical force or the threat of it is used to obtain the other party's agreement. The legal effect of duress is also to make the transaction voidable.

It has emerged from decided cases that the law considers that undue influence may be presumed to exist in certain relationships. These have long included parent/child (when it is the child raising undue influence by the parent), doctor/patient, solicitor/client, religious leader/disciple and more recently the relationship between members of a particularly tightly knit immigrant group was added to the list. In these relationships undue influence is presumed to exist but the court will hear evidence which may rebut that presumption. These relationships are known as Class 2A relationships.

The relationships of banker/customer, husband/wife and parent/child (when it is the parent who is raising undue influence) are amongst those capable of being considered ones of presumed undue influence if it is shown that in the particular relationship, there is the appropriate degree of trust, confidence or influence. Any cohabiting relationship is included in this category, whether heterosexual or homosexual, as is a non-cohabiting relationship where the couple have a long-standing emotional relationship and have two children. It is also now confirmed that this category includes a husband who claims undue influence by his wife. Such relationships where undue influence is presumed because of the special nature of the relationship are labelled Class 2B.

Whether the relationship of presumed undue influence falls into the Class 2A category or the Class 2B, it is necessary for the claimant to prove that the disputed transaction was manifestly disadvantageous to him or her before a claim for undue influence will be upheld. A number of cases have examined this requirement.

In *Lloyds Bank v Bundy*, Mr B provided a series of guarantees, backed by charges on his sole property, to secure the bank's business loans to his son. It was a feature of the case that the bank allowed the loan to increase beyond the agreed limit (and the limit on the guarantee) and then approached Mr B to increase his limit. Mr B was elderly, did not understand business matters well and placed a degree of trust in his bank. When the son defaulted, the bank sought a possession order against Mr B which the court refused on the basis that, due to the trust placed in the bank by Mr B, the bank had failed to recognize a conflict of interest. It should have declined to accept the guarantee until Mr B had obtained independent advice. The transaction was manifestly disadvantageous to Mr B and he also had shown that there was the necessary degree of trust in his relationship with the bank.

In *Goode Durrant Administration v Biddulph*, a wife's indirect advantage in the potential profit to her husband's company (the loan to which she guaranteed) was not taken into account and her personal 2.5% shareholding in the company was considered too small to justify the risk she assumed by signing the guarantee. In *Bank of Scotland v Bennett*, the wife in this case also could show the transactions were not to her advantage when she owned 11.8% of the shares in the company at the time she signed the guarantee and owned 45.1% by the time she charged her house to back up the guarantee. In *Barclays Bank v Sumner*, however, a wife's 50% holding in the relevant company appears to have been considered sufficient to deny manifest disadvantage.

When the guarantee or charge secures a loan that is made in the joint names of husband and wife, there is on the face of things nothing to indicate disadvantage to the wife, since she is jointly entitled to the borrowed funds. In *CIBC Mortgages v Pitt*, the husband influenced his wife to jointly mortgage their home to raise funds which the husband used to speculate on the stock market. However, the lender was told the funds were required for the purchase of a holiday home for the couple and the charge was upheld. The mere fact that the loan is made in joint names would not save the lender, however, if he in fact knows that the funds will be used for the exclusive benefit of the husband.

Where a Class 2A or Class 2B relationship of presumed undue influence is established, the presumption is rebuttable. The onus is on the bank to prove that there has not been any undue influence. In order to do this, the bank may be able to point to the fact that the claimant received independent legal advice before entering into the transaction. The law relating to this and other methods of rebutting the presumption is considered below.

If a claimant is unable to establish presumed undue influence, it is open to him or her to try to prove actual undue influence, known as Class 1 undue influence. This requires it to be shown that the other party had the capacity to influence the complainant, that he did so influence him or her, that the influence was undue, and that it caused the complainant to enter into the transaction. It is not necessary for the complainant to show manifest disadvantage.

In *Barclays Bank v O'Brien*, the defendant's wife claimed undue influence had been exerted on her by her husband. The court found that theirs was not the kind of relationship where undue influence was presumed (ie it did not fall into Class 2B). The court also held that she had failed to establish evidence of actual undue influence (Class 1). She did, however, establish misrepresentation by her husband (this is discussed in the following section).

18.13.3 Misrepresentation

This takes the form of some misrepresentation that is made to the provider of the security which induces him to sign, something he would not otherwise have done. The effect is akin to undue influence in that the victim may void the transaction if the other party to the contract is the maker of the misrepresentation or that other party is somehow tainted by the misrepresentation made by another person.

In *MacKenzie v Royal Bank of Canada*, the plaintiff wife had mortgaged some shares to provide security for loans to her husband's company. She was misled by both her husband and by the defendant as to the effect of the documents she signed, and as the misrepresentation was deemed material, it was held she could void the charge over the shares.

In *Barclays Bank v O'Brien*, the defendant wife had been told by her husband that the charge over the matrimonial home which she was being asked to sign was limited in value to £60,000 and limited in time to a short period. The charge secured a loan to a company with which her husband was involved and in which she had no direct involvement. It was held that the misrepresentation as to the financial limit (the charge was in fact expressed

to be unlimited) had induced the wife to sign and therefore the wife was not liable beyond the limit she had been led to believe existed. It appears the wife had only claimed to limit the charge on the basis of the misrepresentation, and had not sought to invalidate it on this basis. In *TSB Bank v Camfield*, the court invalidated the charge entirely on the basis of a similar misrepresentation by the husband as to the financial limit of the charge.

It appears that in addition to the kind of misrepresentation described above, which has the effect of voiding the security, there can be a negligent misstatement, the effect of which falls short of influencing the person to sign the document but which does lead him to misunderstand the effect of it. The security will not be voidable but the bank will be liable in negligence if it is the maker of the statement. In *Cornish v Midland Bank*, a Mr and Mrs H purchased a farm and approached the bank for finance to renovate it. The bank agreed to do so, subject to a limit of £2,000 and to it taking a second mortgage. Mrs H was left with the impression that the bank had agreed not to lend more than the limit, whilst in reality the charge form included the standard "all-moneys" clause. Furthermore, she was unaware that she had executed any form of mortgage. Soon after, Mr and Mrs H separated (to the bank's knowledge), and Mr H alone operated the account until it was overdrawn well beyond the limit. The court held that the mortgage was valid but that the bank had been negligent in misleading Mrs H (now named Cornish) as to the limit, and it was therefore liable to compensate her for her loss resulting from this. It was also suggested that the bank owed her a duty not to allow Mr H to continue to borrow on the account and to notify her if he did. Further suggestions that, as she was also a personal customer, the bank owed her a duty to advise her as to the nature and effect of the document she was about to sign, have since been disapproved in *Midland Bank v Khaira*, although the point was not addressed by the House of Lords in *Barclays Bank v O'Brien*. It has been suggested that a bank owes a customer a duty of care when some special trust or confidence is being placed in the bank by the security-giver.

18.13.4 How a Bank can be Affected by Undue Influence

A bank's rights against a security-giver can be affected in the following ways:

(a) it exerts the undue influence itself against the security-giver;

(b) it used another person as its agent and that person so exerted undue influence on the security-giver;

(c) it has actual notice that another person so exerted undue influence on him or her;

(d) it has constructive notice that another person did so;

Lloyds Bank v Bundy and *MacKenzie v Royal Bank of Canada* are two cases where the bank involved itself exerted the undue influence on the security-giver. Such a conclusion may be reached from deeming the banker-customer relationship to be Class 2B presumed undue influence which the bank has failed to rebut or from finding that there is evidence of actual undue influence (Class 1).

In some cases it may be shown that the bank used another person as its agent and that that person exerted undue influence. Prior to the decision in *O'Brien*, this method was successfully used to invalidate charges, for instance by pleading that the bank had given the charge forms to the husband through whom the wife signed them, but in *O'Brien* this was considered artificial. In any case lenders soon learned that security forms should not be handed to intermediaries for conveying to the security-giver. It could still happen that the bank is deemed to use another as an agent such as where the bank has virtually recruited the agent to get the charge forms signed by the security-giver.

In the vast majority of cases, however, the bank is entirely innocent of exerting undue influence, either directly or through an agent, and the security-giver is claiming that another person did so, such as the husband in *Barclays Bank v O'Brien*. The security-giver may then be able to show that the bank had actual knowledge of the undue influence. This also is rare in practice, it is much more likely that the bank had constructive notice of it. This requires it to be shown that:

(a) there is an emotional relationship between the security-giver and his or her cohabitee or other close person (this appears to be identical to the category of relationships which are capable of constituting ones of Class 2B undue influence); and

(b) the transaction on its face was not to the financial advantage of the security-giver (this is analogous to the requirement in establishing Class 2B undue influence that the transaction was manifestly disadvantageous to the security-giver and the cases discussed above are therefore relevant here also) and that there is a substantial risk a wrong has been committed by the other person in the emotional relationship.

Once the security-giver has shown that he or she was unduly influenced, the burden of proof is on the bank to show that it did not have constructive notice of it.

Usually the bank is aware of the nature of the relationship between the parties, so condition (a) is not contentious. Most guarantors are in an emotional relationship with the other party and that is why they are prepared to enter into a disadvantageous transaction. *Credit Lyonnais Bank Nederland NV v Burch* was a rare case where there was no such obvious relationship as the guarantor was an employee of the company whose debt was secured and she denied an emotional relationship with the director of the company. The transaction was so disadvantageous to her that the court was able to find in her favour.

Sometimes the bank does not know enough facts to establish condition (b) but a solicitor involved in the transaction does know these facts. Where the solicitor has not passed on what he knows to the bank, it becomes crucial to the question of constructive notice whether the bank is deemed to know what the solicitor knew. In *Midland Bank v Serter*, a solicitor acted for a wife and her husband as well as for the bank, who had instructed him to register its charge. The wife claimed the solicitor knew of the undue influence exerted on her by her husband and therefore that the bank was also deemed to know it. It was held that the bank was only deemed to know what the solicitor knew in his capacity of registering the charge, and found in favour of the bank. The decision would have been different, it seems, if the bank had instructed the solicitor to advise the wife on whether she should give the security.

In another case the loan was being made to a joint account and thus the transaction was not on its face to the wife's disadvantage. The solicitor involved knew, however, that the loan was really to pay off the husband's debts. It was held the solicitor could not convey this to the lender without the couple's consent. Without such consent, the solicitor should have ceased to act for the lender but given that he continued to do so, his knowledge could not be imputed to the lender unless he was acting fraudulently. On appeal this case upheld the lender's victory, but on the grounds of s 199(1)(ii)(b) of the Law of Property Act 1925 which limits what a purchaser of land (and therefore also a legal mortgagee) is deemed to know through his solicitor.

If the necessary conditions are established for a bank to be deemed to have constructive notice, that notice can be negatived by the bank following a procedure laid down by the House of Lords in *O'Brien*. This consists of the bank seeing the wife (or whoever is the security-giver) on her own and explaining:

(a)   the extent of her liability; and

(b)   the nature of the risk she is incurring by signing the security, eg she might lose her home; and

(c)   that she should take independent legal advice.

It was said that the above would suffice in the normal case but that if the bank knew facts which made undue influence probable rather than possible, it should go further and insist on her obtaining independent legal advice.

The danger for a bank in adopting this procedure as routine is that the wife may reveal some facts in the meeting which indicate that undue influence is probable or that a misrepresentation has taken place and a bank would then be obliged to see that she receives independent legal advice. The employee who attends the meeting would need to be able to judge this matter accurately. Alternatively, the wife might later claim that she did not understand the explanations given to her at the meeting. While a strict reading of the dicta in *O'Brien* appear to render it irrelevant whether she under stood any of the explanation, a bank might have a weakness on these facts, especially if it was considered that it was clear she did not understand.

In some cases a bank may insist on independent legal advice; in others the wife or other security-giver may obtain it voluntarily. When it is given, other issues arise. Cases discussed above concern whether a bank is struck with the knowledge of the facts that the solicitor had. Another issue is whether the bank need be concerned as to the adequacy of the advice given by the solicitor. In *Barclays Bank v Thompson*, the husband and wife were told by the bank to take legal advice before granting the charge over their home which was to be security for the husband's debts. The bank itself instructed solicitors to register its charge and it also specifically asked these solicitors to advise the wife. The wife was seen on her own and the solicitors confirmed to the bank that the advice had been given to her. The wife later claimed that the explanation was inadequate. It appears that a failure to adhere to the suggested procedure laid down by the House of Lords in *O'Brien* (ie not seeing the wife on her own) will not matter if the wife does in fact receive independent legal advice. Nor will it matter to the bank if that advice is defective if the solicitor confirms it was given. This has the effect of shifting the risk in transactions where independent advice is given to the solicitor.

In *Massey v Midland Bank*, the couple in that case were also jointly told by the bank that the wife should be independently advised. She was advised by a solicitor but her partner was present during the meeting. This did not prevent the charge from being upheld. In *Banco Exterior Internacional v Mann*, the wife was advised by a solicitor who acted for her husband and her husband's company. This also did not prevent the charge from being upheld. In *Bank Melli Iran v Samadi-Rad*, however, it was suggested that an assurance given by solicitors that the wife would be independently advised was insufficient for the bank to rely on. An undertaking that she had been so advised would, however, be sufficient.

In *Credit Lyonnais Bank Nederland NV v Burch*, the defendant was a not very highly paid employee of the company whose debt she charged her home to guarantee. The controller of the company persuaded her to sign an unlimited guarantee securing the company's overdraft which had a limit of £270,000. The defendant was advised in a letter from the bank that she should seek independent advice and warning her that the guarantee would be unlimited. She was not told the planned overdraft limit for the company nor that its debts at that time already stood at £163,000. The defendant did not claim to have had an emotional relationship with the controller of the company. The court still felt able to conclude that the bank had constructive notice of a Class 2B type of presumed undue influence on the facts. This was decided on the basis that the bank knew she was only a junior employee of the company, who had no interest in it as director or shareholder and that the transaction was manifestly disadvantageous to her. Two members of the court held it was the category of case where independent legal advice must be obtained if the bank's charge is to be upheld. One member went further and suggested that it would have made no difference even if she had been independently advised.

Finally, in *Royal Bank of Scotland v Etridge* (2001), the House of Lords laid down minimum requirements to protect a guarantors wife and reduce the risk of such indulgence to an acceptable level. From this case emerged the principles that the bank should:

1. check with her the name of the solicitor she wishes to act;

2. provide the solicitor with the financial information needed to advise her;

3. the bank must inform the solicitor if they suspect anything untoward;

4. the bank should obtain confirmation from the solicitor.

Finally, it is pertinent to recall that in the *Morgan* case, Lord Scarman issued a warning to the effect that the law leaves the dividing line, between mere folly on the one hand and unconscionable transactions on the other hand, deliberately uncertain. He said there is no precisely defined law setting limits to the equitable jurisdiction of a court to relieve against undue influence.

19

GOODS AND PRODUCE AS SECURITY (PRODUCE ADVANCES)

19.1 General Features

The use of goods and produce as security is widely seen in international trade and is a somewhat specialized area.

Lenders frequently provide finance to exporters (those selling goods abroad) and importers (those buying goods from abroad). As a scenario, a lender may grant a produce loan for imported goods such as wool, cotton, wheat, etc. The importer issues specialized documents and is financed by the lender until the goods are sold. The bank takes constructive possession of the goods being used as security by having them warehoused in its name or by taking possession of the title documents. There is very little in the way of formal security procedures and the quality of the security largely rests upon the customer, the shipper and the level of insurance attached to the goods.

Given the nature of most goods and produce, these types of loan are essentially short-term and repayment comes from the sale of the goods. Thus the lender is earning money quickly and repeatedly. It is not unusual to see a company with a revolving credit facility for its import/export activities in addition to their other facilities. Their short-term nature means that, while such things as inflation and interest rates will not directly affect the sale price, there might be other factors (especially with perishable goods) that could cause price fluctuations. Thus wide security margins in this field are common.

19.2 Advantages

1. The bank has recourse to the underlying goods in the event of default.

2. The documentation is simple to execute.

19.3 Disadvantages

1.   Initial valuation can be difficult. The importer will be buying and probably on-selling at a mark-up. The importer will often seek finance against the higher price.

2.   Insurance of the goods is essential and can be expensive, and a well known insurer is a must.

3.   Warehousing of goods is usually necessary and this is an extra expense. The warehouser has a lien on the goods for unpaid costs.

19.4 Type of Charge

The main type of charge that is taken in connection with a produce advance is a pledge which involves either actual or constructive delivery of goods to a lender. Constructive delivery is achieved by giving the corporate customer a key to a warehouse in which the goods are stored.

The bank is the pledgor of the goods who has legal title to the goods, and the pledgee is the customer who becomes a bailee and who must return the goods or repayment as agreed. The bank is entitled to demand a receipt for deposit of the goods.

The customer owes a duty of care for the goods while in his possession and if they are lost or damaged through negligence then the customer must make good the loss to the bank.

Banks usually prefer to exercise more control over the customer having access to the goods and usually require control to be done through a warehouser of the goods. A "Trust Receipt" will be issued by a warehouse on deposit of the goods and will constitute the document of title to the goods which must remain in the possession of the bank until the loan facility is repaid.

Another rare form of charge for a bank to take is a "Chattel Mortgage" of the goods or item by way of a conditional bill of sale. Such a bill must be registered at the High Court within seven days otherwise such a charge is void.

19.5 Valuation

Banks need to ensure that there is a ready market for the goods outside the confines of the particular transaction. This may not be the case with perishable products or fashion or other specialist goods may not be easily realisable by a bank in a forced sale situation. The difference between invoice value and a forced sale valuation must be considered by a bank and lend only up to a particular margin of the goods. The bank may need to have goods valued by a professional but no matter what valuation is obtained a bank should only lend no more than 75% by way of a protective charge.

19.6 Safe to Lend Considerations

It is a dangerous assumption that a banker should regard produce advances as less risky than other forms of security as it can look at the underlying goods as security. As has been said above the produce advance can be secured by the goods being imported, provided only that control can be exercised over them should the importing customer not be bale to meet the obligation.

A banker must consider the following issues before considering a produce advance.

(a) The terms of any accompanying letter of credit must provide for documents to be released against payment and not against acceptance, as in the latter case the bank would loose control of the goods when they are released to the importer on acceptance of a bill.

(b) There must be a ready market for the goods outside the confines of the particular transaction. This may not be the case with perishable products or fashion or other specialist goods may not be easily realizable by a bank in a forced sale situation. The difference between invoice value and a forced sale valuation must be considered by a bank and lend only up to a particular margin.

(c) The bank must consider its liability for any storage and selling costs that may be involved in a forced sale which must also be built in to any protective lending margin. Only in this way can a bank regard a produce advance as being fully secured and self-liquidating.

(d) The documents must enable a bank to acquire title to the goods. Title may be acquired by a negotiable bill of lading or a trust receipt issued by a warehouse. Shipments covered by airway bills or lorry consignment notes cannot be regarded as secured as such documents do not constitute documents of title.

(e) A bank must be satisfied that any overseas supplier will ship the goods and so some sort of credit check may need to be done. Also, as the bank does not deal in the actual goods it may be prudent to require a certificate of inspection as part of the loan documentation.

(f) The goods must be fully insured and the bank must see sight of the policy and/or consider assigning such a policy.

(g) The bank must ensure that all import requirements such as licences will be obtained.

(h) Finally, if the loan is in foreign currency the bank must consider the currency exchange risks involved as part of its protective margin.

20

GUARANTEES

20.1 Personal Guarantees

A guarantee is a promise made (to a lender), to the effect that if the borrower does not repay a debt then the guarantor will. Guarantees can be given by individuals, two or more people – when liability is joint and several – and by companies (if the Articles of association permit). In groups of companies, the cross-guarantee is one of the most common forms of security given. A cross-guarantee is where one company within a group provides a guarantee for the debt of another group company. Modern forms of bank guarantee incorporate an indemnity clause. This effectively binds the guarantor so that he or she is not able to avoid the debt on a technicality. Generally speaking, guarantees are among the simplest forms of security to take because they are effected by simply signing the guarantee form. However, when taking guarantees the lender must be certain of a number of points.

1. *Does the guarantor have the legal capacity to enter into the guarantee?* For example, minors and those deemed mentally incompetent are not able to give guarantees.

2. *Whose laws apply?* Most domestic guarantee forms contain a statement that the law of England and Wales governs the contract. In most cases this will suffice, however, there can be difficulties if the guarantor is a foreign national. These difficulties primarily revolve around the capacity to contract which may be defined differently in other countries. For instance, the age of maturity in the UK is 18 whereas in some other countries it is 21 or 25.

3. *Has undue influence been placed on the guarantor?* *Lloyds Bank Ltd. v Bundy* (1975) – undue influence of a son on his father. The father gave a guarantee for the son's bank account. Bundy Senior gave a guarantee for £1,500 in favour of Lloyds Bank to secure the business account of Bundy Junior. The guarantee was supported by a mortgage over a domestic property. At a subsequent meeting of Bundy Senior, Junior and a bank official, the guarantee was increased to £11,000. The son was made bankrupt by the bank who called on the guarantee. The High Court set the guarantee, and the mortgage, aside as Mr Bundy Senior was deemed to have been influenced to enter into a contract that benefited others. Subsequent to this landmark ruling (and the ruling in *Barclays v O'Brien* which involved misrepresentation), lenders have invariably insisted that any guarantor has independent legal advice prior to entering into the guarantee. This prevents guarantors avoiding a guarantee on the

grounds that they did not understand what they were doing or did not appreciate the level of liability they were agreeing to guarantee. The legal adviser would normally make enquiries on the lender as to the current situation of the debtor which, providing the debtor agreed, would be disclosed. This enables the legal adviser to advise the potential guarantor that "the debtor is currently £45,000 overdrawn" or "the debtor is currently in credit". If the guarantee was for £50,000 this might have an influence on the guarantor.

4   *Is the guarantee actually worth anything?* Guarantees are normally all moneys, in which case the guarantor is covering all borrowing of the debtor, or limited to a specific maximum, but is the guarantor sufficiently financially strong to meet the liability? How then, can a lender determine the value, if any, of a guarantee? If the guarantor is a customer of the lender the problem is somewhat less because the lender will probably know something of the financial standing of the guarantor. If the guarantor is a customer of another financial institution a status enquiry would be the easiest method of trying to quantify financial standing. In many cases the lender seeks to have the guarantee supported by a legal mortgage over other assets that are easy to value. Normally this is by way of a charge over property owned by the guarantor.

The value of the guarantee would in fact be the value of the tangibility of the security.

	No prior mortgage	Prior Mortgage
Value of property	100,000	100,000
Discount 75%	75,000	75,000
First mortgage	nil	50,000
Value of guarantee	75,000	25,000

If the second mortgage is taken to support the guarantee then the usual considerations and formalities will need to be followed.

Once the guarantee is in place the lender can operate the account up to the extent of the guarantee. While the guarantee is in force, the lender needs to remember that a duty of confidentiality is still owed to the debtor and the guarantor does not have rights, for example, to see statements or know how the account is being conducted. Of course, the guarantor can ask the lender to what extent the guarantee is being relied upon and there will one of three possible replies:

(a)   The guarantee is being fully relied upon – debt equals guarantee.

(b)   The guarantee is being relied upon to the extent of £X plus interest and charges but the position can change from day-to-day – debt less than guarantee.

(c)   The guarantee is not currently being relied upon but the situation can change day by day – debtor's account in credit.

The guarantor may decide on receipt of replies (b) or (c) to inform the lender that he or she is withdrawing the guarantee. However, such notice takes three months to become effective. Most guarantee forms contain a clause stating that the guarantee remains effective for three months after the death or mental incapacity of the guarantor. In such circumstances a claim can be made under the guarantee if the borrower cannot find alternative security.

The lender obviously has the right to call upon the guarantor for the full amount as and when required, or upon a lesser amount if he or she decides to terminate support to the debtor.

To summarize: guarantees are easy to take but difficult to value and often require additional security to make the guarantee worth anything.

20.2 Corporate Guarantees

20.2.1 Introduction

In the UK, guarantees are noted in a company's annual report as contingent liabilities. Analysts may add these into the borrowings figure to calculate gearing. However, in reality, only guarantees given in respect of the performance of third parties should be added in, as guarantees of inter-company indebtedness would already be included in the total borrowings figure, as shown on the balance sheet. The difference lies in the guarantor obligation falling on the company, not the consolidated group. It is therefore the gearing level of the company that is affected by the contingent liabilities – a fact that is sometime miscalculated.

The policy to guarantee or not will vary by company and industry type. Many companies will wish, for management purposes, to ensure that subsidiaries are viewed on a stand-alone basis, and will maintain the subsidiary's capital base to that effect. Other companies will take a group approach, seeing the subsidiaries or divisions forming a part of the whole, and therefore be more "relaxed" about giving guarantees to lenders as support for indebtedness.

20.2.2 Purpose of Guarantees

● To ensure if principal debtor does not pay then recovery can be from another person.

● Secondly one may take a guarantee to ensure a supervisory function, ie parent and subsidiary.

● Secure non-interference, ie in the case of a central bank with power to impose exchange controls.

20.2.3 Forms of Guarantee

- *Guarantee* – an obligation of secondary liability where demand must be made on the principal debtor or borrower first before making demand on the guarantor.

- *Primary* – indemnity liability. No consideration is needed with an indemnity obligation as opposed to a guarantee in as much as the indemnifier must pay even if the underlying transaction is void or unenforceable. Thus as with an indemnity the liability of the indemnifier does not depend upon the liability of the principal debtor.

- *Letter of comfort* – not necessarily legally binding but can vary in wording as to be guarantees or indemnities.

20.2.4 Inter-company Guarantees

In large international companies with many subsidiaries and associated companies the pattern of financing can often be very complex. The fact that Subsidiary A requires funds does not necessarily mean that it is the best vehicle through which the group should obtain the relevant finance. On the other hand, it may be that Subsidiary B, which is highly liquid, will nevertheless be the most economic unit through which to source a new group borrowing. For the most part, decisions in this area are tax-driven but there are other considerations, such as access to domestic markets, which might cause the corporate to route a borrowing indirectly. Looked at on a unilateral basis, it is not to be expected that all the units in a group will have the same credit standing and it is accordingly normal for such transactions to be supported, where necessary, by inter-company guarantees. The bank will want to look very closely at the implications of these while, in turn, the corporate must ensure that it does not agree to anything which might constrain the corporate's ability to finance itself in the most satisfactory way in the future.

20.3 Consideration

It is not unusual for one company to guarantee the liabilities of a second company. Quite often this will happen within a group situation where each company provides cross guarantees for each others members of the group. In order for such a guarantee to be effective, there must be commercial justification for the company to enter into this (or indeed any) contract, see: *Charterbridge Corporation v Lloyds Bank* (1969). Although s 238(5) of the Insolvency Act 1986 will protect the bank if the guarantor acted "in good faith and for the benefit of carrying on its business" and that at that time, there were grounds for believing that the transaction would benefit the company.

20.3.1 "Upstream", "Downstream" and "Cross-stream" Guarantees

The credit strength of a group of companies lies where the assets are. If the group is structured with a parent company which is merely a holding company then the various subsidiaries will be the only assets to which a bank can look to for security if it is lending to the parent company. Any guarantee given by one of those subsidiaries to the bank will result in the subsidiary's creditors ranking ahead of the parent company in the event of the subsidiary's liquidation – they will thus rank ahead of the bank which has lent to the parent company. Accordingly, the bank would require an extension of the restrictions of the negative pledge to the subsidiaries in which the real strength of the company lay. Where the bank is lending to one of the subsidiary companies, the need for protection may be equally acute. One particular danger that the bank will perceive is that the subsidiary might give what are known as *"upstream"* or *"cross-stream"* guarantees for indebtedness of the parent company or of a fellow subsidiary. The existence of such guarantees can change the order or ranking in a liquidation situation to the disadvantage of the bank and in an extreme situation could possibly be used to defraud it. Thus, the parent company lends money to Subsidiary A under the guarantee of Subsidiary B which has, in turn, borrowed from the bank. The parent then deliberately strips all assets out of Subsidiary A and forces it into liquidation using the upstream guarantee to tank ahead of the bank in the consequent liquidation of Subsidiary B. You will find it instructive to review the matrix of possibilities in this area. Therefore, banks should lend money to directly to subsidiaries where the assets are held and not through a layer or structure of guarantees. In the case of upstream or cross-stream guarantees there must be some commercial benefit to the company providing the guarantee, otherwise it can be struck out in the event of a legal challenge by a liquidator.

When negotiating these points, the corporate's primary concern must be to ensure that none of the constraints that have been introduced into the loan agreement to protect the bank will, in turn, place unacceptable constraints on the company's financing flexibility. In particular he should not agree to any prohibition of "downstream" guarantees (that is, parent guarantees of subsidiary or associate company borrowings) even though it is possible to demonstrate that, in certain circumstances, the bank could be disadvantaged thereby. Such a restriction could prevent the use of borrowing-vehicle companies to achieve a tax advantage or circumvent foreign exchange control restrictions. Similarly it could impede the financing of a joint venture operation with adverse commercial consequences.

20.3.2 Possible Problems for the Guarantor

Dependent again on the credit status of the parties, the bank may wish to obtain similar covenants from the guarantor that it has required from the borrower. This will be the case particularly if the borrower is a vehicle company so that it is only in the guarantor that credit of any substance lies. In such a situation the bank will be negotiating directly with the guarantor and will behave much as if it were making a direct loan. The borrowers position in all this should be to ensure that the covenants his company accepts in the capacity of guarantor are no stronger than those he would accept were the company itself borrowing. While it is prudent financial management to regard a guarantee as a real rather than as a contingent liability, for purposes of internal housekeeping, it is certainly not sensible to allow the company's financing flexibility to be reduced in order to obtain off-balance sheet finance.

Any guarantee given for a loan will be required to cover not only its capital value but also outstanding interest charges and any other payments due by the borrower under the loan agreement. Where the borrower is not a wholly-owned subsidiary, this could put the guarantor into a situation in which it was compelled to continue supporting the borrower even though it did not wish to do so. It is therefore advisable to specify, in the guarantee agreement, a limit to the amount of interest to be covered; one year's interest or one period's interest. What the guarantor does not want is to be forced, against its will, to continue to meet routine interest payments because the bank has elected not to call a default and the guarantor has no powers to force the bank to do so. This is an unlikely situation but one which should be guarded against when the borrower is a joint venture company. While the bank will not normally fail to call a default if the guarantor asks it to do so, it could be in a difficult situation were it to receive conflicting request from two parent guarantors which could not agree on how to treat their failed associate.

20.3.3 The Effect of Time-limited Guarantees

In this connection you should note that, while it is possible to write a time-limited guarantee, its only effect is to bring the bank to a point at which it must either call the underlying loan or insist on the guarantee being renewed. In all normal circumstances it will do the latter, but it will certainly insist that the agreement specifies that expiry of the guarantee constitutes a default, so that it is in a position to do the former should it be appropriate. More important, the existence of such a covenant will give it the leverage to obtain a continuing guarantee. Thus the commonly-heard statement that there is no such thing as a time-limited guarantee, while not strictly true, is a sensible axiom for the treasurer to work to.

20.3.3.1 Joint or Several Guarantees

Particular care needs to be taken where a guarantee is given in association with a third party, as may frequently occur when the borrower is a joint venture operation owned by two or more otherwise unconnected parents.

A company should not normally be willing to guarantee more of a subsidiary or associate company's debt than is properly attributable to its share of the ownership. If a corporate only owns 50% of the associate then it should only guarantee 50%, unless there are specific reasons for doing otherwise – perhaps the existence of a separate profit-sharing agreement. Where the guarantee is to be given by more than one party it can be given in one of three forms.

- *Joint*: the partners are jointly responsible for the whole debt in the event of default by the borrower. The effect is that, if for any reason one of the parties is not able to meet the liability, then the guarantee becomes unenforceable against the others. This situation is, understandably, unacceptable to the banks – were one partner to fail then the bank would become dependent on the goodwill of the others to recover anything.

- *Several*: the partners are severally or individually liable for a specific amount, regardless of the actions of the others. Clearly no partner should ever give a several guarantee for more than its appropriate proportion of the debt, nor will it be necessary to do so. This is the normal form in which guarantees should be given. The effect is that the guarantor has a clearly-defined obligation which is restricted in any eventuality to the proportion of the borrower's debt properly attributable to it.

- *Joint and several*: under this form of guarantee each guarantor becomes individually liable for the whole amount of the debt. In the event of the guarantee being called the co-guarantors will share equally in the obligation because the guarantee is joint. However, in the event that one of them is, for any reason, unable to unwilling to pay, then the bank can turn to the other guarantors who are individually liable for the whole of the debt. Banks will frequently seek joint and several guarantees, particularly in situations where one guarantor is stronger than another. The corporate should think hard before agreeing to such a proposal which has evident dangers, the most obvious being that the "strongest" guarantor is required to make full payment, and seek contribution form its co-guarantors afterwards... an unsatisfactory situation.

20.3.4 Guarantor's Rights

Where a guarantor has met its obligation to the bank under a guarantee in full, it would automatically be entitled under the doctrine of subrogation to stand in the bank's position as regards recovering all or some part of its resultant loss from the borrower and be entitled to any security that the banks hold. The right of subrogation can be varied in the guarantee and in the case of joint or several guarantees, whatever its form, the situation should be specified to this effect in the terms of the guarantee.

In the normal course of events, the bank will expect to maintain its full rights against the borrower unless and until it has recovered the whole of its debt. Thus if companies A and B each guarantee one half of a $100 million borrowing by company z, which subsequently defaults, the position will be as follows.

20.3.4.1 Under a Joint Guarantee

A and B will each be liable for $50 million but, if one fails to pay, the other may be able to avoid its obligation at law. Note that the consequences of doing so would be so severe as to make such action unthinkable in any but the most critical circumstances. If A pays and B does not, then the bank will normally claim against the liquidator of Z for $100 million even though it has already recovered $50 million under the guarantee. Only if it should recover more than $100 million will it reimburse company A in respect of the excess.

20.3.4.2 Under Several Guarantees

A and B will each be liable for $50 million. Failure of one to pay will not affect the position of the other. The situation as regards subsequent claims against the liquidator of company Z is the same as in the case of a joint guarantee.

20.3.4.3 Under Joint and Several Guarantees

Should A fail to pay, then B becomes liable for $100 million and vice versa. Given that the bank has recovered in full, A and B (or whichever of them has paid) can rank against the liquidator of company Z for whatever they have paid in meeting their respective guarantees.

20.3.5 Guarantee Documentation

The wording of guarantees will differ in each instance, and is therefore difficult to generalize, but standard clauses should include:

- the names of the guarantor and the names of those guaranteed;

- the amount, or reference to a loan schedule, in order to limit the guarantor's obligation;

- the situations covered by the guarantee, such as non-payment of principal and interest (after grace periods) or liquidation of the company;

- a clause stating that the guarantee is continuing;

- protection clauses which allow the lender to modify obligation of the debtor without discharging the guarantor otherwise the guarantee would be discharged;

- clauses enabling the lender receive sums from guarantor into a suspense account;

- the terms of cancellation of the guarantee;

- the rights of remedy of the lender;

- no variation without written consent of the guarantor;

- subrogation rights;

- rights of the company to sue its subsidiary in competition to the bank if it has paid up under the guarantee; and

- governing law, jurisdiction should be same as that governing transaction.

Consideration should also be stated – *Re Lee Behrens & Co* (1932). No implied power and the possibility that the guarantee may be ultra vires.

Additionally, a guarantor in a term loan may give similar covenants to those given by the

20 – Guarantees

borrower including negative pledge, undertaking to give financial or other information. Representations and warranties, grossing up clauses, pari passu and sharing clauses may also be drafted.

20.3.6 Legal Problems

1. If the debtor is not liable, then under English law, neither is the guarantor unless he is indemnifying or the guarantee contains an indemnity clause.

2. The problem of capacity of the guarantor with the possibility of the guarantee being held to be ultra vires. This is especially true of non-corporates or entities in other jurisdictions.

3. Consideration in the sense that there must be some commercial benefit to the guarantor for giving a guarantee which should be stated such as if the guarantee is being given in consideration of the bank lending the borrower a sum of £5m and the bank in the event only lends £4m, then the guarantee may be ineffective.

20.3.7 Letters of Comfort

20.3.7.1 Introduction

A letter of comfort is a letter, usually written by a parent company, to a lender giving comfort to a lender about a loan made to a subsidiary. Parent companies will often argue strongly with lenders to give a letter of comfort as opposed to a full guarantee. A letter of comfort, or letter of awareness, is not legally binding on the giver of it, unlike a guarantor of a guarantee. However, in dealing with relationship bankers there can be said to be a moral obligation attached to such a letter. As such, therefore, they should not be given lightly, and should be negotiated as would any formal, legally-binding agreement. However, views vary from company-to-company on this. Given because the person giving them does not intend legally to be bound by them but perhaps to give approval to a proposed loan or transaction.

20.3.7.2 Legal Problems

English law presumes that a commercial agreement is legally binding unless otherwise clearly stated (*Edwards v Skyways Ltd* (1964)). Under English law the courts construe that letters of comfort are intended to create a contract but lean against converting comfort letters into guarantees and construe them against a lender. However, some comfort letters may be binding but this will depend on the drafting of such letters and different jurisdictions react differently to letters of comfort.

The weakest form of wording is commonly called a letter of awareness, where the parent company acknowledges its relationship with another group company, and its awareness of a loan being made to the company by the lender.

In the case of *Kleinwort Benson Ltd v Malaysian Mining Corporation* (1989) All ER 785 it was held that that the parent company was not liable as the parent had stated in its comfort letter that "it is our policy to ensure that the business of our subsidiary is at all times in a position to meet its liabilities to you". This was not held to be binding because it merely stated its present policy which thus be changed at any time. A letter of comfort therefore tries to state a policy or intention to do something but if it contained a promise or guarantee it may well constitute a legally binding agreement.

Whilst, as stated, letters of comfort do not have a legal standing in English law, the corporate should be aware that in other countries, the use of certain wording does raise what is, in English law terms, a comfort letter to a guarantee under the foreign jurisdictions. Legal advice through a legal opinion should therefore be sought in such instances.

A comfort letter in its stronger form will, in addition to acknowledging the situation, indicate the company's willingness to accept some responsibility to honour the borrowing obligations of the subsidiary, without legally binding itself so to do – such wording as using "its rights as a shareholder", or "best endeavours" so that the company conducts its business in a prudent manner. There are many variations on the theme, but the letter should refrain from making positive statements that the company "will ensure" etc, which could then transform the letter to being a guarantee. Legal advice should be sought on the matter.

20.4 Safe to Lend Considerations

A guarantee is easy to take from someone but can be difficult to enforce in practice. The value or benefit of a guarantee depends upon the guarantor. A guarantee is worthless if the guarantor is insolvent or not of sufficient means.

A banker must enquire into the creditworthiness of any potential guarantor whether it be personal or corporate. In the case of corporate guarantees the bank must be alert to the problems of lending to holding companies against the security of upstream guarantees which in effect may be worthless and banks should lend direct to the asset holding subsidiaries instead. In the case of corporate guarantees a bank must ensure that the issue of consideration is duly addressed in the taking of any guarantee.

As has been seen at 18.13.4 above the bank must assess the risks of undue influence where the guarantor is a partner or spouse of the customer. The bank in such circumstances must insist without exception on independent legal advice being taken by the guarantor. Failure to assess such risks will potentially render a guarantee void.

21

STOCKS AND SHARES

21.1 Forms of Company Security

21.1.1 Types of Shares

A company can issue different types of shares; the one thing that they all have in common is that in the UK the law requires them to have a nominal value. The nominal value is completely irrelevant when assessing the value of a company's shares.

The Companies Act defines equity shares as "shares in the company other than shares which as respects dividends and capital carry a right to participate only up to a specified amount in a distribution".

A company can issue various shares with different rights attaching to them, particularly with regard to voting. The rights attaching to each type of share would be specified in the issue documents and/or Articles of Association.

21.1.1.1 Ordinary Shares

This is what most people think of under the heading "equity". Ordinary shareholders are often thought of as being the main risk-takers as there is no certainty of income. If the company succeeds there is no upper limit on the amount of dividend paid, but it is never under any obligation to pay one. It is also the case that the share price of the ordinary shares will be most volatile in response to changing market conditions and perceptions of the company's future prospects. Companies can issue different types of ordinary shares, such as deferred shares which only receive dividends after other shareholders have received a set amount – these are very rare. Finally, it should be remembered that ordinary shares carry voting rights in the company which may be a valuable benefit.

21.1.1.2 "A" Shares

Ordinary shares that do not carry voting rights are often called "A" shares. The Stock Exchange is not happy to admit new non-voting shares to listing as it believes that it is more equitable for all ordinary shares to carry voting rights. In the early 1990s, some companies announced decisions to enfranchise their non-voting "A" shares. Amongst the better known companies that did this was GUS, the stores group.

21.1.1.3 Preference Shares

This term is not defined in the Companies Acts and each issue must provide its exact details of rights attached to preference shares. Investing in preference shares is often seen as an alternative to investing in bonds as they usually provide a fixed rate of dividend which is expressed as a percentage of the nominal value. Due to the tax structure of dividends there may be an advantage for institutional investors but not for private investors. The following facts about preference shares should be emphasised:

- the company cannot pay an ordinary dividend until it has paid the preference;

- the dividend only becomes payable when it is declared by the company which it will not do if it makes insufficient profits;

- if arrears have built up they only need to be paid if the shares are cumulative (which is the presumption);

- in a winding up they receive the nominal value before ordinary shareholders get anything; and

- participating preference shares can be issued where they share in surplus profits both annually and on winding up.

21.1.2 Security over Shares

As with every form of security, a key aspect is the ability to prove that Mr X is in fact the owner and thus has the power to create the charge. With this type of financial asset there are several ways in which ownership can be proved.

The most common is the share (or loan stock) certificate. This details the name of the owner, the type of share and the nominal value of the share. The share certificate is issued by the company registrar. This is usually a bank or insurance company that keeps the details of shareholders for the company. The registrar amends the records of ownership only in receipt of a stock transfer form signed by the owner transferring his or her rights to a third party. Recent developments in the stock exchange have introduced a non-paper based system of ownership registration via CREST. Within CREST, ownership is recorded electronically – the term dematerialized is used to differentiate this form of recording from the paper-based system. Again, ownership is transferred on the receipt of a CREST transfer form.

The majority of shareowners choose to have the shares registered in their own name but there are a few alternatives. Perhaps the most common alternative is to have the shares registered in a nominee name. Effectively, the nominee is the registered holder of the shares and receives all the dividends due. The nominee ultimately remits all the due dividends to the real owner. The main stated advantage for a nominee company is that an individual with a number of shareholdings need not be concerned with paperwork and tax calculations. Each nominee company obviously keeps records as to who owns what. If shares are registered in the name of a nominee, the owner loses the ancillary benefits that often accompany share ownership. Ownership in bearer form is also available, but this is becoming less popular as proof in the possession of a tangible document. Shares and loan stocks issued in bearer form have the same drawbacks but are easy to transfer and mortgage.

21.2 Mortgages over Securities

21.2.1 Legal Mortgage

A legal mortgage is effected by transferring title to the security from customer to the bank, in much the same way as if the bank had purchased it. The bank mortgagee thus becomes the registered holder of shares which are mortgaged to it. Assuming the mortgage is of company shares, the bank will take from the customer:

(a)   the share certificate; and

(b)   a signed and completed share transfer form.

The above documents are sufficient to create a valid legal mortgage and there is no requirement for any further mortgage form, nor for any documents to be executed as deeds. However, it is invariably bank practice to take a memorandum of deposit from the customer incorporating various protective clauses and confirming that the shares are transferred by way of security rather than sale.

21.2.2 Equitable Mortgage

In law, an equitable mortgage requires a minimum only of an intention for the bank to assume an equitable interest in the shares, in return for some valuable consideration provided to the customer to be effected. Unless clearly deposited by way of safe custody, the mere deposit of a share certificate will create an equitable mortgage over the shares. In practice, the bank will require deposit of the share certificate and a signed memorandum of deposit in order to clarify the terms of the mortgage. A transfer form signed by the customer but otherwise left blank is often taken and whilst in this case legal title to the shares remains with the mortgagor until the form is completed and submitted for transfer, for purposes of determining priority over other equitable interests, the relevant time is when the mortgagee advances funds.

A memorandum of deposit will normally include the following clauses:

(a)   a continuing security clause to cover further advances and to exclude the decision in *Clayton's* case;

(b)   a clause excluding the waiting periods after default, which would otherwise apply under s 103 of the Law of Property Act 1925;

(c) a statement that dividends from the shares will form part of the security;

(d) a statement that the bank holds the shares as security. Otherwise, it might be argued in the case of an equitable mortgage that the customer had merely deposited the shares under safe deposit arrangements, or in the case of a legal mortgage that the bank had purchased the shares;

(e) in an equitable mortgage, the customer agrees to execute any transfer which the bank requests him to complete.

21.3 Realising the Mortgage

21.3.1 Legal Mortgages

Once the customer is in default, the bank has a power of sale of the shares, which it can easily exercise since the shares are registered in its name.

21.3.2 Equitable Mortgages

A court order would be required for the bank to sell shares held under an equitable mortgage. However, the bank normally holds a blank, signed transfer form which it may complete and thereby effect a sale. Alternatively, a sale will be possible if the equitable mortgage is under seal and the bank holds irrevocable power of attorney granted by the customer. Otherwise the bank can seek to enforce the clause in the memorandum of deposit by which the mortgagor promises to grant a legal mortgage if so requested.

21.4 Risks for the Lender

21.4.1 Legal Mortgages

Shares in a private limited company may be difficult to transfer or to sell at a satisfactory price. The company's Articles of Association may prohibit registration of a transfer of shares save in the directors' absolute discretion. Alternatively, the Articles may require a selling shareholder to offer his shares to existing members of the company.

There is no system of registering equitable or beneficial interests in shares, and therefore any such interest will only bind a legal mortgagee if he has notice of it. Such notice must be actual or constructive, in the sense that it is clear from the situation that a beneficial interest may exist. In other words, when a customer presents a genuine share certificate in his name, this proves that he holds the legal title to the shares. It is quite possible that he holds the legal title as trustee, so that some other person has a beneficial interest. However, it is only if the bank knows or ought to surmise from the situation that this is a nominee holding (and knows this at the time it takes its legal mortgage), that its title is defective. There is, however, a risk from a forged transfer document, and it will not assist if the shares have since been registered in the bank's name or even if the shares have been sold. In *Sheffield Corporation v. Barclay*, a genuine but stolen share certificate was presented to the bank with a forged transfer document. The bank sent these in for registration and obtained a share certificate in its own name. Later the shares were sold by the bank to an innocent purchaser. When the original owner realized his loss, he sued the company. Naturally, the company had two innocent persons claiming ownership of the same block of shares, and had to recognize both. The bank was held liable to the company for having misrepresented the situation by submitting a forged transfer. It was considered irrelevant whether or not the bank had been negligent. In the event of the share certificate also being forged, the company will presumably bear at least part of the responsibility if it completes the transfer.

Where the shares are partly paid, the bank holding a legal mortgage will be liable for further calls from the company. However, demand may be made of the customer at this time and the shares sold if a default occurs. It could only involve the bank in a loss if the company were in insolvent liquidation.

As legal owner of the shares, the bank will receive dividends, bonus and rights issues, the memorandum of deposit typically provides that these accrue to the bank in partial discharge of the mortgagor's debt.

A variety of consequences may flow from the legal mortgage for the company whose shares are mortgaged to the bank. If the bank's holding in the company exceeds 50%, the company may be considered a subsidiary of the bank for certain purposes, and thus the company will cease to be a member of its original group. Thus a company's Value Added Tax grouping may be jeopardized and there may also be complications in connection with group accounting. Of interest to the bank is the consideration that much smaller holdings may come within the disclosure of interests rules. A solution to these problems can be found if the bank mortgagee disclaims all voting rights in the company whose shares are mortgaged to it until the bank makes demand.

21.4.2 Equitable Mortgages

Unlike a legal mortgagee, the equitable mortgagee takes subject to prior equitable interests of which he has no notice, actual or constructive (such interests are very possible with shares because it is so common for shares to be held by a nominee or trustee). Contrast this with the legal mortgagee whose title defeats prior equitable interests unless he had actual or constructive notice of them at the time he took his legal mortgage. It is now the position that a mortgagee who advances funds on the security of a share certificate and a blank signed transfer, since he has it within his power to become a legal mortgagee, enjoys the same priority as an actual legal mortgagee. This was held in *Macmillan Inc v. Bishopsgate Investment Trust*, where shares in a US company which beneficially belonged to the plaintiff were mortgaged by companies in the Maxwell group as security for loans. Since the mortgagees had no notice, actual or constructive, of the equitable interest at the time they advanced the funds and since at that time they held the share certificates and a blank signed transfer, they took priority over the equitable interest. It was also held in this case that when shares in a foreign company are mortgaged, the matter of priority is governed by the law of the place of incorporation of the company. That law also determines what formalities are necessary to perfect a transfer of title.

A different risk is that a fraudulent customer may deposit the share certificate with an equitable mortgagee, and then claim to the company that the certificate is lost, obtain a new certificate and sell the shares. The bank's title will be inferior to that of an innocent purchaser. There is a procedure whereby the equitable mortgagee may utilize the Civil Procedure Rules to serve a "Stop Notice" on the company, which will then be obliged to give the mortgagee 14 days' notice before registering any transfer of ownership. In this time, the bank can seek an injunction from the court to stop its customer from selling the shares. This procedure is not appropriate as a matter of routine, however, and if there is any concern about fraud on the part of the customer, it would be far simpler to take a legal mortgage from the start.

As the bank does not hold legal title to the shares, any dividend or rights or bonus issue will go to the mortgagor, although the bank can require that these be mandated to his account with the bank. Rights and bonus issues, of course, may dilute the equity, making the block of shares held under the bank's charge less valuable. The memorandum of deposit can specify that the mortgagor agrees to charge these to the bank if requested to do so.

21.5 Valuation

The main advantages of these assets are that, like life policies, the procedure is reasonably simple (especially compared to land). They can be easy to value: shares of plc's are often quoted on the stock exchange and it is thus possible to sell them without restriction and the share prices can be ascertained daily. However, as we are all aware, prices on stock exchanges can vary greatly and while it is simple to get today's value there is no guarantee that the value will be the same in seven days. A large price increase is obviously not a problem for a lender who is relying on the shares; a large fall is. A prudent lender will discount the value and each lender has its own discount rates. Unless the company is a blue-chip company, 50% discount is considered prudent.

Unfortunately shares of unquoted (limited) companies are less easy to value, far more volatile in price, and may be covered by restrictions in transferability. This obviously means that assessing a security value can be very, very difficult.

Loan stocks are also tradable on capital markets and prices can be obtained easily. Just as some shares are perceived to be of better quality than others (British Telecom plc is better than Dodgy Mobiles plc), some loan stocks are considered better than others. The best form of loan stock to take as security is not debt issued by a company, but rather that which has been issued by the UK government. These are universally known as gilt-edged stock (gilts for short). Gilts are extremely marketable, and while their market value can fluctuate, they have guaranteed income payments and guaranteed capital repayment at a fixed point in the future. For example, if we were offered £15,000 nominal of 7% Treasury Stock 2003 as security we would know the following with absolute certainty:

1.   income of £1,050 (£15,000 x 7%) paid in two instalments – ignoring tax; and

2.   a capital repayment of £15,000 in 2003 (in practice we know the precise date).

Although we can calculate the interest due with the same precision for company loan stock, we can never have the same absolute certainty of receipt. Similarly, there will always be some element of doubt with regards to the capital repayment with company debt, because both interest and capital repayment depend on the continued existence of the company.

The value of loan stock is calculated by multiplying the nominal value by the market price. Therefore, as the market price changes, the value of the security changes. Again, prudent lenders will discount the market value. The level of discount depends on the quality of the debt. Obviously gilts will have the lowest discount rate while the much maligned Dodgy plc will be discounted the most.

21.6 Advantages of Security over Stocks and Shares

1.   Absolute legal title available.

2.   Esay and inexpensive to take.

3.   Easy to realize.

4.   Notice of rights and bonus issues come to the bank.

21.7 Disadvantages of Security over Stocks and Shares

1.   Stocks and shares fluctuate in value.

2.   There can be problems in realising securities issued by a private company.

3.   If a legal charge is taken problems can arise, a such as forgery, administration involved in dividends and corporate actions.

4.   In the case of an equitable mortgage the charge can be defeated by a prior equitable

charge, the problem of the bank receiving a duplicate share certificate, a bonus or rights issue can affect the value.

5. In the case of a memorandum of deposit should the customer die the blank transfer form is unenforceable and the bank will need to approach the courts for enforcement.

21.8 Overseas Equities

Investment in overseas equities is now a major factor present in the construction and operation of many portfolios.

Investment on overseas stock markets is now largely unrestricted, and London market-makers have reciprocal arrangements with their counterparts all over the world. London is ideally placed for trading in overseas markets due to its location in the so-called "Golden Triangle", namely New York, London, Tokyo. London can transact business with Tokyo during normal working hours at the start of the day, and at the end of the day, the close on the London market overlaps with the opening of the New York market.

Several hundred large overseas companies have their shares quoted on the London Stock Exchange thereby making valuation and security of such shares easy for a bank.

21.9 Considerations for Taking Security

Taking a mortgage over stocks and shares is simplicity itself. Stage one is to take possession of the share certificate. A memorandum of deposit and a signed undated stock transfer form are also taken. After these two stages an equitable mortgage has been created. This can be converted to a legal mortgage by depositing all the documents with the company registrar, who will issue a new certificate in the name of the lender.

As discussed above, realizing the security is again very easy. Because the transfer form is signed and undated, the shares can be sold at any time or simply passed into the ownership of the nominee company.

21.10 Safe to Lend Considerations

When considering an advance against the security of stocks and shares a bank must consider the following issues.

(a) The value of the shares should be checked by looking at the *Financial Times* or the relevant stock index and a bank must continue to monitor the value of the shares to ensure that they to not depreciate to the point where the lending becomes unsecured. In the case of unquoted shares a professional valuation must be sought and a higher protective margin of lending must also be done.

(b) The bank must consider that the customer is the registered holder of the stocks and shares and must consider the risks of forgery or duplication as discussed above.

(c) The bank should check that the shares are fully-paid and not partly-paid.

(d) The bank needs to consider whether a legal or equitable assignment should be taken and much will depend on the amount of the advance as to what charge is taken. In the case of an equitable mortgage the bank must ensure that a power of attorney clause is incorporated in the documentation in the event of non-cooperation by the customer in selling the shares.

22

LIFE POLICIES

22.1 Types of Life Policy

Life assurance policies may take one of four different forms:

1. *Whole life policy*. This matures on death of the life assured. But may acquire a surrender value prior to death.

2. *Endowment policy*. This matures on expiration of a fixed term or on earlier death of the life assured. Endowment policies may be either low-cost or full-cost. The former is commonly used in conjunction with a house-purchase mortgage loan. During the term of the mortgage loan, interest only is paid to the lender, and at the end of the term the endowment policy matures in order to repay the principal. These too may acquire a surrender value prior to death.

3. *Term policy*. This provides cover against death of the life assured during a fixed term. If the life assured survives this term, no moneys are paid.

4. *Key man insurance*. This is a policy taken out by a company on the life of a director or key employee. A company may also take out health insurance for the same individual(s). This is to protect the company from potential losses arising from the death or failing health of a director/employee.

When a lender is using a life policy as security for a loan, it is a simple matter to discover the present surrender value of the policy, ie what it can be cashed in for. Assuming premiums are paid, the surrender value should increase as time passes. A policy with no surrender value, such as a term policy or a newly enacted policy, may still be assigned in order to protect the lender against death of the borrower.

22.2 Parties Involved in a Life Policy Contract

(a) The insurer, ie the life company.

(b) The policyholder, usually he takes out cover on his own life for his own benefit (or for the benefit of his beneficiaries on his death).

(c) The life assured. It may be that the policyholder takes out cover on the life of another (see discussion on insurable interest below).

(d) The beneficiary. It may be that the policyholder has declared that some other person will receive payment when the policy matures. This is a policy written in trust, and includes settlement policies made under the provisions of the Married Women's Property Act 1882.

Mortgages of life policies are truly assignments of the debt owed by the insurer. As before, there are two types and in both the policyholder (or such other beneficiary as may exist) assigns to the lender the benefit he is entitled to receive at some future date from the insurer. The assignee can only receive as good an interest as the assignor holds; life policies are not negotiable instruments.

22.3 Advantages and Disadvantages as Security

Advantages	Disadvantages
Easy to complete formalities	Uberrimae fidei considerations
Easy to value	May need to make premiums if debtor does not.
Easy to realize	

22.4 General Points on Life Policies and Taking Security

When taking a life policy as security a number of points need to be borne in mind.

1. Is the insurer a UK-based company?

2. Has the policy been set up properly? A prudent lender will check that the correct age has been detailed on the policy document and that the policy has been endorsed age admitted. The age of the person being insured is the primary factor an insurance company uses to set the sum assured and the premium. Had a customer taken out a policy and used the wrong date of birth the policy would be voided under the principal of *uberrimae fidei*.

3. Is the policy in trust? If it is, the beneficiary will not receive the proceeds on death or maturity. These will be paid directly to the trustee. The solution is to ensure that the beneficiary and trustee sign the charge form. The most common form of trust is created when a policy has been effected under the Married Women's Property Act 1882. The normal scenario is where a man takes out a policy on his own life in favour of his wife and/or his wife and children. This wording creates the trust and may cause problems for taking the policy as an effective security. The problems are:

- Wife: what happens in divorce situations? At the time of creation of the trust the wife may have been Mandy but on death the wife might be Alison. Does a charge form sign by Mandy bind Alison? No. The wife needs to be named.

- Children: Are the children named? Are they over 18? If not can minors enter into a charge? No. For a valid charge the children need to be named and over eighteen.

The signing of the charge form by the beneficiaries must be witnessed and that witness should, ideally, be able to provide the beneficiaries with independent legal advice. This is to avoid the possibility of undue emotional pressure or influence being put on one or more of the beneficiaries. There are three famous cases where the question of undue influence has been examined.

Lloyds Bank Ltd v Bundy (1975) concerned undue influence of a son on his father. The father gave a guarantee for the son's bank account which the court eventually set aside.

Barclays Bank plc v O'Brien (1993) concerned misrepresentation of the facts by Mr O'Brien to Mrs O'Brien. Mrs O'Brien entered into a legal charge jointly with her husband over the matrimonial home. This charge secured the overdraft of her husband's limited company. Although it could not be proven that Mr O'Brien had put his wife under emotional pressure, the House of Lords believed Mrs O'Brien's contention that she had been told that the sum involved was £60,000 (it was £130,000) and that it was for a period of three weeks which it was not. Mrs O'Brien was able to set aside the charge, because Barclays Bank had not insisted that she take independent legal advice.

The bank having got the assignment executed will write to the insurance company to give notice of its assignment.

If the debt has been repaid and the customer wants the life policy returned the bank will reassign the policy back top the policy holder by signing the receipt in the form of assignment and giving notice to the insurance company.

In the case of *Royal Bank of Scotland v Etridge* (1998) it was held by the House of Lords that if a bank has material information not available to the advising solicitor or if the transaction is one which no competent solicitor could advise the security-giver to enter, the taking of independent legal advice by the security-giver would not prevent the bank being fixed with constructive notice of undue influence.

22.5 Valuation

The valuation of a life policy by a lender is determined by the surrender value of the policy which is ascertained by the bank writing to the insurance company concerned to obtain a valuation. The general rule on life policy valuation is as follows.

The value of a policy is much lower at start of policy than the premiums paid due to commission. However, it is possible to do other things if you cannot afford to continue paying the premiums:

- borrow on the value of the fund from the life office;

- convert into a fully-paid policy; and

- sell policy on second-hand market.

Endowments are much more expensive than simple term assurance.

22.6 Safe to Lend Considerations

Taking life policies as security against a corporate loan is not common. There are two exceptions to this, namely key man term insurance and key man private health insurance policies in which the premiums are paid by the corporate on the life of key directors or employees whose death or illness would have a detrimental effect on the finances of the corporate.

A bank that wishes to use a life policy as security for an advance must consider the following issues.

(a) Ensure that the premiums are paid up-to-date and continue to monitor to ensure that they continue to be paid.

(b) Ascertain an up-to-date surrender value of the policy which will normally be the limit of an advance.

(c) Give notice to the insure of the banks interest and ensure that age is admitted on the policy.

(d) Check that there are no previous notices of assignment from the insurer.

(e) Look at the policy to check that there are no undesireable conditions like suicide or that the beneficiaries of the policy are minors or that the beneficiary is a spouse or partner in which case their consent is required.

23

CASH COVER – CHARGES OVER BANK BALANCES

23.1 Legal Rights

In practice it is quite common for a bank to wish to use a customer's credit balance as a form of security for some liability which the customer owes or might in the future owe to the bank.

The concepts of combination of accounts and set-off normally permit, for example, a bank which has lent money on current account to set this off against a credit balance held on a current account in the same name, and thus provide an ideal form of security for the bank since no formal procedures are involved such as application to the court; the bank can simply combine the accounts. Nor is any advance documentation necessary. In the event of insolvency of the customer, the statutory set-off rules in the Insolvency Act 1986 apply, with the same effect.

A simple reliance on common law and statutory set-off will not always be sufficient, however. For instance, the customer may be able to withdraw the funds from the credit balance because the debt owed on the other account is not yet due, or he may assign the credit balance to some third party, or the bank may wish to look to the deposit as security for the debt of a third party, or may wish it to secure a contingent liability (such as liability under a guarantee, which will only become operative if the principal debtor defaults). In these events the right of set-off may not be available to the bank.

There is a clear commercial need, therefore, for a simple and effective form of charging a bank deposit to the bank where it is deposited, in the same way that other property of the customer, such as shares, can be charged. Much the same need arises in the insurance industry, where companies lend money to their policyholders against the security of the life policy issued by themselves. Unfortunately, the law has struggled to meet these needs and something which ought in theory to be quite simple becomes labyrinthine in practice.

The following discussion assumes that a bank wishes (in effect) to take a charge over a credit balance, so that it may prevent the customer from withdrawing it and so that it will be a good security in the event of the customer's insolvency. There are three recognized means of attempting to do so, and in true belt and braces fashion, banks commonly adopt all three in combination (a device known as the "triple cocktail").

The key to understanding what follows is to remember that when a customer has "money in a bank account", the law analyzes this as the bank owning the money but owing a debt to the customer, who, therefore, owns the right to receive that debt from the bank (called a chose in action).

As explained earlier, the rights of combination and set-off prior to insolvency are based on common law and, subsequent to insolvency, on statute. Common law will not permit (without documentation) a contingent liability, an unmatured liability nor a third party liability to be set-off against a cash balance. Furthermore, the bank may at any time receive notice that the benefit of the credit balance has been assigned to some third party or attached under a garnishee order of the court, and this will prevent a set-off of contingent or subsequent liabilities when they mature or crystallize. Common law is also prepared to perceive an implied agreement between bank and customer not to set off, for instance when the debit balance is on a loan account but not in the case of a frozen current account.

A properly drafted deposit agreement or letter of set-off will deal with all of the above concerns, with the possible exceptions that it may not permit future and contingent debts to be unaffected by notice of garnishee, (once a bank has received notice of the garnishee order, set-off could not of course be extended to further debts not covered by the original set-off agreement). The agreement should precisely specify which deposits and which liabilities are to be the basis of the set-off (including contingent and future liabilities). The bank will be granted irrevocable authority to debit the credit balance with the debts, and the depositor will be restrained from drawing from the account. If the depositor's credit balance is to be set-off against a debt owed by a different legal entity, a guarantee must also be taken.

On the onset of the depositor's insolvency, garnishee orders will not be a concern as judgment debts cannot be pursued. The chief concern for the bank at that time, therefore, is whether set-off is available in respect of unmatured and contingent debts of the customer. Statutory set-off under s 323 of the Insolvency Act 1986 will apply (for insolvent companies the Insolvency Rules 1986, rule 4.90 has similar effect). This provides for the setting-off of mutual credits and debts. Any unmatured debts are accelerated and contingent liabilities may also be set off. This is helpful since any contractual provision which seeks to improve the position of an unsecured creditor in the event of insolvency is void.

In summary, a well-drafted letter of set-off will cover the various pre-insolvency risks (such as assignment of the deposit by the customer) and extend the prevailing right to combine and set-off to future and contingent debts as well as to third-party debts. On insolvency of the customer, the mandatory statutory set-off will replace the terms of the set-off agreement (and serve the bank equally well).

Notwithstanding the prevailing assumption that a letter of set-off does not create a charge, it is conceivable that a court might analyse it as such. If this occurred with a corporate customer then there might be a requirement to register the "charge" under the terms of ss 395 and 396 of the Companies Act 1985, and failure to do so within 21 days of its creation would render it void as against a liquidator and other creditors. As it would be far too late to register when the case came to court, it may seem a sensible precaution to register all set-off agreements as charges within 21 days of their being made.

The set-off agreement, if it is a charge, is one that requires registration if the credit balance constitutes a "segregated fund" which seems to apply if the money is held in a separate account.

23.2 Taking a Charge over the Credit Balance

In *Morris v Rayners Enterprises*, the House of Lords held that it is possible to take a charge over a credit balance Prior to this, it was stated in *Halesowen Presswork* and *Assemblies Ltd v Westminster Bank* that a bank could not take a lien over a deposit with it, and this was applied in the first instance decision of *Re Charge Card Services Ltd* to conclude that a debtor could not take a charge over a debt owed to itself since this would involve the debt owed by the bank being appropriated to itself, and the bank could not sue itself.

In *Morris v Rayners Enterprises*, Lord Hoffmann distinguished between a lien and the broader concept of proprietary interests. He revisited the well-established law that a deposit with a bank is a form of property known as a chose in action, and he declared that an equitable charge is a form of proprietary interest which is granted by way of security and as such it

> entitles the holder to resort to the property only for the purpose of satisfying some liability due to him. and the owner of the property retains an equity of redemption to have the property restored to him when the liability has been discharged. A charge is a security interest created without any transfer of title or possession to the beneficiary.

He noted that it is accepted that a charge over a bank deposit can validly be given to a third party and he held that if a charge by a bank over a deposit with it were taken

> there would be no merger of interests because the depositor would retain title to the deposit subject only to the bank's charge. The creation of the charge would be consensual and not require any formal assignment or vesting of title in the bank. If all these features can exist despite the fact that the beneficiary of the charge is the debtor, I cannot see why it cannot properly be said that the debtor has a proprietary interest by way of charge over the debt.

The application of this conclusion had an interesting effect on the facts in *Morris*. A company had borrowed from BCCI and a depositor with BCCI had charged his deposit as security for the company's borrowing. The depositor had not given a guarantee. BCCI went into insolvent liquidation and its liquidator sought to recover the loan from the company leaving the depositor to claim for his deposit from the insolvent bank (which claim would of course only be partially met). The depositor, on the other hand, argued that insolvent set-off applied with the effect that his deposit would be lost but the liquidator would not reclaim the loan from the company. The depositor's main argument was that since charging his deposit to the bank was legally impossible, the effect of the document he signed had to be to make him personally liable for the company's debt, which would have led to a set-off. The decision went with the liquidator.

If a charge is taken over the credit balance, the question arises as to whether it requires registration as a charge over a book debt under s 395 of the Companies Act 1985, if the chargor is a company. Once again, there is some doubt as to whether the law does require registration, this time because it is not clear whether the credit balance constitutes a "book debt". In *Morris*, Lord Hoffmann expressed no view on the matter but he recorded the view of Lord Hutton in *Northern Bank v Ross* that an obligation to register is unlikely to arise.

A cash deposit is, in legal terms, a debt due from one party (usually in this context the bank) to another (the customer). The decision in the *Charge Card Services* case in 1987 placed severe doubts on the ability of the bank to rely on a charge over a cash deposit which was, in effect, a charge over one of its own debts.

Neither s 395 of the Companies Act 1985 nor the *Morris v Agrichemicals* case in 1997 were helpful as regards whether or not a charge over cash should be registered with the Registrar of Companies. The bank therefore adopts the cautious stance and attempts registration in the usual way, placing any rejection letter with the completed security as evidence that it attempted registration.

In the event that a set-off of a deposit is not available and that a charge taken is not effective, a backstop is provided by an agreement between bank and customer. This is part of the contract of deposit, and restricts the ability of the customer to withdraw his funds until his liability to the bank has been discharged or can no longer arise (if it is contingent), such as a guarantee being determined with no debt due from the principal debtor and thus no liability on the part of the guarantor. Another variation is an agreement that the deposit will not be repaid until the debts of a third party are fully repaid.

23.3 Advantages of Taking Charges over Cash

The clear advantage with cash as security is that it is certain and cash is cash and cannot therefore fall in value. The valuation of the cash balance will be evidenced either by a passbook, certificate or the bank looking at the account records.

There is a question over the effects of a fixed charge over book debts on the third parties by whom those debts are payable. The provisions of the debenture operate, as between the company and the debenture holder, as a fixed equitable charge of each debt as soon as the debt arises. A third party will therefore get a good discharge if he pays the company before receiving notice of the charge, and the debenture holder cannot make him pay again, even if the company fails to comply with a term of the debenture requiring payment of the debt into the company's account with the debenture holder. It is thought that registration of a charge does not amount to notice to the third party for this purpose. For cash payments it is suggested that for notice to be given in the debenture instrument to appoint the company as the debenture holder's agent to receive the book debts subject to the fixed charge, thus putting third parties on notice that the charge is in place.

23.4 Disadvantages of Taking Charges over Cash

The only disadvantage is to ensure that the customer has a clear title to the moneys and that it is not shared with anyone else otherwise their consent is required.

In the case of companies it is imperative that registration of any charge is registered at Companies House within 21 days of creation.

23.5 Safe to Lend Considerations

Providing that a banker is satisfied that the title to any credit balance is absolute then cash is perfect security. If the credit balance is shared with someone else then their consent is required. In the case of companies a bank must ensure that a charge is registered at Companies House.

24

MANAGING RISK

24.1 Managing Risk

24.1.1 Introduction to Managing Risks and Exposures

Business activity inevitably involves a number of risks and exposures which potentially could undermine the financial stability and future performance of the organization. The key issue is that the relevant personnel within the organization are actually aware of all areas of potential exposure. Without the knowledge of such risks and exposure, management cannot take place.

The purpose of this unit is to give you an appreciation of how and where exposures arise and why it is important that "exposure management" takes place. Towards the end of this section we shall look at a typical process of managing exposures.

24.1.2 Examples

Let us look at a fairly typical trading transaction:

ABC plc (a UK company) sells goods to D (a company based in Germany). D places an order for 10,000 units at a price of 600 Euros each. Agreed payment terms are 90 days following shipment.

This is a larger than usual order and consequently ABC plc will require materials specifically to meet the order. Raw materials will be imported from the US at a cost of US$2 million. Payment is due in this respect three months after the order has been placed.

The finished goods will be ready for shipment three months after the raw materials have been ordered. The German company is happy with the timescales involved.

Total attributable overheads and production costs, but excluding finance charges, will be no more than £1/2 million. Finance will be required for the whole transaction, repayable in full from the sale proceeds.

ABC plc are keen to pursue further exporting opportunities to Germany. They feel they can produce goods competitively for this market, and intend to take additional stocks of raw materials in anticipation of this increased demand.

We shall assume that ABC plc is your customer, and ABC's treasurer calls to see you to discuss borrowing the money from your bank to finance the transaction. You will naturally need to be convinced that repayment will be forthcoming to clear the borrowing. Similarly, ABC's treasurer will need to be convinced that the transaction will generate sufficient cash to enable the company to do so, and make a profit. For him to do this he will need to appreciate the various risks and exposures involved so that he can take any necessary action to eliminate these, or at least monitor and control them.

24.1.2 Main Areas of Exposure

So what then are the main areas of exposure to ABC plc in this transaction?

(a) How firm is D's commitment to see the deal through? Have contracts been signed?

(b) Is D a good credit risk, ie will it be able to pay for the goods?

(c) As this is a larger than usual order, is ABC plc absolutely certain that it has sufficient productive capacity/manpower and knowhow to produce the goods to the required standard?

(d) Is the US supplier a good risk, ie

 (i) Is it sufficiently sound financially to see the transaction through?

 (ii) Can it meet the time scales required?

 (iii) Will the goods be of the required quality?

(e) Is the cost of raw materials definitely fixed?

(f) What is the risk of damage (pilferage of raw materials and finished goods during transportation from US to Germany and whilst held in the UK), and more importantly, as to whether it is the US supplier's responsibility to insure the goods?

(g) Has any allowance been made for possible transportation delays, for example, strikes, or is there a clause to cover this in any contract/documentation?

(h) Is ABC plc happy with its estimates or costs/overheads?

(i) What measures is the company taking to protect itself against adverse exchange rate movements, ie

 – future Euro/£ conversion

 – future US$/£ conversion?

(j) What effect could there be from competitor activity if exchange rate fluctuations made ABC plc's product more expensive than something similar available from, say, France?

(k) Has any allowance been made for possible interest rate fluctuations? ABC plc has two exposures:

There may also be political and economic factors to consider that would either prevent or delay materials, or payment from D, for example, local legislation, taxes/duties, war, political unrest, Exchange Control – although these factors carry less weight in this specific transaction as ABC plc is dealing with Germany and USA. However, it may be that materials/goods pass through other less stable countries at some stage.

24.1.2.2 Future Transactions

As regards future transactions, it is assumed that ABC plc has undertaken adequate research to ensure that a market exists, at the right price, for its goods, particularly as it intends to take on additional stocks in anticipation of this. Are future orders firm? Has the company fully considered the full costs of holding stocks, for example, premises, insurance, pilferage?

From all of the above you will see that there are a number of risks involved, indeed you may have identified more than those main areas listed.

24.1.3 Risks/Exposures

Having identified the risk areas, if we categorize these, then it will be possible to see what the company can do to minimize, or in some cases eliminate them.

24.1.3.1 Internal

These are the areas of exposure that are directly under the control of the company, for example, manpower, training, production capacity.

24.1.3.2 External

24.1.3.2.1 "Insurable"

These are the areas that the company can take out some form of cover for, either EGCD, or similar, or normal commercial insurance, for example, to cover against damage of goods.

24.1.3.2.2 "Uninsurable"

There would be, for example, changes in customers' needs due to social/cultural reasons and to competitor activities.

24.1.3.3 Exposure Management

This term, which is one of the corporate treasurer's main responsibilities, relates to the company's exposures due to *interest rate* and *exchange rate* volatility. There are a number of products/techniques available to control such exposures. A broad explanation of the types of exposure is as follows.

24.1.3.4 Interest Rate Risk

Interest rate risk is frequently overlooked despite the fact that this type of exposure can have quite dramatic repercussions on the corporate's performance. What then are the risks?

(a) Exposure to potentially higher cost of finance for borrowing companies due to rate increases either during the offer/tender to contract stage, or during the term of the borrowing if it is variable rate.

(b) Exposure to potentially lower return on investments, for investors, due to a fall in rates.

(c) Where a company chooses to lock into a rate for a period it runs the risk that rates may in fact more favourably and thus it forgoes the opportunity to benefit, either from cheaper finance or increased investment return. (This may be quite acceptable since the downside risk is eliminated, depending on the company's policy (philosophy).)

If you refer back to the example shown at 24.1.2, you can see that ABC plc has an interest rate exposure. This particular exposure is over two quite separate, although consecutive, time scales.

First, it does not need finance for the US supply transaction until three months after the order has been placed. If we assume ABC plc places the order today, it therefore has an initial exposure to interest rate volatility for the three months that follow. Having costed/budgeted the transaction, if the company takes no further action it may be faced with a higher financing cost at the time of draw down if rates, in the meantime, move adversely. (Similarly, of course, in three months' time rates could have gone down.)

Secondly, in three months' time the company will actually borrow the money, by some means, to pay the US company which has supplied the raw materials. This "loan" will be repaid after a further three months, ie in six months' time, on receipt of the proceeds from D. Therefore, ABC plc runs the risk that:

(a) If it borrows fixed rate for the period it may be paying higher financing costs than necessary should rates fall between the three-months and six-months period, and

(b) It borrows variable rate the converse would apply should rates rise during the time the advance is outstanding.

As already mentioned, interest rate exposure does not only relate to borrowers: investors, too, are also clearly vulnerable to movements in interest rates. For example, a company is involved in a business operation that is very seasonal. For six months it operates on a virtual net nil basis, ie income matches expenditure. In month seven its income increases dramatically and this continues for three months, to the extent that it is several million pounds in surplus. This position continues for another three months at which time expenditure increases and purchases are made for the cycle to begin again at the end of month 12 – back to a net nil situation.

This company has no borrowing requirement, yet it is still exposed to interest rate movements. This is particularly the case when it is preparing cash flow forecasts. Perhaps it operates in a very competitive market and may need to rely on investment return during the period it is very cash risk, to help keep its prices down.

24.1.3.5 Exchange Rate Risk

Exchange rate risk arises from transactions which necessitate the conversion of one currency to another, normally, but not always, being to/from the "home" currency.

Exchange rate risk can be broadly defined as vulnerability to movements in exchange rates that would have an adverse effect on:

(a) the value of present and future cash inflows;

(b) the cost of current and future liability commitments, ie increasing the cost of cash outflows;

(c) the underlying value of assets owned by the corporate but based in different countries and liabilities; and

(d) the corporate's trading activity generally, for example, making its goods more expensive, and these are less competitive, than those manufactured in other countries.

These can be classified as (explained further in 24.3.1):

(a) Transaction Exposure;

(b) Translation Exposure;

(c) Economic Exposure.

24.1.4 Managing the Exposures

We have seen above that there are different types of "exposure", and the risks involved in simply ignoring these could be dramatic because of the possible adverse impact on performance. These areas most likely to be affected are:

(a) profitability;

(b) balance sheet (such translation exposures may give rise to some tax considerations); and

(c) competitiveness.

Let us now take a look at what process, typically, the corporate treasurer will go through when undertaking "exposure management".

24.1.4.1 Establishing Policy/Philosophy

As always, two-way effective communication is vital if an organization's various operations are to succeed in achieving the overall corporate objectives. The board of directors policy must be clearly stated, particularly as regards risk avoidance, for example, do they simply want to "lock in" to rates for all transactions, thus fixing costs but foregoing the opportunity to gain from any favourable rate movements? Likewise, their philosophy, or indeed policy, may not allow the use of certain of the techniques/products available.

24.1.4.2 Framework

Within the group's policies/philosophies, a framework needs to be established outlining the practical day-to-day administration aspects involved in identifying and managing exposures. This will include delegated responsibilities and reporting mechanisms.

24.1.4.3 Determining Areas for Monitoring

Having established the framework it is vital that it is sufficient to cover all areas of the organization's activities that, potentially, could create exposures. In this way it is possible to clearly determine those areas requiring monitoring.

24.1.4.4 Forecasting

Depending on the level or sophistication, some organizations undertake quite complex processes of forecasting rate movements. It has to be said that markets tend to fluctuate between volatile and very volatile, so accurate forecasting in the current environment is difficult. However, most organizations will need to have at least "a view".

24.1.4.5 Quantifying

Having determined the exposed areas and then using the organization's "view" as regards possible fluctuations, it is then possible to quantify the exposure. Some companies may build in safety-net margins to allow for any extraordinary circumstances that may arise and affect rates more than anticipated. Any action taken to control the exposure identified must be considered to be cost-effective.

24.1.4.6 Reporting

Reporting systems must be implemented to ensure such identified exposures are brought to the attention of the treasurer, for action as appropriate.

24.1.4.7 Strategies

These "strategies" are, effectively, general courses available to the treasurer. These are eventually threefold:

(i)   do nothing;

(ii) hedge everything;

(iii) hedge selectively.

To elaborate:

(i)   "Doing nothing" has to be a positive decision, ie for reasons known to the corporate the identified exposure is to be left uncovered. The implication is that the downside risk, as forecast by the corporate, does not outweigh the costs incurred in mitigating against it.

(ii) The term "hedging" is probably the most common expression in exposure management. "Hedging" is the action taken to control/minimize/eliminate the impact or adverse movements in interest/exchange rates. The action which can be taken may include a number of alternatives and these are covered in the next two lectures.

(iii) By hedging everything the company must of course consider the costs involved and time/costs of monitoring and the fact that upside potential is limited or with some instruments removed entirely.

Selective hedging is probably the most common strategy. In such a situation, action will be taken to manage identified risks where the exposure has been qualified as being "a reasonable amount" and where the company's view is that it is vulnerable to adverse rate movements, ie rates could move in such a way that outflows would increase and inflows reduce or there could be translation/economic exposures.

Selective hedging can be defined as passive and aggressive/speculative. The former is where exposures are simply covered, possibly to allow for gains to be made of rates more favourably. In the case of aggressive/speculative hedging, action could actually be taken to increase exposures to take advantage or any anticipated favourable movements in rates.

24.1.4.8 Instruments

In the light of the foregoing, the treasurer will then undertake a full appraisal and comparison of the alternative hedging techniques/products available to him. Most will be suitable for different purposes – and these will be clarified in the next two lectures.

24.1.4.9 Implement

The treasurer will then need to select the most appropriate instrument/product, depending on the given circumstances, and implement it.

24.1.4.10 Monitor/Review

Having implemented his chosen course the treasurer cannot simply forget the exposure. He will have to monitor and review the position regularly to ensure the exposure is being covered as desired. Market movements may change the position considerably and it may be that the action taken will prove to be inappropriate.

24.1.4.11 Corrective Action

Following on from the above, if necessary corrective action should be taken to bring matters in line with the current market position.

24.1.5 Summary

If you are faced with an exposure management situation you will find it useful to consider the following:

(a) Identifying the type(s) of exposure, ie interest rate and/or exchange rate (transaction/translation/economic).

(b) What are the company's objectives, particularly as regards:

    (i) Strategy (hedge all/selectively/nothing)?

    (ii) Fee, ie is a product for which a fee is payable likely to be acceptable?

    (iii) Does the company's policy/philosophy prevent the use of certain, more speculative, methods?

    (iv) Is the treasury function sophisticated or sufficiently knowledgeable to handle some of the more complex products?

    (v) Is the company interested in purely eliminating downside risks or does it wish to be able to benefit, even if only partially, from favourable rate movements?

(c) Consider the alternative techniques and instruments available that could be used, in the light of the circumstances. For each pay attention to:

    (i) Amount

    (ii) Term/period (including flexibility)

    (iii) Fee and any other costs

    (iv) Operation (complexity)

    (v) Documentation

    (vi) Currency

    (vii) Availability

(d) Then ask yourself: "Does it meet the company's needs"?

(e) If you are required to make a recommendation make it clear why you prefer your selected course of action

24.2 Currency Exposure Management

24.2.1 Currencies

24.2.1.1 The Currency Market

The currency market (also called the Foreign Exchange Market, FX market or Forex market) for buying and selling quantities of one currency in exchange for another, is dominated by the "forex" or "FX" traders of large banks, using phones and screens. Relatively few of the transactions, perhaps less than 10%, involve end-users (ie clients who will actually need the relevant currency). Most deals are either inter-bank or forms of speculative trading.

The major "products", ie FX deals are between US dollars and the euro (EUR/USD) and the dollar and the yen (USD/JPY).

24.2.1.2 Currency Dealing

The market is over the phone between dealers (usually acting for banks) and brokers (matching up institutions). There are two types of contract:

(a) **Spot** deals, for settlement two business days later (T+2)

A spot rate is the rate of exchange (selling or buying) which is used for currency dealing "now", with delivery of the currency to the buyer (usually) two working days later. This is known as the spot date, ie the date when the currency is delivered and settlement is made.

(b) **Forward** settlement contracts.

A forward exchange contract is a contract to sell or buy a quantity of foreign currency at a fixed future date, at a rate of exchange that is determined "now", ie when the forward contract is made. For example, a one-month forward contract is settled two business days after the date in one month's time after the transaction is made.

Prices for currencies are quoted against the US dollar, eg USD 1 = JPY 120, USD1 = 7 Hong Kong dollars, etc. (Two exceptions are the sterling/US dollar exchange rate, eg GBP 1 = USD 1.60 and the euro/US dollar rate, eg EUR 1 = USD 1.15).

Traders in FX quote a price at which they will buy a currency and the price at which they will sell that currency. The difference between these prices (the bid and the offer prices) is known as the spread. For example, for GBP/USD, a trader might quote price of 1.6120-1.6130. It will sell dollars in exchange for sterling at GBP 1 = USD 1.6120. It will buy dollars at GBP 1 = USD 1.6130.

Prices for forward FX contracts are usually quoted at a premium (pm) or a discount (dis) to the spot price. Premiums are subtracted from the spot rate and discounts are added. For example, if a bank quotes a spot rate of 1.6100 and the one month forward rate is at a premium of 0.0025, the one month forward rate will be 1.6075.

24.2.1.3 Spot Rate Computations

The dealer may quote a dollar spot rate against sterling as follows:

Bank sells   *Bank buys*

USD 1.6850   USD 1.6890

This means that the dealer will sell dollars (buy pounds) at $1.6850 and buy dollars (sell pounds) at USD 1.6890.

$$\text{Converting USD to GBP} = \frac{\text{Number of dollars}}{\text{Spot rate}}$$

Converting GBP to USD = Number of GBP x spot rate.

Examples

(a)   GBP 10,000 to USD = £10,000 x 1.6850 = USD 16,850

(b)   USD 3,000 to GBP = USD 3,000 (1.6890 = GBP 1,776

(c)   to buy USD 9,000 costs USD 9,000 (1.6850 = GBP 5,341.

24.2.1.4 Forward Rate Computations

Rather than quote "forward rates" a dealer will quote a forward premium (pm) or discount (dis). The spot rate is adjusted by the amount of the premium or discount.

The rule is **deduct premiums** and **add discounts**

	Bank sells	*Bank buys*
Spot	USD 1.6850	USD 1.6890
1 mth	0.2 cents pm.	0.18 cents pm.
3 mth	0.8 cents pm.	0.75 cents pm.

Note

1 cent = $0.01, so 0.2 cents = USD 0.0020 (or 20 "pips")

24.2.2 Exchange Rate Forecasting

In order to be able to make informed decisions on currency exposure and overseas investment, it is important to appreciate the factors affecting exchange rates and the likely future direction of exchange rates.

24.2.2.1 Shorter-term Factors Affecting Exchange Rates

24.2.2.1.1 Interest Rates

In the short-term, high interest rates will attract "hot money" from around the world seeking high yields into a currency. This will create demand for the currency and increase the exchange rate.

Interest rate differentials are also relevant in the International Fisher Effect, covered at 24.2.2.3.

24.2.2.1.2 Balance of Payments

If the UK has a balance of payments surplus then it is exporting goods with a higher value than it is importing. In order to pay for these goods, overseas customers will need to purchase sterling. Demand for sterling will increase, meaning that the currency will strengthen. Alternatively, as is unfortunately more likely to be the case, if the UK has a balance of payments deficit, then UK companies will need to sell sterling to buy overseas currencies to fund their purchases. This will cause sterling to weaken.

24.2.2.1.3 Economic Growth

Economic growth will stimulate demand for a currency both through capital flows into the country, due to attractive investment opportunities, and current account flows, due to increased supply and demand for the country's traded goods and services. Alternatively, a credit boom, which causes demand for overseas goods and services, will cause the currency to weaken.

24.2.2.1.4 Fiscal and Monetary Policies

Taxation and public spending policies have a direct impact on economic growth. Government borrowing plans will impact on interest rates, as will monetary policies which aims to reduce or increase money supply through changes in interest rates.

24.2.2.1.5 Natural Resources

The discovery or existence of valuable natural resources, such as oil, can cause a currency to strengthen dramatically.

24.2.2.1.6 Currency Block Membership

Some currencies are pegged to the US dollar, such as certain Middle Eastern currencies. Such formal or informal relationships should be noted since they will have a key impact on the exchange rate.

24.2.2.1.7 Political Events

Central bank intervention can affect exchange rates, although experience has shown that it is sometimes the speculators who win the day rather than the central authorities. On top of this, events such as elections, public opinion polls, government ministers' statements and press releases can all affect the exchange rate.

24.2.2.2 Longer Term Factors – Inflation and Purchasing Power Parity

In the shorter term, the exchange rate is determined by supply and demand factors and, to a greater or lesser extend, market sentiment. Longer term exchange rates are determined by purchasing power parity, which is a relationship between economies and the levels of inflation they suffer. Purchasing power parity is best explained by way of a small example.

If a basket of goods costs £100 in London and the same basket of goods costs 200 euros in Paris, this predicts the exchange rate between the two countries will be £1–2 Euros. However, if the two economies suffer differing rates of inflation then, over time, the exchange rate will alter.

If, after a number of years, the basket of goods costs £115 in London, due to the impact of inflation on UK prices, and yet remains at 200 Euros in Paris, this would suggest that the exchange rate between the two currencies is now £1–1.74 Euros – a decline in the value of sterling. This theory of exchange rate behaviour can also be referred to as The Law of One Price.

Short-term supply and demand features may well mask this overall trend, but purchasing power parity gives an underlying theme to the foreign exchange markets. If one economy consistently has an inflation rate in excess of its competitors, then its currency will deteriorate against its trading partners.

24.2.2.3 The International Fisher Effect

We have seen above that longer term exchange rates are theoretically determined by purchasing power parity and the inflation differential between two currencies. We have also seen in relation to currency rates above that forward rates are determined by reference to interest rate differentials. These two concepts are brought together in the Fisher theorem which links together interest rates, inflation and the foreign exchange markets.

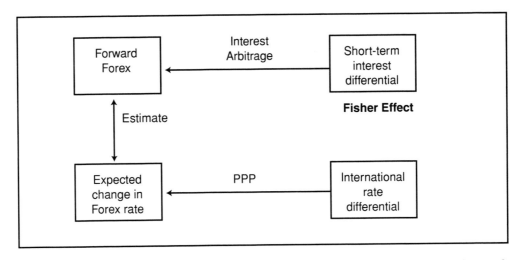

Forward foreign exchange prices are derived from the short-term interest rate differentials between two economies. The expected foreign exchange spot rate in future is given by the purchasing power parity theorem which we developed above.

24.3 The Management of Currency Risk

Following on from the previous section you will be aware that exchange rate risk can arise from any of the following variables:

1. Value of present and future cash flows

2. Cost of current and future liability commitments, ie cost of cash outflows

3. Underlying value of cash outflows

4. Corporates general trading

24.3.1 Transaction Risk

It may be defined as the risk that the domestic currency value of a foreign currency denominated transaction will vary as a direct result of changes in exchange rates.

– Payments to creditors

– Receipts from debtors

– Dividends, interest payments, royalties, management charges

24.3.1.1 Problems – Borrowing in Hard Currency

To take the example of Laker Airways in 1981 which company arranged lease finance in US Dollars for bulk of the aircraft. When $ strengthened, the company's Balance sheet and cash flow ability to service debt came under excessive strain. Similarly, J. Lyons in the 1970s had Swiss Franc borrowings – £ weakened against SFr and its plight similar to Laker. There was uncovered hard currency debt. This is a good example of transaction risk.

24.3.2 Translation Risk

This is the risk when translated at the foreign exchange rates which will apply at a future accounting date, the domestic currency values of the assets and liabilities on a company's existing balance sheet will alter, giving rise to a reported gain or loss.

24.3.3 Economic Risk

This is the risk that future cashflows generated by a company's activities in its domestic currency will fluctuate as a result of changes in exchange rates.

Vulnerability to long-term movements in rates will arise from the following factors:

Internal

(a)   Sourcing decisions (eg where raw materials are bought in from).

(b)   Price lists (overseas).

(c)   Contractual commitments with uncertain timing, ie royalties or licence payments.

External

(a)   Competitors' currency risk.

(b)   General effect of currency values on general economic environment.

24.3.4 Strategy

The information that the corporate treasurer needs before evaluating his strategy is as follows:

–   identify the exposed positions;

–   forecast of future exchange market movements;

–   analysis of post-tax cash movements on the company;

–   the level of acceptable risk that can be taken; and

–   implementation of the strategy.

The strategies are as follows.

1.   Doing nothing – implication is that rates as forecast by the corporate will not move adversely.

2. 100% Hedging – eliminates downside risk but no upside – opportunity cost loss.

3. Selective Hedging – most common and this is a specific percentage between, say 20–60%.

Exposure

(1) The treasurer will assess risks – such as exchange rate.

(2) The treasurer will establish the policy, framework and strategy.

The treasurer's decision will be affected by his/her:

(a) attitude to risk;

(b) previous experience;

(c) confidence in ability to forecast;

(d) reaction of competitors;

(e) the balance sheet capacity of the corporate, ie strength ability to withstand losses; and

(f) the corporate's overall risk strategy.

The strategy may either be defensive or aggressive and varies according to the nature of the company concerned and also against the general economic climate.

24.3.5 Managing The Currency Risks

24.3.5.1 Transaction Risk

Not covering is an extremely dangerous policy. A firm may incur a vast loss on a single very large receivable or payable, leading to financial distress. Transaction risk must be managed effectively.

24.3.5.2 Translation Risk

Translation risk is the process of consolidation of foreign currency and only becomes problematical if company affected by its gearing ratio or related financial covenants, or if it is an issue to investors shareholders.

24.3.5.3 Economic

Operating responses consist of alteration to sourcing, product, plant location, market selection, credit, pricing and currency of invoicing policies. By their very nature these are much longer-term strategic decisions.

24.3.6 Internal Methods of Hedging Exchange Rate Risk

24.3.6.1 Leading and Lagging

"Leading and lagging" is accelerating/delaying payments to take advantage or perceived appreciation or depreciation of currency.

It concerns either the timing of imports (payables) or exports (sales).

24.3.6.2 Currency Accounts

24.3.6.3 Basket Currencies

For example – using the Euro for transactions in Europe.

24.3.6.4 Matching

Matching is the practice of balancing receivables and payables denominated in the same currency, thus avoiding the need to convert currency. One can offset all company or group receivables and payables by currency.

Such a system would require a central treasury and also requires highly sophisticated on line cashflow tracking abilities for each currency.

24.3.6.5 Netting

Netting is applying an internal rate of exchange for all inter-group transactions but cover the risks that group companies don't co-operate in the group's interest when market rates make external selling more attractive than meeting the needs of other group businesses. This is similar to matching but is inter-company only and excludes third-party cashflows.

24.3.6.6 Pricing Policies

This is concerned with pricing goods in the most efficient way either in the:

- currency of costs;

- currency of the customer; or

- currency of competitors.

24.3.6.7 Invoice in Own Currency

Match revenue and costs.

But this may not be acceptable to your customer. This does protect the profit margin but does not provide protection against changes in relative competitiveness of price due to exchange rate movements.

This technique depends on the marketing/bargaining power.

24.3.6.8 Exchange Rate Variation Clause ("ERV")

In contacts quoting a price using an ERV clause can be used to protect the profit margin of the business from exchange rates are movements during the tender period.

24.3.6.9 Protective Margin

Price set includes a margin to provide a degree of protection against a weakening in the chosen currency relative to your own currency during the tender period. However, it results in a less competitive price and it may present negotiation difficulties.

24.3.6.10 Withdraw from the Markets

The corporate may withdraw from markets and return when exchange rate has improved.

(1) Existence of replacement markets.

(2) Effect of loss of contribution to profits on withdrawal.

(3) Marketing disadvantages – relaunch costs.

24.3.7 Borrowing

Borrowing in the same currency may match interest and repayment costs with dividend flows. Currency borrowings are excellent for controlling translation risk as by matching there are no cash effects and no charge or credit to the profit and loss or balance sheet reserves.

The asset will of course only be hedged if the borrowing remains permanently in place and to the extent that the values are matched.

The treasurer will have to consider the problems of exchange controls and tax treatment of nominal and accrual currency losses.

24.4 External Methods of Hedging Exchange Rate Risk

24.4.1 Forward Foreign Exchange Contracts (Forward Contracts)

24.4.1.1 Introduction

24.4.1.1.1 Definition

A forward contract is a legally binding agreement between two parties, to exchange an agreed sum of one currency for another on a specified future date at a rate determined when the contract is entered into. The important thing to remember is that once the contract is entered into both parties are legally bound to see it through and are committed to carrying out the exchange at the rate agreed at the outset, irrespective of the spot rate prevailing at that time.

24.4.1.1.2 Operation

A typical transaction could arise as follows:

"A company will be receiving US$5 million in one month's time and wishes to establish now how much sterling this will realize on conversion."

The company can use a fixed future date forward contract to establish the conversion rate now. The process of establishing this is simple and involves the company telephoning its bank and obtaining a quotation. Acceptance from the company will put the contract in place. No fee is payable; the bank will make allowance for this in the rate it has quoted. In one month's time the company will receive the US$ and will exercise the forward contract at the rate agreed.

Because it is a fixed future date contract, exercise can only take place on that nominated date, and in fact it *must* be exercised then irrespective of whether or not the underlying proceeds are received.

In the event that the underlying transaction is delayed, or just does not materialize, the contract will be "closed out". In such circumstances the company will have to buy, or sell (depending on the contract) the necessary currency at the prevailing spot rate in order to see the contract through. In our example, if the US$5 million did not materialize, then the company would have to buy that sum at spot to meet its obligations under the contract, through which it had sold in the forward market.

The bank/contract provider carries a contingent risk that the customer is unable to close out the deal should the market have moved detrimentally from the contract rate. This is ordinarily assessed as a percentage of the total contract price at, say, 5 to 10% depending on the maturity of the currencies involved.

In certain circumstances extensions or early settlement may be accepted by the bank but at a penalty cost.

24.4.1.2 Features of Fixed Future Date Contracts

This relates purely to the *traditional* fixed future date contracts.

Amounts:	Flexible, but subject to market availability.
Term/Period:	Most major currencies are available for periods of up to five years (exceptionally longer), with the lesser traded currencies being to 12 months.
Documentation:	None – mandatory authority to transact – assuming relationship exists with the provider of the contract.
Fees:	None – built into rate.
Currencies:	All traded currencies.
Availability:	Widespread, all major banks.
Flexibility:	Very flexible as to period, amount and currency. (Has to be exercised though, ie it is not an "option".)
Protection:	Establishes rate at outset thus protects against adverse movements. (Variations are available to give some benefit for favourable rate movements.)

24.4.1.3 Benefits

(a) Protection against adverse rate movements.

(b) Establishes conversion rate at the outset which assists future budgeting/ forecasts.

(c) Amounts, term and currency may be tailored to suit precise needs.

(d) Widely available – assists in obtaining competitive quotes.

(e) Easy access and simple to deal in.

(f) No fee.

(g) No documentation necessary.

(h) The variations available allow some benefit to be obtained from favourable movements in rates.

24.4.1.3 Disadvantages

(a) An obligation to exercise irrespective of how rates have moved and how the underlying transaction proceeds.

(b) Fixed future date contracts rely on definite delivery dates, which may be difficult to determine.

(c) Rates quoted for the variations may appear unrealistic with the market and thus seem expensive.

(d) May be expensive to seek early settlement or an extension if necessary.

(e) No upside potential.

24.4.1.3 Conclusion

The importance of the traditional fixed future date forward contract market cannot be overemphasised. It is recognized by many corporates as the simplest, most flexible and cheapest means of managing currency exposure. The market is much more widely used than any other techniques available.

24.4.2 Currency Options

The concept is exactly the same as for interest rate options, ie for the payment of an up-front premises the buyer is not obliged to see the contract through if he does not wish.

24.4.2.1 Definition

A currency option is an agreement between two parties under which the buyer has the right, but not the obligation, to buy/sell a specified sum of currency at an agreed rate of exchange either on a specified expiration date (European Option) or at any time within a pre-determined future period (American Option).

A "Call Option" is where the buyer of the option is acquiring the right to buy a currency. A "Put Option" is where the buyer's right is to sell the stipulated currency.

As in the case of interest rate options, there are two types.

(a) Traded options are those available, in standardised contract form, from recognized exchanges around the world, for example, LIFFE.

(b) Over-the-counter options are available from banks and are much more flexible. They are tailored to meet the needs of individual customers, within broad criteria which we shall look at later.

24.4.2.2 Operation

The operation is similar to that of the Interest Rate Option.

For the payment of an up-front premium the buyer acquires the right to exercise the option, if it is in his favour to do so, on the nominated expiration date or within the agreed option period prior to this (in the case of an American Option). As already mentioned, the exchange rate is agreed at the outset, and this is known as the "Strike Price" (sometimes called the "exercise price"). In this way the purchaser:

(a) has peace of mind that he has established a definite rate in case the market moves adversely;

(b) is able to take advantage of any favourable rate movements; and

(c) has the comfort that if, for example, the underlying transaction falls through, the option can just be allowed to lapse (unlike in the case of a Forward Contract where the customer is bound to see it through).

To demonstrate the use of a currency option we can use the same example as we did for the forward break option contract.

You will remember that the company was looking to hedge its exposure in connection with an anticipated inflow of US$5 million, in three months' time. If we assume that it has taken a decision to "do something" and needs the assurance of establishing the worst possible position, ie by fixing a rate now. From the methods we have looked at so far, there are potentially a number of courses he could take.

24.4.2.2.1 Matching

Does this match an exposure of similar currency, account and timing, ie an outflow of US$ around the same time? Alternatively he could borrow US$5 million now, invest the proceeds or use them otherwise, and repay the loan in three months from the proceeds due. (This latter action does not enable him to benefit from any favourable rate movements and ties up borrowing lines unnecessarily.)

24.4.2.2.2 Forward Contracts

The different types of forward contracts are available for consideration. Such a contract will enable him to lock into a definite rate, with varying degrees of flexibility and the benefit to take at least some advantage of any favourable rate movements that should occur. (This will be a binding agreement which he usually must complete, or pay a severe penalty. The variations which allow him to take advantage of favourable rate movements will have a higher "fee" built into the rate quoted thus valuing them effectively more expensive and adversely affecting the benefit of potential gain, or even deliminating it.)

24.4.2.2.3 Financial Futures

Essentially, financial futures are a tradeable version of a forward contract executed in standard terms and for standard amounts and maturities. They enable "lock-in" if held until delivery/expiry, and the opportunity to gain if favourable movements in the contract price occur and it is sold prior to expiry. (They require regular monitoring, margin payments, and standard delivery dates (March, June, September and December) might not suit the customer's needs therefore the contract would have to be sold prior to expiry and the customer would carry the risk that the prevailing rate at that time might be unattractive.)

24.4.2.2.4 Currency Option

For payment of an up-front premium the company is able to set a "strike price" to suit its needs. The "strike price" could be set:

(i)   "at the money" – where the "strike price" is set at the same as the prevailing spot rate;

(ii)   "in the money" – where a rate more favourable than the spot rate is set; or

(iii) "out of the money" – where the "strike price" is less favourable to the company than the current spot rate.

In our example, where the company is selling US$ in three months' time, let us assume that spot is currently 1.80 and that this is the "Strike Price" the company wishes to set (ie "at the money"). If the company is certain as to dates it will use the European Option, which, you will recall, can be exercised on the expiry date only. Alternatively, if dates are uncertain, then the American Option would be better suited as the exercise can take place, if required, any time up to the expiry date. Because of this greater flexibility, the premium payable for an American Option will be higher.

In three months' time:

(i)   The spot rate is 1.75; this is more favourable to the company therefore the Option will be allowed to lapse and the prevailing spot rate used.

(ii)   The spot rate is 1.85; this is a worse rate than the Option rate so therefore the contract will be exercised. This is the essence of an Option; the holder only needs to exercise it when it is in his favour to do so.

24.4.2.2.5 Cylinder Options

Cylinder options set an upper and lower rate, similar to the interest rate collar. It is made up of two separate option contracts, for the same currency/amount/ term, but one is written by the bank (to the customer) and the other by the customer (to the bank). Cylinder options are available in both American and European style.

We shall again use our example of selling US$5 million in three months' time. In order to eliminate the risk of adverse movements the company wishes to fix a rate "at the money", say 1.80. However, the company is happy to set a lower rate representing the extent of any potential gain from favourable movements to the level set, say, 1.70.

The company does this by:

(i)   Purchasing from a bank an Option at 1.80, ie company sells US$.

(ii)   Selling to a bank an Option at 1.70, ie bank purchases US$. Depending on the "Strike Prices" set it may be possible to eliminate totally any premium payable in this way.

In three months' time, at maturity of the contract, a number of things could happen:

(i)   The spot rate is below 1.70 – the bank exercises its option to purchase US$ at the "strike price" agreed, ie 1.70. However, the company allows its option, set at 1.80, to lapse and converts at the prevailing spot rate.

(ii)   The spot rate is between 1.70 and 1.80 – the bank and company both allow their options to lapse and use the favourable prevailing spot rate.

(iii) The spot rate is more than 1.80 – the company will make use of lower rate available under the option and exercise the contract. The bank, however, will use the more favourable prevailing spot rate.

In all of the above scenarios, the company has the flexibility to gain from favourable movements, but by restricting this to a pre-agreed level it is able to reduce, or maybe even eliminate, the fee payable.

24.4.2.3 Pricing of Currency Options

We have already seen that an up-front premium is payable and this will depend on a number of aspects:

(a)   American or European (the former will be more expensive);

(b)   maturity;

(c)   the "strike price" set, and whether it is at/in/out of the money;

(d)   prevailing market rates; and

(e)   volatility of the currency involved.

Potentially, a further factor may be any additional cost to the bank in hedging its own position.

24.4.2.3.1 Options delta

If the market rises (ie if the market value of the underlying asset rises), the value of a call option will also rise. The amount of the change in the option's premium as a proportion of the change in the underlying price is known as its delta.

The effect is magnified or geared (gearing). In other words the return on investment for a holder of options will be greater than the return on investment for a holder of the underlying assets themselves. This is because options only cost their premium, whereas the underlying investments cost their full market price.

The seller or writer of a call would have to make delivery of the product in question if a holder requires it. Consequently the seller can incur large losses. When a person sells exchange-traded options, the exchange will require margin (or collateral) to be deposited with the exchange/clearing house, to cover foreseeable potential losses. Additional margin will be called for if the price of the underlying asset moves in favour of the option holder and against the option writer.

Call holders can make unlimited profits, while their losses are limited to the premium paid (call holders have a bullish view of the security in question).

In contrast writers (or sellers) can make only limited profits (premiums) and unlimited losses if they do not own the underlying asset.

24.4.2.4 Features

Amounts:	Flexible, usually a minimum of £25/£50,000, or currency equivalent.
Term/Period:	The market is liquid to 12 months, although contracts beyond may be catered for on an individual basis.
Documentation:	Agreement between buyer and seller.
Fees:	Up-front premium payable which varies, as we have seen, depending on a number of factors. As a general rule between 5% – 3% of contract amount.
Currencies:	Major currencies against Sterling. Major currencies against US$. Restricted availability for others, eg Euro against SWFr.
Availability:	Widespread, all major banks.
Flexibility:	Very flexible as to amount, period and currency. Choice of American/European Options.
Protection:	Sets maximum rate whilst allowing holder to gain from any favourable rate movements.

24.4.2.5 Benefits

(a) Protection against adverse movements by fixing rate that can be applied in such circumstances.

(b)   Ability to gain from favourable rate movements.

(c)   Known premium amount up-front.

(d)   Flexible contracts, can be tailored to meet needs.

(e)   Useful if timing is uncertain (American Option).

(f)   Useful in tender situations, as if the contract is not even, the option is simply allowed to lapse.

(g)   "Strike Price" can be set to suit needs.

(h)   Ability to reduce/eliminate premium, by use of Cylinder Option.

24.4.2.6 Disadvantages

(a)   Premium may appear excessive.

(b)   Short-term market only – may be difficult to go out beyond twelve months.

24.4.3 SWAP

A SWAP is the name given to an agreement made between two parties who agree to exchange an item one of them possesses for an item the other possesses.

The most common SWAPs are:

1.   Interest rate SWAPs

2.   Currency SWAPs

3.   Gilts for cash SWAPs

As well as raising money, companies might want to rationalize/improve their interest costs and risks, eg by hedging their exposure to interest rate risk or currency risk.

For the two parties involved in an interest rate swap, it is a contractual agreement whereby they exchange a series of "interest" payments for the term of the swap on a notional amount of principal. Typically, one party agrees to pay a floating rate of interest (eg six-month LIBOR) and the other agrees to pay a fixed rate of interest in return. The "interest" is calculated on an agreed notional amount of principal. If the swap is in the same currency this is known as a "plain vanilla" swap.

No exchange of principal amount is involved with interest rate swaps, only of interest obligations (ie it is not a means of raising capital).

Swaps are not tradeable instruments nor transferable securities. They are "over-the-counter" transactions.

For example, X and Y might arrange a five-year interest rate swap, on a notional principal of £10 million, whereby every six months, X pays floating interest at LIBOR to Y, and Y pays fixed interest of 6% pa to X.

Swaps are also used for currencies (currency swaps). For example, X and Y might arrange a three-year currency swap in which X pays interest at sterling six-month LIBOR on Principal of £10 million and Y pays interest at US six-month LIBOR on principal of $16 million. Swaps can therefore be used to hedge both interest rate and currency exposures.

Benefits

● Lower cost of funds – a swap can give two companies more efficient access to capital markets by enabling them to raise fixed or floating rate funds more cheaply (eg it might be cheaper to borrow fixed rate funds and swap into floating rate, than to borrow floating rate funds direct).

● Active debt management (ie managing the organization's debt financing profile).

● A swap can be used to lock in refinancing costs.

Swaps Trading

In the same way that a bookmaker, having taken a large bet, will lay off some of the risk, so too may a swap bank lay off some of its exposure.

24.4.4 Currency Swaps

24.4.4.1 Definition

A currency swap involves two parties (counterparties), usually through a bank acting as intermediary, who agrees to:

(a) exchange at the outset a principal sum denominated in one currency for another at a specified rate;

(b) to reverse the transaction, at the same rate, as a predetermined date; and

(c) in the meantime, cover each other's interest commitments during the term of the swap.

A currency swap is a legally binding exchange which both parties are committed to, unless by mutual consent (including the intermediary bank). A currency "swaption" may be obtained, on an individually tailored basis.

As in the case of interest-rate swaps, the essence of the market is "comparative advantage" and the benefits companies can obtain in different markets.

24.4.4.2 Operation

There are two companies. Company A is British and Company B is an American operation. Company A is well known in the UK and can therefore raise sterling more cheaply, although it requires US$ finance. The opposite is the case for Company B. In order to take advantage of their relative strengths in their home currencies Company A borrows in Sterling and Company B in US$.

Company A has borrowed £50 million. It is agreed that A and B will enter a swap transaction whereby A received US$ and B Sterling. The current spot rate is 1.80 and this is the exchange rate that is agreed between both parties. Thus Company B receives £50 million and Company A US$90 million. During the term of the swap, Company A pays the interest costs relating to the US$90 million and Company B does likewise in connection with the finance arranged by Company A. These payments are made in the respective currencies.

At the end of the swap the principal sums are repaid. Most textbooks explain this by a series of boxes and arrows, as follows:

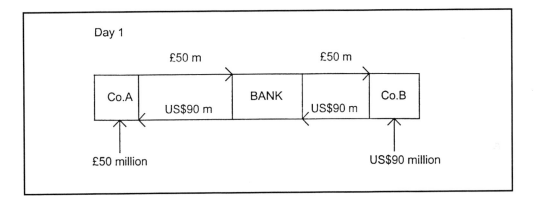

24.4.4.2.1 During Swap (Interest)

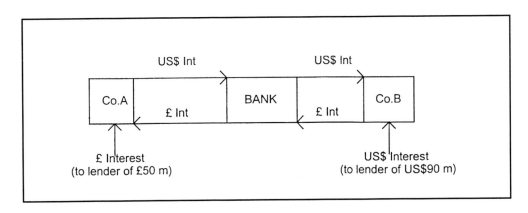

2.4.4.2.2 *Expiry of Swap*

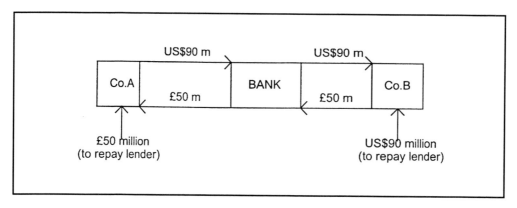

(In reality, the bank will take a loss by way of its fee.)

Thus it is possible to obtain currency finance at competitive rates by raising in the "cheapest" and then swapping to the currency required.

24.4.4.3 Features

Accounts:	Generally a minimum of £3/£5 million, or currently equivalent, but smaller amounts may be accommodated on an individual basis. No maximum, subject to counterparty availability.
Term/Period:	Usually minimum two years, maximum ten/12 years.
Documentation:	Swap agreement, generally ISDA (International Swap Dealers Association).
Fees:	The intermediary bank may have taken an arrangement fee, although most commonly this is achieved by way of a loss on the rates allowed between counterparties.
Currencies:	Major currencies.
Availability:	Financial institutions (particularly merchant banks).
Flexibility:	Subject to counterparty availability, or desire of intermediary bank, the swap market provides a flexible means of raising currency finance to suit a varied range of needs.
Protection:	A means of establishing a rate to apply now, for the initial exchange, and on expiry of the swap.

24.4.4.4 Benefits

(a)   Cheap currency finance is possible by using "comparative advantage".

(b) A useful means of managing "translation" exposure by converting foreign currency items into "home" currency.

(c) Flexibility of the market enables a wide range of needs to be met.

(d) Establishes exchange rate at outset.

(e) Off-balance sheet.

(f) Private, ie no publicity.

(g) Generally no up-front fee payable.

(h) Terms clearly established through standard documentation and counterparties have the comfort of the standing of a bank as intermediary.

(i) Available to meet medium-long-term needs.

24.4.4.5 Disadvantages

(a) A definite commitment (may be difficult/impossible to break).

(b) Not available for short-term purposes.

(c) Can appear complex.

(d) Security depends on the standing of the intermediary bank.

24.5.1 Product Types: Other Derivatives

The main exchange traded derivatives are on interest rate products.

- **Bond Products** are based on underlying domestic bonds (US Treasury Bonds, UK gilts, German Bunds, etc). These are physically deliverable. Like the underlying bond in the cash market, their price will vary inversely with interest rates.

- **Short-term Interest Rate Products.** These are based on a notional amount of money for a deposit term of three-months, eg the Short Sterling contract is based on a notional deposit of £500,000 for three months.

The price of a short-term interest rate future is expressed as 100 less the interest rate. If the market believes that three month interest rates *will* be 6% in six months' time, the price of a future for delivery in six months would be 94.00 (= 100-6.00). This pricing method preserves the inverse relationship between price and interest rates. Thus if we now believe that three-month interest rates (for delivery in six-months) *will* be 5% the price of the short-term interest rate future will rise from 94.00 to 95.00.

Short-term interest rate products are known as "Euro" or "three-month", eg the Eurodollar is the contract on the three-month US interest rate, etc. As they represent an index of interest rates, they are cash settled.

24.5.1.1 Equity Indices and Equity Options

These are available on major stock market indexes (both as a future and an option), eg FT-SE, S&P 100, DAX, Nikkei-Dow. Individual share options (but not futures) are available on a company's shares. For large companies, equity options and their shares are exchange-traded.

Whereas options on stock market indices are cash settled, options on individual shares may result in delivery of the underlying share, when the options are exercized.

24.5.1.2 Currencies

Most currency derivatives are traded "over the counter" (OTC) rather than exchange traded. Because of this, the only exchanges with successful currency contracts are the well-established ones, such as the Philadelphia Stock Exchange (PHLX) which trades options on currencies and the Chicago Mercantile Exchange (CME) which trades futures and options on futures.

Futures are often said to provide a perfect hedge. Hedging is the method of using instruments to protect an existing position or known commitment. Futures can achieve this. With futures there are unlimited profits available but there is also the possibility of unlimited losses. When entering into a futures contract it is not known in which direction the price will move, but both the buyer and seller are committed to the agreed price. Investors must be made aware that they are obliged to supply margin as a form of good faith deposit. It is a small proportion of the value of the contract but is recalculated daily. If the price has moved against them, they will be required to supply more margin each day.

24.5.2 Futures

An agreement to buy or sell a standard quantity of a specified asset on a fixed date at a price agreed today.

These are very usually two parties to the futures contract:

● the buyer of a future enters into an obligation to buy on a specified date;

● the seller of a future is under an obligation to sell on a future date

These obligations relate to a standard quantity of a specified asset on a fixed future date at a price agreed today. Exchange traded futures are traded in standardized parcels known as contracts. This is to ensure buyers and sellers know exactly what quantity will be delivered.

Example

A future contract on a gilt might be £100,000 nominal of a 7% gilt. If you sold one gilt future you would know you were obligated to sell £100,000 nominal of gilts. Futures are only traded on whole numbers of contracts, therefore if you wished to by £200,000 nominal of gilts you would have to buy two gilt futures.

In many cases a physical delivery does not take place on delivery day. The exchange calculates how much has been lost or gained by the parties to the contract and it is only the monetary gain or loss which changes hands.

What happens if the farmer's crop is hit by a drought and it is impossible to delivery the potatoes? Because futures can be traded the obligation can be offset by undertaking an equal trade in the market.

Example

Let us suppose a farmer has *sold* one August potato future at £130 per tonne. If he later decides he does not want to sell his potato, but use it to feed his cattle, he simply *buys* one August future at the then prevailing price. His original position is offset by a bought position, leaving him with no outstanding delivery obligations.

Offsetting is common, very few contracts run through to delivery (cut losses).

Some people use futures to reduce risk, others to seek high returns – and for this they must be willing to take high risk. They are categorized as:

● Hedger – someone seeking to reduce risk (sitting on the hedge).

● Speculator – a risk-taker, seeking large profits (gambler).

● Arbitrageur – seeks riskless profits from exploiting market inefficiencies.

Financial Futures and Options Exchange. Futures on indices are officially described as contracts for difference.

Futures and options are classed as derivatives – their value is derived from an underlying asset traded in the cash market.

A futures contract is an agreement, transacted through an exchange, to buy or sell a standard quantity of an underlying asset (currency, interest rate, gilt, equity index or commodity) at a future date, at a price agreed today.

Futures merely represent an agreement to buy or sell at a future date. As the contract is standard, it can be readily traded until a set date. The standardising allows *fungibility*, ie all futures are substitutable.

A buyer of a futures contract (who is long in futures) has the following choices:

● to actually receive the asset from the futures exchange when the contract stops trading. This is very rare. Another term for receiving the asset at maturity/ expiry in the futures market is "take delivery" of the asset. The obligation to buy the asset only arises if the contract is held to expiry; or

● to sell the future before trading in the future stops. This "offsets" or "squares" his position. The offset is performed by executing an equal and opposite trade in the same underlying asset and future month. He would crystallize or realize any profit or loss that had arisen at that point.

For example, if I buy 1,000 June futures contracts at one price, I might sell 1,000 June futures (at another price) at any time before the contract stops trading in June. This will square my position, leaving me with a gain or loss on the original purchase and subsequent sale.

A unique aspect of futures is that one can *enter* the market *either* by buying or selling contracts. In other words, it is possible to take a "short" position by selling futures before buying any. For example, I can sell 1,000 September sterling interest rate futures contracts, and later square my position (before the contract expires in September) by buying 1,000 September contracts. I will make a gain or loss on the difference between the original sale price and the subsequent purchase price.

Note: Futures prices

The price of a future depends on the nature of the underlying asset. Prices in futures move in standard price units or multiples of price units. A price unit for futures contacts is called a "tick". For any given futures contract (eg a sterling short-term interest rate future) a tick has a fixed value. It is therefore easy to calculate the value of a change in price as x ticks at £y per tick per contract.

24.5.2.1 Uses of Futures

The prime function of a futures market is the provision of insurance cover (or "hedging") against the risks of adverse price fluctuation.

Futures prices today

5770   5740

Futures prices next week?

5725   5745

The solid line shows the value of futures contracts on the FT-SE 100 Index. Most futures will have lower values for the nearer month than the far months.

An investor who is concerned that his portfolio of shares might fall in value within the next month can hedge, or insure, himself by selling the one-month future. Suppose he sells 1,000 futures.

Suppose that a few days later the value of the FT-SE 100 has fallen, and the one-month price is now, say, 5730. The investor sold futures at 5750 and can now close his position by making a closing purchase. For each futures contract he sold then purchased, he has made a profit of 20 (ie 5750 – 5730) multiplied by the value per point for the futures contract which for the FT-SE 100 future is £10. (a half point is a tick which is worth £5).

Profit = 20 x £10 = £200 per future.

Profit for 1,000 futures = £200 x 1,000 = £200,000.

For the investor, his actual portfolio of shares has declined in value, so he has made a loss on the portfolio. However, he has made a profit on the futures trading. This will help soften the blow of the decline in the value of his shares – in other words, the futures have provided the investor with a "hedge" against a fall in the price of the FT-SE 100 shares.

For the market to work however, some of the risk being offset by hedging has to be absorbed by someone else. This is the function of speculators who buy or sell futures hoping to profit from the movement in the contract.

A speculator buys if he thinks the market is going to rise ("bullish") or sells if he thinks there will be a fall ("bearish").

24.6 Interest Rate Exposure Management

24.6.1 Introduction

In this unit we will look at the methods of managing exposure to interest rate movements.

It is important to the lender to understand:

● what the customer wants to achieve, ie what his/her requirements/objectives are;

● how the product(s) work(s);

● what the respective benefits/disadvantages are of each alternative available.

24.6.2 Internal Treasury Techniques

These are not "products" but actions that can be taken internally to reduce exposure.

24.6.2.1 Smoothing

This is the process of distributing fixed and variable rate exposure in order to spread the risk.

If, for example, a company took all of its debt finance at fixed rate, without taking any other action, it would:

● be protected against any adverse rate movements since by taking fixed rate borrowing it would have locked in to a rate to cover its future financing needs; but

● incur higher financing costs than necessary if rates were to fall, ie where the cost of variable rate finance would have been lower.

(It is important to appreciate that the impact of rate movements can be quite dramatic where large sums are involved.)

With a "smoothing" operation, the treasurer would maintain a balance between fixed and variable rate borrowings, thus maintaining an element of protection against increasing rates (by fixed rate) while still retaining the ability to take advantage of falling rates (in the case of variable rate finance).

Do not forget that investors will also consider such a process.

There may be very sound underlying reasons, however, why corporates do not maintain a 50/50 split between fixed and variable rate financing, and in fact few do. For example, they may command finer rates in the fixed market.

Consequently, this strategy cannot be regarded as a prime hedging tool as the underlying exposures remain. It is more a method of striking a balance overall to minimise the impact of rate movements.

24.6.2.2 Matching

This term relates to the internal matching of liabilities and assets denominated in the same, or similar, reference rate. For example, in a decentralised group it could be that one subsidiary company is investing in the money market whereas another is borrowing through the same medium. Therefore an increase in the reference rate, LIBOR (London Interbank Offered Rate), will affect both sides, ie the borrowing costs move but the interest received on the deposit also increases.

However, this may prove expensive compared with say an effective cash management system and use of hedging products to control interest rate exposure.

24.6.3 FRAs (Forward or Future Rate Agreements)

24.6.3.1 Definition

This means a contractual obligation between two parties through which an interest rate is fixed to apply to a "notional" account for a specific period commencing on a stated future date.

24.6.3.2 Operation

If the company's borrowing requirement is £5 million for three months from June, and assuming that it has a short-term LIBOR; a loan facility in place and intends to borrow using this, on a three-month rollover drawn in June, in order to establish the cost of the borrowing now, the company could use an FRA.

For example:

- *Day 1 – March:* purchase FRA for £5 million notional amount at, say, 10% per annum. (The price will simply be quoted by the institution selling the FRA and will reflect current rates, volatility, supply/demand and the seller's return.)

- *June:* £5 million drawn on three-month LIBOR rollover, the latter being, say, 11 % per annum at that time, ie the interest that will be paid in September on maturity will be £137,500 (plus lender's margin, which the company would have known at the outset).

- *June:* settlement under the FRA takes place and this will involve either:

  - the purchaser paying the bank of the FRA if market rates are lower than the FRA rate; or

  - the bank paying the purchaser if rates are higher.

In this case the cost of the loan is 1% per annum more than the FRA rate (11% against 10%, ie the borrower will be paying 1% per annum more than it had budgeted and therefore the seller of the FRA will compensate the company accordingly. (Note: the FRA is a totally independent contract from the underlying loan/deposit. It may be purchased from a different bank or, indeed, may even be used by speculators with no loan/deposit to protect.)

2.6.3.3 Settlement

(1)	(2)	(3)
Agreement Date	Settlement Date	Maturity Date

(1) This is the date the FRA is taken out (March in our example) and is called the "agreement date".

(2) This is when settlement is made under the IRA and will relate to when the loan/deposit is taken (June in our example).

(3) This is when the FRA matures (period (2) to (3) is called the "contract period".

The operation of FRAs in the United Kingdom is regulated by terms laid down by the British Bankers Association (these terms are called FRABBA) and it is the reference rate set by the BBA that is used to calculate any settlement necessary. From an approved panel of banks, the BBA establishes average reference rates for the LIBOR settings at 11.00 am daily.

This represents the prevailing "market" rate and will be established on the settlement date of the FRA, in the case of sterling (two business days before if there are currencies involved).

However, since settlement is being paid up front while interest on market loans/deposits is paid/received on maturity, the settlement account will be discounted to reflect the time value of money. In our example the bank will pay the company on the settlement date:

$$\pounds5 \text{ million} \times (11\% - 10\%) \times \frac{3 \text{ months}}{12 \text{ months}} = \pounds12,500 \text{ less discount, ie}$$

$$\pounds12.500 \times \frac{100}{100 + (11 \times \frac{3}{12})} = \pounds12,165.45$$

24.6.3.4 Features

(a) *Amounts:* can be tailored to suit individual requirements. The market is liquid between the range £1 million and £50/£75 million. Banks may look at deals outside of this on an individual basis.

(b) *Term/Period:* generally for any forward "market" period, with the start or the contract period (ie when settlement takes place) within 12/18 months and maturity one year later. (Banks may be prepared to consider different periods but on a one-off basis only.)

(c) *Documentation:* standard document – FRABBA terms apply.

(d) *Fees:* none as such – built into rate quoted.

(e) *Currencies:* the main markets are in sterling and US dollars although FRAs denominated in Euros, Swiss francs, D-Marks and yen are obtainable.

(f) *Availability:* widespread, from financial institutions.

(g) *Flexibility:* Within broad criteria, contracts can be tailored to suit requirements.

(h) *Protection:* fixed interest cost/return to supply, thus eliminates downside risk. Linked to LMOR.

24.6.3.5 Benefits

(a) FRAs establish a definite rate to be applied for a future need, borrowing or investing. This eliminates the risk of higher financing costs or lower investment return of rates more adversely.

(b) There is no fee payable.

(c) There is no balance sheet impact.

(d) There are no margins to pay, thus no impact on working capital (ie cash is not tied up in margins).

(e) As they relate to interest element only, FRAs are not tied to the underlying loan/deposit.

(f) They can be tailored to meet needs (within the criteria).

(g) Protection is available for certain currency transactions.

(h) They are not tied to exchange "open hours".

(i) They are available from a range of sources.

(j) Standard documentation applies.

(k) Once they are in place, there is nothing further the company has to do pending settlement, ie no concerns about reversing early or margin payments.

24.6.3.6 Disadvantages

(a) Settlement has to take place, so the purchaser of the FRA has to be certain of amounts and timing (maybe unwound in some circumstances, but against penalty).

(b) Advantage cannot be taken of any favourable movements; FRAs *fix the rate* to be applied.

(c) There will be a basis risk if the underlying borrowing/deposit is not against LIBOR.

(d) It is difficult to obtain a perfect match for any non-market recognized periods.

24.6.4 Interest rate options

There are various types of option contracts available, and these can be split between:

- *traded options* those quoted as standardized contracts and purchased from exchanges, for example, LIFFE

- *OTC ("over the counter") options*, OTC which can be purchased from financial institutions and thus tailored more specifically to meet varying needs.

It is the OTC options that we shall be looking at here given the greater flexibility compared with traded options.

24.6.4.1 Definition

Any form of "option" contract is an arrangement between two parties under which the buyer (or holder) has the right, but not the obligation, to perform with the seller (or writer) in accordance with the stated terms of the contract. The terms of an interest rate option will include:

- interest rate;

- underlying notional amount; and

- the time during which the option can be exercised.

The essence of the option is that the holder is not obliged to exercise it and is thus able to benefit from favourable rate movements. It does not "lock-in" or fix rates as in the case of forward forwards, financial futures and forward rate agreements. However, there will usually be a premium to pay for the privilege. You will not be far wrong if you consider options as a form of insurance, to be exercised if the worst happens, otherwise simply allowed to lapse taking the benefit of favourable movements in the market. It is important to understand this concept of having the right to exercise but not the obligation.

There are different types of OTC interest rate options, including: caps, floors, collars and interest rate guarantees.

24.6.4.2 Caps

An interest rate cap is an agreement between the seller and the buyer, through which the former agrees to reimburse the latter should interest rates rise above a specified level during an agreed period of time. Reimbursement is made on the basis of a pre-determined underlying notional amount. The option, in this case a cap, is a separate contract to the underlying borrowing. Finance may or may not be provided by the seller of the cap, or indeed there may even be no underlying amount if the buyer is a speculator.

Caps are available referenced against both LIBOR, usually three or six months, and base rate.

A premium is payable to the seller and in the case of caps this will be a one-off fee paid up front. In the case of base rate caps, the premium may be paid quarterly, or at another frequency agreed with the seller.

The figure below showing movements in three-month periods between, for example, 1999 and 2001, demonstrates how a cap works.

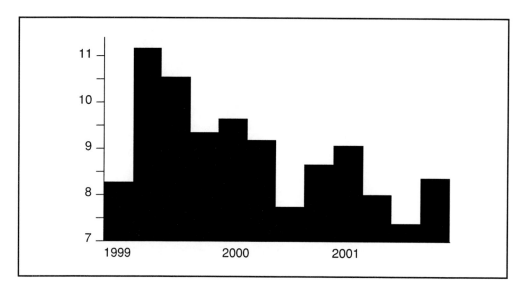

During that period a company will be borrowing £10 million on a floating rate loan facility, with drawdown/maturity on a three-month basis. The current rate (ie in January 1999) is 8%. The treasurer has no particular views as to how rates are likely to move, but cannot run the risk that the rate will increase beyond 10% during the term in question. Some assurance is therefore needed that the maximum cost will be 10% plus the agreed margin with the lender. However, the company still wishes to benefit from any favourable movements in the rate below that maximum ceiling.

At the beginning of 1999 the treasurer purchases a cap at 10% per annum for three years, linked to the three month LIBOR rate, and based on a notional amount of £10 million. The affect is shown in the figure below.

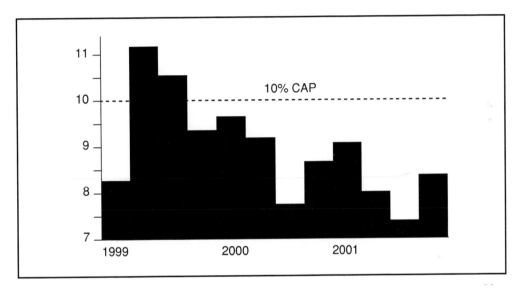

During the second and third quarters in 1999, three month LIBOR leaps to more than 10% and during those periods the company is reimbursed by the seller of the cap for the excess amount of interest. Thus, during that time the borrowing cost is restricted to 10%. Throughout the remainder of the borrowing period the company is able to take advantage of lower rates.

24.6.4.3 Floors

An interest rate floor is essentially the opposite of a cap in that the seller undertakes to pay the buyer compensation if interest rates fall below an agreed minimum during a predetermined period. In this way, an investor can establish a guaranteed minimum return while retaining the right to take advantage of any favourable rate movements.

24.6.4.4 Collars

An interest rate collar is simply the combination of a cap and a floor. Of the parties involved in the transaction, one will sell the cap and the other will sell the floor.

In this way, a borrower can buy the cap and in so doing will set its maximum borrowing cost. It can then sell a floor, to cover the same amount and period, in order to establish its minimum cost. The main purpose of this will be to reduce, or in some cases even eliminate, the fee payable. But it must be remembered that by setting a floor the company will not benefit if rates fall below the level nominated.

Investors are also exposed to movements in interest rates. Similarly therefore, an investor could use a collar to establish maximum and minimum returns, choosing to forgoe some potential gains, in excess of the cap, in return for a reduced premium, or none at all.

In the example above, the company could have nominated to set a floor of 10%, thus restricting its borrowing cost to between 10% and 12%, as shown in the next diagram.

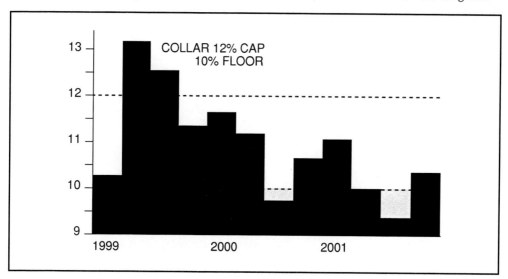

Where rates exceed 12%, the seller of the cap will reimburse the company, as we have already seen. The company then benefits from any reductions down to 10%. Any further reductions are forgone in respect of the floor.

24.6.4.5 Pricing of Options

All the options above involve:

● a nominated price ("strike price");

● a determined notional amount;

● a specific period, with an agreed expiry.

The "strike price" is the rate that the option is based on; for example, the "strike price" in the cap was 12%. The buyer of the option may nominate the "strike price" and this will have an impact on the premium payable. A number of factors affect the premium. These are:

- the relationship between strike price and current market price;

- maturity;

- volatility;

- supply and demand;

- is there a floor or is it "participating"?

A number of option type products are called "participating". The concept of participation means that should there be a favourable movement in rates, then this will be shared between the buyer and seller on a basis determined at the outset, say 50/50. This will, at least, reduce the premium payable, and very often eliminate it.

24.6.4.6 Features of interest rate options

(a) *Amounts:* LIBOR caps/floors/collars – minimum £1 million, maximum £100 million.

Base rate caps – minimum £250,000, maximum £10 million.

Interest rate guarantees – minimum £1 million, maximum £100 million.

(LIBOR caps/floors/collars and interest rate guarantee may be on more restrictive availability below £5 million.

Sums in excess of the maximums shown may be considered.)

(b) *Term/Period:* LIBOR caps/floors/collars – minimum twelve months, maximum five/seven years.

Base rate caps – one or two years.

Interest rate guarantees – minimum one month, maximum twelve/eighteen months.

(c) *Documentation:* Agreement form, setting out obligations of buyer/seller.

(d) *Fees:* Up front fee payable (see earlier comments).

(e) *Currencies:*   Sterling and US$ – restricted availability for other major currencies.

(f) *Availability:*   Widespread, from financial institutions.

(g) *Flexibility:*   Very flexible, can be tailored to suit needs, within the above broad criteria.

(h) *Protection:*   Caps – set a maximum ceiling

Floors – set a minimum

Collars – combine <cap and floor

The beauty of the option is that the holder is not obliged to see it through if rates move favourably.

24.6.4.7 Benefits

As to the individual benefits of each type, these are covered in the text. The major benefits of interest rate options generally are summarized below.

(a) They are very flexible and can be tailored to meet precise requirements.

(b) They are a form of insurance, giving protection if needed, yet there is the flexibility of being able to benefit from any favourable rate movements.

(c) The cost is known at the outset so this can easily be included in future budgets/projections.

(d) They are unrelated to underlying loans/deposits.

(e) They are simple to establish and widely available.

The price of the premium can be reduced by setting higher strike price or using a floor/collar.

24.6.4.8 Disadvantages

(a) The premium may be considered high, certainly when compared to FRAs where there is no fee payable.

(b) The market is mainly restricted to cover against fluctuations in LIBOR (apart from some availability of base rate caps) thus there may be a basis risk if the underlying loan/deposit is against a different sequence.

24.6.5 Interest Rate Swaps

Although there is a degree of mystique surrounding swaps, the concept really is quite simple.

24.6.5.1 Definition

An interest rate swap is an agreement between two parties who agree to exchange differing interest commitments on a notional sum throughout a predeferred period. Essentially, interest rate swaps are most commonly used as a method of converting fixed rate debt to floating rate debt, or vice versa. The transaction involves no exchange of principal, but simply transfers the interest obligations between the parties involved.

The backbone of the market is the concept of "comparative advantage". This is because some companies can command their finest rates in, say, the fixed rate market, whilst others are best placed in floating. So a company can raise funds in the cheapest possible way, say fixed rate, and then, if necessary, swap with a counterpart in a similar situation but whose comparative advantage is in floating. The benefit can be shared between the two and in this way both have raised finance cheaper than they could have achieved themselves direct from the market.

Protection is given to the counterparties as a bank will act as intermediary and put the swap transactions together, assuming the credit risk of both parties.

24.6.5.2 Swaption

A swap is a binding agreement which all parties are obliged to see through. A swaption is where the buyer has the right but not the obligation to site into a swap transaction at some future date, like a typical "options", an up-front premium is payable.

24.6.5.3 Features

Amounts:	Minimum £1 million, no maximum.
Term/Period:	Minimum one year, maximum usually ten years. (Longer subject to availability of counterparty.)
Documentation:	A swap agreement – standard terms have been established by ISDA (International Swap Dealers Association).
Fees:	Arrangement fee may be taken by bank acting as intermediary, ie matching counterparties although most commonly the fee is "hidden" in the spread of rates quoted.
Currencies:	The bulk of the interest rate swap market is in US$ and Sterling, other currencies are subject to availability.
Availability:	Financial institutions (particularly merchant banks).

Protection: Provides the opportunity to switch from fixed to floating and vice versa, to suit requirements and perception of future movements.

24.6.5.4 Benefits

(a)   A means of managing existing debt, ie by swapping if necessary.

(b)   Access to cheaper finance through comparative advantage.

(c)   The swap market is sufficiently liquid to enable reversals of positions if necessary.

(d)   Counterparty risk is assumed by the bank acting as intermediary (underlying loan does not have to be with the latter).

(e)   Discrete, ie not made public.

(f)   Flexible as to amount and period, subject to intermediary's ability to match terms or otherwise hold a mis-match position itself.

24.6.5.5 Disadvantages

(a)   Positions can be unwound, however, it may be more expensive than in the case of alternative hedging techniques.

(b)   Other alternatives may be more flexible and less expensive.

(c)   A swap involves "locking in" and therefore loses the benefits of the option type products.

(d)   Can appear to be complex.

25

CASE STUDIES

Case Study 1– Milner Construction Ltd

Milner Construction Ltd is a firm of contracting builders. The company was established in 1977 and has banked with you since its formation. The founders of the company, Michael Milner and Patrick Greenwood, own all the shares. They are both now in their 40s. They were originally bricklayers and, at first, the company supplied bricklaying services to house builders. As the business grew, the company undertook a wider range of activities – supplying materials, scaffolding, etc, as well as labour. It now works mainly for large building companies as a subcontractor on major construction contracts, such as office blocks and shopping centres. Milner's normal minimum contract size is £300,000.

Although, at one stage, the company had 120 employees, most labour is now self-employed working on a subcontract basis for Milner. There are now only ten full-time employees.

The company currently has the following facilities from the bank:

Overdraft	£500,000
Bonds/guarantees	£300,000

As security, the bank has a debenture that includes a first charge over the company's freehold office building, which was valued at £250,000 three years ago. There are also directors' unlimited guarantees, supported by the equities in their houses of £180,000 and £80,000. Six years ago, the company decided to expand into Europe and established a subsidiary in France. However, this venture was not a success and, earlier this year, the company closed down the subsidiary and wrote off its investment.

The 2001 audited accounts are now available. The directors call to see you to discuss their requirements for the next 12 months. The company has never produced management accounts or formal forecasts, although its "back of the envelope" assessments have, in the past, been reasonably accurate.

The company currently has underway, or has won, contracts to the value of £1.6 million which the directors believe will produce a net profit of £250,000 in the current financial year. In addition, they have a good chance of winning a contract worth £1 million in the next 12 months as a subcontractor to one of the UK's largest building developers.

This contract will require a performance bond of 15% of the contract value. The company is utilizing fully the current £300,000 bonding facility, and is also making full use of the overdraft facility. The directors ask the bank to increase the overdraft limit to £600,000 and the bonds/guarantees limit to £450,000. (The company has never had a claim under any performance bond issued on its behalf.)

Required:

Analyze the current position of the company and give, with reasons, the response you would make to the request.

Profit and Loss Summary

Year to 31 July	1999 £	2000 £	2001 £
Turnover	2,102,849	2,213,071	3,637,515
Gross profit	367,850	406,706	757,988
Depreciation	27,420	37,902	47,469
Directors' remuneration	96,487	130,350	222,160
Interest paid	51,320	63,815	78,682
Profit before tax	129,841	120,061	291,594
Extraordinary item (Write off of investment in subsidiary)	–	–	359,418
Tax paid	35,550	49,594	162,154
Retained profit (loss)	94,291	70,467	(229,978)

Balance Sheets as at 31 July

Year to 31 July	1999 £		2000 £		2001 £	
Current assets:						
Cash	157		1,000		501	
Debtors	341,485		562,286		796,446	
Work in progress	132,050	473,692	188,624	751,910	411,913	1,208,860
Current liabilities:						
Creditors	226,802		232,323		457,266	
Hire purchase	22,008		17,810		24,748	
Bank overdraft	225,678		444,526		539,541	
Current taxation	82,686	(557,174)	100,722	(795,381)	117,659	1,139,214
		(83,482)		(43,471)		69,646
Net current assets/(liabilities):						
Fixed assets:						
Land and buildings	134,764		134,931		132,586	
Plant and machinery	135,009		110,116		130,776	
Investment in subsidiary	290,165	559,938	329,471	574,518		–263,362
Term liability:						
Hire purchase		(99,806)		(83,229)		(115,168)
Net assets		376,650		447,818		217,840
Financed by:						
Share capital		100		100		100
Profit and loss account		376,550		447,718		217,740
		376,650		447,818		217,840

Accounting Ratios

	1999	2000	2001
Gross margin (%)	17.5	18.4	20.8
Net margin (%)	6.2	5.4	8.0
Interest cover (times)	3.5	2.9	4.7
Net gearing (%)	92	122	312
Current ratio	0.85:1	0.95:1	1.06:1
Acid test	0.61:1	0.71:1	0.70:1
Credit given (days)	59	93	80
Credit taken (days)	48	47	58
Work-in-progress turnover (days)	28	38	52

Suggested Answer: Milner Construction Ltd

The company is a long-standing customer of the bank which would want to help if possible. The management are experienced in the business but they do not have an unblemished track record. The French venture seems to have been a disaster. Despite this the core business has performed well recently The steady sales increase suggests the directors can get business from major builders so their reputation must be good, and in the absence of any claim on the bond indicates a high degree of technical competence.

The directors appear to be financially naive as indicated by the lack of management accounts and forecasts. However, they have proved that they can take hard decisions. for example the closure of the French business cannot have been very palatable.

Not least because of the French subsidiary write off, the capital structure of the business has weakened significantly. However when assessing the capital needs of the business it must be appreciated that the company has been living without the capital invested in the French venture for some time. The current liquidity pressure is more to do with the rapid expansion in turnover rather than the write off.

There is a hidden reserve in the property if the old valuation still holds good.

One of the problems for the business is that the directors have been taking too much cash out recently. They do need to be questioned about whether some of the cash previously taken out can be reinvested.

Given the nature of the debtors – large builders – the company may not have a great deal of control over the credit given.

There is also likely to be a significant element of "retentions" in the debtor figure which will increase the locked-up cash as turnover expands. The bank needs to see a detailed breakdown of debtors, with retentions shown separately. There is probably some scope to squeeze creditors who are mainly the company's own subcontractors but it also needs to be recognized that these cannot be stretched too far because the subcontractors' own liquidity is likely to be tight. Fundamentally in this business there is a limited scope to improve liquidity if they want to undertake the desired level of turnover without a capital injection. They now need to produce a good detailed cash forecast and also a detailed forecast of bond movements. It seems likely that sonic bonds must be due to run off soon.

Underlying profitability is excellent as is shown in the impressive trend in the gross margin, and performance at the bottom line level is solid, especially in 1999 if the exceptional directors' remuneration is discounted. Basically this is a very good business which has made one serious error in France.

Looking at the security available, the freehold deeds need revaluing. However, assuming that there is little change from the balance sheet figures the main security is a second charge on the freehold office, in which there is an equity of £510,000. This has to cover over £1M of facilities. The debenture must have some value but this is a business engaged in large contracts and the debtors and work in progress would break up badly in a receivership. The bank's receiver would almost certainly have to trade on to complete contracts with the risks that it involves of further potential loss for the bank.

The decision is finely balanced with the fundamental strength of the business being matched against the thin security. The directors have already committed all their personal assets, although they should reinject any cash which is available from their large drawings. A detailed financial plan is needed and a good monitoring system put in place. This might be a situation where the bank would want to use a firm of accountants to design the monitoring package and to review the actuals. Provided this is done and is satisfactory, the previous good track record of the UK business and the good track record with previous bonds make a positive decision on balance the right one.

Case Study 2 – Lewis Willis

Lewis Willis is a successful property developer who, jointly with his brother, owns a group of private property companies which have an estimated net worth of around £25 million. Willis is 52 years old and has been a customer of your bank for 30 years in both a personal and business capacity.

Willis calls to see you. He wants to undertake a property development on his own and has set up a brand new company for the purpose. He has identified a site that has planning permission for 60,000 square feet of offices.

He has already found three large companies which have expressed keen interest in taking all the office space when built. He has also had discussions with a number of institutions (pension funds and insurance companies) which would be interested in buying the building from him once let.

Willis has produced a detailed feasibility study for the project which he leaves with you. He asks if you would be prepared to recommend that your bank lend him the £6.5M needed to complete the development.

Required:

Consider the proposition and give details of the risks involved. Indicate your response to the request made by Willis.

Corporate Lending and Securities

Lewis Willis – Project Appraisal (Feasibility Study)

	£	£
Sales		
Net useable space 60,000 sq. ft @ £12.50 per sq. ft rent		750,000 p.a.
Income capitalized at 9% yield		333,333
Less 2.75% purchasers' costs		229,167
Sales value		8,104,166
Costs		
Site cost	1,300,000	
Stamp duty on site @ 1%	13,000	
Legal fees on site @ 0.5%	6,500	
Agents' fees on site @ 1%	13,000	
Total site costs		1,332,500
Building 60,000 sq ft @ £47.50 per sq ft	2,850,000	
Access roads	750,000	
Site clearance	50,000	
Contingency @ 2.5%	91,250	
Professional fees @ 12%	438,000	
Total building costs		4,179,250
Interest at 12.5% compounded quarterly (13.1% APR)		
Site costs + fees 15 months to end of build	221,629	
Construction + fees 12 months (50% weighted)	265,284	
Void period (complete but empty) 9 months	589,369	
Total interest costs		1,076,282
Agents' letting fees @ 15% of rent	112,500	
Legal fees on letting @ 1%	7,500	
Agents' capital sale fees @ 0.5%	40,521	
Promotion	25,000	
Total disposal fees and end costs		185,521
Total costs		6,773,553
Sales value		8,104,166
Less total costs		6,773,553
Profit		1,330,613
Profit on cost		19.6%
Rent yield on cost		11.1%

Suggested Response: Lewis Willis

Willis is a good customer and if possible the bank would want to help him. He has an excellent track record in the business (but then so did a number of property developers who have gone bust recently). This is a business where past track record is not necessarily a guide to future success if the marketplace fundamentals relating to property go against you.

Despite all the indications about future tenants, the development is not yet pre-let or sold, so it is open-ended and therefore speculative. Willis has deliberately avoided putting the project through one of his existing companies. Whatever the reason for this, it reduces the risk of loss to him and increases the risk to the bank. This is because the bank cannot look to assets outside the project if things go wrong. Moreover, Willis is putting in no stake and the bank will be lending 100%, including rolling up interest for two years.

Although there is an apparent 19.6% margin on the project, this is unlikely to be sufficient if things go significantly wrong.

Case Study 3 – M Group Ltd

M Group was involved in cash-and-carry wines and spirits, with three warehouses and six retail shops. The business commenced in 1960 and had grown rapidly in recent years. The board of four directors included the proprietor and his wife, a sales director and a chartered accountant acting as finance director.

You have been unable to obtain recent debenture figures, due to the company transferring records to computer. There has been pressure of late on the bank account and you have had to report temporary excess positions to the control department. The company directors have told you that the bank account problem is only temporary and is mainly caused by the cost of a move of premises.

However, draft accounts have just been produced to the company year-end 31 March, and when you compare them with previous years, the following is revealed:

	Draft Accounts	Audited Accounts		
	2002	1999	2000	2001
Sales	£36.1 m	£30.4m	£19m	£9.3m
Gross profit	1.2 m	£1.3 m	£909,000	£586,000
Gross profit %	3.4%	4.2%	4.8%	6.2%
Overheads	1.7m	£1.1m	£689,000	£485,000
Profit (Loss)	(£484,000)	£147,000	£220,000	£101,000

The group results indicate the rapid growth of the business in the last four years, with sales going from £9.3 million to £36.1 million, and with a fine (and deteriorating) gross margin, down from 6.2 % to 3.4 %. The draft accounts reveal both a drop in gross margin and at the same time increased overheads, to £1.7 million, resulting in a loss of £484,000.

With the move of premises and transfer to computer, no management accounts were prepared during the latter part of the year to 31.3.98, and consequently the considerable loss came as a shock to the directors.

The directors agreed to the appointment of investigating accountants to try to pinpoint the current trading position and cash flow requirement. The accountants subsequently reported:

(a) a serious imbalance of trade between volume of sales, gross margins and overheads incurred;

(b) that the accounting records maintained were most inadequate for a business of this nature with fine gross margins and high volume of turnover.

The following figures were provided to illustrate the bank's position:

	At 31.3.98		At 20.5.98	
	Estimated Draft balance sheet £000	Estimated break-up balance sheet £000	Estimated balance sheet £000	Estimated break-up balance sheet £000
Assets subject to fixed charge:				
Freehold deeds	283	175	283	175
Leasehold	9	–	9	–
Goodwill	70	–	70	–
Trade debtors	1,318	1,197	1,102	956
(A)	1,680	1,372	1,464	1,131
Assets subject to floating charge:				
Fixtures and equipment	420	50	420	50
Motor vehicles	60	30	60	30
Stock	5,568	4,202	4,150	3,058
	6,048	4,282	4,630	3,138

	At 31.3.98		At 20.5.98	
	Estimated Draft balance sheet £000	Estimated break-up balance sheet £000	Estimated balance sheet £000	Estimated break-up balance sheet £000
Less: Preferential creditors:				
PAYE/NIC	(28)	(28)	(58)	(58)
VAT	(299)	(299)	(799)	(799)
Wages and holiday pay	(10)	(23)	(10)	(23)
Other preferential debts	(3)	(3)	(66)	(66)
	(340)	(353)	(933)	(946)
Net floating charge (B) assets	5,708	3,929	3,697	2,192
Total realizable (A+ B)	7,388	5,301	5,161	3,323
Bank	2,510	2,510	2,743	2,743
Surplus on bank's (C) charge	4,878	2,791	2,418	580
Unsecured creditors	4,459	3,759	1,999	1,399
Net assets/(liabilities)	19	(968)	419	(819)

The accountants also made the following report:

The group business has such a high turnover of stocks, with very short periods of credit given and taken, that the balance sheet can change dramatically in short periods of time. This is highlighted by the reduction of surplus on the bank's charge on a going-concern basis between 31/3 and 20/5 from £4.8 million to £2.4 million. [See also break-up basis, £2.8 million to £580,000: line (C).]

In our view the bank's position is not satisfactory ... the bank can never be sure as to what the position is ... Losses are highly likely to be continuing.

A few weeks later a receiver was appointed.

Case Study 4 – Company X

Company X were UK distributors for domestic kitchen appliances. Sales were mainly to electrical wholesalers and kitchen specialists. The goods carried no manufacturer's guarantee, but were distributed by Company X with their own 12 months' warranty. Company X traded profitably in their early years, but later incurred substantial losses due to abortive ventures into new kitchen and bathroom products. At the same time, high warranty charges were encountered with one major product line and business overheads also increased during 1996 and 1992.

Year Ended December:	1994	1995	1996	1997
Sales	£2.57 m	£3.56 m	£4.23 m	£2.3 m
Gross Profit %	19%	18%	18%	17%
Overheads	£493,000	£641,000	£965,000	£783,000
Overheads/Sales %	19%	18%	23%	34%
Net profit/(loss)	–	–	(£202,000)	(£323,000)

Investigating accountants went in in September (after the bank received the disastrous trading figures) and reported that the bank debt should be covered on a break-up basis:

Estimated Statement of Affairs as at 30.9.98

	Book Value £000	Break-up Value £000
Assets subject to fixed charge:		
Debtors	425	335
Less: Bank	(393)	(393)
Surplus/(Shortfall) to debenture holder under fixed charge	32	(58)
Assets subject to floating charge:		
Stock	497	251
Plant/Machinery/Motor Vehicles	33	15
	530	266

		Book Value £000	Break-up Value £000
Preferential creditors:			
PAYE/NI	36		
Rates	12		
VAT	130		
Employees (Holding Pay)	3	(181)	(181)
Surplus/(Shortfall) under floating charge		349	85
Surplus/(Shortfall) to debenture holder		32	(58)
		381	27
Unsecured Creditors		(553)	(553)
Shortfall to Unsecured Creditors		(172)	(526)

(You will see that most of the bank's cover was on book debts as a fixed charge.)

When receivership took place later in December, the bank's cover on debtors was quickly dissipated with many counterclaims from customers to set off on warranty work and retentions in case of future complaints on warranty work. Finally, by 2001 the total recovery from book debts amounted to only £134,000 as against the initial book value of £425,000. Stock also suffered, although previously discounted by 50% to £251,000. Eventual realization was only £125,000 (50% of the discounted figure).

Case Study 5 – Sparks Ltd

Sparks Ltd have banked with your bank for over 20 years and act as wholesalers and suppliers of a range of electrical components to industrial customers. The directors, Richard Lee (aged 49) and Charles Proctor (aged 52) own 50% of the company each, and draw remuneration in the same proportions. Lee looks after sales and Proctor is responsible for finance and administration.

The company currently has overdraft facilities of £300,000 secured by a debenture.

The overdraft was renewed for 12 months a short while ago, at which time the company supplied a profit and loss forecast for the year to 30 September 1997.

Richard Lee calls to see you. He tells you that Proctor has recently suffered a mild heart attack and is seriously considering giving up work. He wants Lee to buy him out of the business and has put a value of £400,000 on his shares. Lee wishes to go ahead and buy the shares at this figure, and his initial thoughts are as follows:

1. He can raise £100,000 himself – £50,000 from savings and £50,000 by increasing the mortgage on his house (value £300,000, existing mortgage £40,000).

2. The company buys back sufficient shares to cover the remaining £300,000. He sees this being financed by:

    (a) a ten-year loan of £200,000;

    (b) utilizing the existing overdraft facility to provide the balance of £100,000.

3. A book-keeper will be employed to replace Proctor at a salary of £25,000 per annum.

Required:

Set out, with reasons, your response to this request.

SPARKS LTD: Profit and Loss Summary

Year to 30 September	1999 £	2000 £	Draft 2001 £	Forecast 2002 £
Sales	1,731,672	1,909,452	2,024,434	2,250,000
Gross profit	626,400	611,970	649,378	720,000
Directors' remuneration	136,066	171,753	172,500	180,000
Interest paid	21,180	23,830	20,714	22,500
Profit before tax	87,372	30,042	21,437	112,500
Retained profit	78,372	18,042	9,887	–

Corporate Lending and Securities

Balance Sheet

As at 30 September	1999		2000		2001	
	£	£	£	£	£	£
Current Assets						
Cash	7,261		7,327		7,402	
Debtors	423,216		474,668		482,925	
Stock	385,998	816,475	359,973	841,968	367,338	857,665
Current Liabilities						
Creditors	255,007		239,677		309,750	
Bank	151,109		167,030		109,311	
Hire Purchase	38,917		48,223		46,179	
Taxation	9,000	(454,033)	12,000	(466,930)	11,550	(476,790)
Net Current Assets		362,442		375,038		380,875
Fixed Assets						
Leasehold Property	13,500		12,000		10,500	
Fixtures and Fittings	24,106		23,831		17,876	
Motor Vehicles	97,212	134,818	104,433	140,264	115,938	144,314
		497,260		515,302		525,189
Financed By:						
Ordinary Shares		2,500		2,500		2,500
Profit and Loss Account		494,760		512,802		522,689
		497,260		515,302		525,189

Accounting Ratios

	1999	2000	2001 (Draft)	2002 (Forecast)
Net gearing (%)	36.8	40.4	28.2	–
Current ratio	1.80:1	1.80:1	1.80:1	–
Acid test	0.95:1	1.03:1	1.04:1	–
Credit given (days)	89	91	87	–
Credit taken (days)	84	67	82	–
Stock turnover (days)	127	101	96	–
Gross margin (%)	36.2	32.0	32.1	32.0
Net margin (%)	5.0	1.6	1.1	5.0
Interest cover (times)	5.1	2.3	2.0	6.0

Operation of Bank Account

	High £'000	Low £'000	Average £000
1994	202 Dr	5 Cr	145 Dr
1995	225 Dr	30 Dr	172 Dr
1996 to date	180 Dr	60 Cr	139 Dr

Interest margin 3% over base.

Suggested Answer Sparks Ltd

This situation concerns a company wanting to buy back its shares and the effect it would have on its balance sheet, etc. Share buybacks are allowed under s162 of the Companies Act 1985 but there must be sufficient undistributed profits to enable the buyback to take place. In this case there are.

The existing proprietors, Lee and Proctor, have built up a good business and they must have been competent managers to do so. However, Proctor will not be there in future and his talents could be missed – who will replace him? If the management become stretched, will Lee be able to devote the same amount of time as before to his marketing role, particularly as the company's projections require sales to increase by over 11%. Weakening the management team at the same time as putting the business under greater financial pressure by reducing the capital it has available is not an ideal situation.

The first issue to be considered is the price being paid. On a net asset basis, £400k looks a high price for 50% of £525k of net assets. On a P/E basis the price is too high, with the price earnings ratio being 81 times on the 2001 figures! The price can only be justified based on the 2002 forecast adjusted for a reduction in costs as a result of the lower directors' remuneration.

Looking at historical financial performance it can be seen that the current balance sheet structure is strong with low gearing. The business is liquid with both current ratio and acid test showing a healthy position, which is also reflected in the good credit given and taken figures and low overdraft usage. However, profitability has been disappointing, particularly at the net level. The last time the business made a decent net profit was two years ago when the gross margin was 36.2% rather than the 32% it is now. At the raw net profit level, it does not look as though the business could carry a lot more debt, but it has to be recognized that the directors have been able to pay themselves high remuneration and this could be regarded as "quasi profit".

If projections for 2002 look optimistic their achievement will require much tighter overhead control than has taken place in the past. Although the sales targets look ambitious, the company has a good track record of achieving good sales increases in the past.

Turning now to the proposition itself. Given his income and despite his age, Lee should be able to raise the extra mortgage he suggests so the main issue is whether the company can carry the extra debt burden. There is headroom within the overdraft facility to accommodate £100k but this will almost certainly create a hard core and it will be better to fund this element by way of loan. The deal will require cash outflow in terms of interest and loan repayments of circa £50k, against which can be set net directors' salary savings of £60k – last year say £85k less a book-keeper's salary of £25k. Repayment does therefore look theoretical possible.

Gearing would rise significantly:

	£
2001 Net Debt	148,088
Add New Debt	300,000
	448,088
2001 NTAs	525,189
Less buy back	300,000
	225,189

So net gearing will be nearly 200%. The new capital structure will be uncomfortable. What is needed is a detailed business plan going forward with sensitivity analysis.

As security in the new scenario only once debtor cover would be available and there would be less than two times current asset cover, so security is thin. Moreover as a wholesaler the business is at high risk of reservation of title in relation to the stock. Given the level of gearing and the thin security cover, Lee's guarantee looks necessary, supported by the equity in his house which will amount to £210k after the re-mortgage.

This is a marginal proposition which could be argued either way. Repayment looks feasible but gearing and security are uncomfortable and this tends to suggest that the price being paid by Lee is too high. He should be advised to go away and renegotiate the price. If an absolute reduction is not achievable some of the consideration could be deferred on to an "earn out" basis.

Whatever the decision, what is required is a detailed business plan, probably produced with the assistance of outside accountants.

Case Study 6 – Advanced Products Ltd

Advanced Products Ltd was established 30 years ago, and manufactures high-specification components for the motor industry. For the last ten years the company has been part of a medium-size industrial group with interests in a number of areas, including plastics and building materials. In recent years Advanced Products has performed poorly despite changes in management and substantial capital expenditure to acquire the latest plant and machinery. Its parent has decided to dispose of the business, and is looking for a buyer.

You have contacts with a firm of venture capitalists, and they have approached you to see if your bank is interested in participating in the financing of a management buy-in of Advanced Products Ltd. The proposed structure of the transaction is:

Finance required	£000
Acquisition price	2,470
Working capital	400
Deal costs	175
	3,075
Funded by	
Deferred consideration	350
Overdraft	500
Medium Term Loan	900
Management shareholding	40
Investor shareholding	1,255
	3,045

The requirement from the bank is the overdraft and five-year medium-term loan.

The main elements of the proposal are:

(a)   The MBI will be undertaken by a William Wallace (age 41), who will operate as managing director on a full-time basis. A new finance director – someone known to Wallace – will also be appointed. Wallace is a graduate engineer and qualified accountant who has been known to the venture capital house for some years. He has a track record as a "company doctor" in making underperforming engineering companies profitable. He has been looking to acquire a business "of his own" for two years, and has identified Advanced Products as a good opportunity.

(b)   Wallace has had full access to the company and its staff for the past three months. He has had the opportunity of examining internal financial information, and has met all the major suppliers and customers.

(c) Quality control has been a problem, and caused the loss of two major customers in the last financial year. Wallace has discussed the possibility of getting this business back with the companies concerned, and believes they will return when he is in charge.

(d) Wallace has drawn up projections for the future. These, together with the recent trading performance and opening balance sheet position, are to be the subject of due diligence by a national firm of accountants on behalf of the venture capitalists.

(e) An experienced industrialist is to be appointed as non-executive chairman to represent the interests of the outside investors.

(f) The preference shares are redeemable from Year G onwards.

(g) The bank is offered a debenture giving a fixed and floating charge over the company's assets.

Advanced Products Limited

Balance Sheet Projections

	Opening (£000s)	Year D (£000s)	Year E (£000s)	Year F (£000s)
Fixed assets				
Plant, machinery & vehicles	2,314	1,952	1,681	1,484
Stock	700	914	986	1,086
Debtors	1,228	1,495	1,688	1,938
Creditors	(911)	(1,015)	(1,133)	(1,283)
Dividends	–	(60)	(60)	(60)
Tax	–	(79)	(179)	(328)
Bank balance	77	195	297	691
Working Capital	1,094	1,450	1,599	2,044
Deferred tax	–	(14)	(17)	(16)
Medium-term loan	(900)	(800)	(600)	(400)
Leasing creditor	(863)	(786)	(695)	(686)
Deferred consideration	(350)	(350)	(175)	–
Net Assets	1,295	1,452	1,793	2,426
Financed by:				
Management equity	40	40	40	40
Institutional equity	60	60	60	60
Institutional cumulative redeemable preference shares	1,195	1,195	1,195	1,195
Profit and loss	–	157	498	1,131
	1,295	1,452	1,793	2,426

Advanced Products Limited

Profit and Loss Summary

12 months to 31 December	Actual Year A (£000s)	Year B (£000s)	Year C (£000s)	3 months to 31 March Year D (£000s)	Budget Year D (£000s)	Year E (£000s)	Year F (£000s)
Sales	5,861	5,740	3,673	1,222	5,600	6,700	7,900
Gross profit	1,371	1,784	1,067	501	2,510	3,014	3,589
Overheads including:	2,598	3,373	3,065	551	2,030	2,270	2,470
Depreciation	307	540	676	147	623	600	533
Repairs under warranty	–	82	45	3	13	13	13
Bad debts	63	46	32	6	25	25	25
Group management charge	88	98	72	15	–	–	–
Salaries (including directors' remuneration)	1,114	1,306	1,123	221	830	990	1,060
Redundancy costs	153	157	49	3	–	–	–
Stock provisions	11	123	350	3	–	–	–
Profit before interest and tax	(1,227)	(1,589)	(1,998)	(50)	480	744	1,119
Interest	316	95	121	24	217	214	184
Profit before tax	(1,543)	(1,684)	(2,119)	(74)	263	530	935
TAX	–	–	–	–	46	129	242
Dividends	–	–	–	–	60	60	60
Retained profit	(1,543)	(1,684)	(2,119)	(74)	157	341	633

Accounting Ratios

	Year A	Year B	Year C	3 months to 31 Mar Year D	Opening balance sheet	Year D	Year E	Year F
Net gearing (%)	–	–	–	–	130	96	56	16
Current ratio	–	–	–	–	2.2:1	2.3:1	2.2:1	2.2:1
Acid test	–	–	–	–	1.4:1	1.5:1	1.4:1	1.6:1
Credit given (days)	–	–	–	–	–	97	92	90
Credit taken (days)	–	–	–	–	–	189	176	169
Stock turnover (days)	–	–	–	–	–	112	98	92
Gross margin %	23	31	29	41	–	45	45	45
Net margin %	(26.3)	(29.3)	(57.7)	(6.1)	–	4.7	7.9	11.8
Interest cover (times)	–	–	–	–	–	2.2	3.5	6.1

This is an example of a Management Buy-In (MBI). MBIs generally are more risky than MBOs because the management of the business is brand new on top of everything else, and they do not have the sort of detailed knowledge of the business that an existing team brings.

The introduction is from a good source and so needs to be taken seriously. The venture capitalists will be persuading investors to take a higher risk than the bank, and their reputation will be on the line. Their willingness to support Wallace is positive. Even so, the bank still needs to have other references on him, particularly in relation to his previous performance as a company doctor.

The fact that there is going to be a non-executive chairman, who will provide an ongoing independent influence on the business, will be in the bank's interest as well as the investors'.

Wallace's time spent in the business will have given him a good picture of it, and he is committing £40,000 of his own money. However, he cannot have that in-depth knowledge that actually being responsible for the business brings. The existing management team and workforce have been associated with failure, and will have to be motivated to turn things around, which may not be easy. This could be particularly crucial in relation to the critical quality problems the company has been facing. Plant and equipment should be up to date, and little capital expenditure should be needed.

The purchase price at £2,470,000 for net assets of £1,295,000 looks high, particularly for a loss-making business. There has to be an underlying strong assumption that the forecast profits can be achieved to justify the price.

The initial gearing looks high but is probably acceptable in view of the medium-term element. The overdraft is not used at the opening or year-ends in the projections, so a monthly cash flow is needed to justify the request.

The three-year gap before the preference shares start to be redeemed seems reasonable. It would be helpful to see audited accounts for the historical business to put the projections into context. The forecasts indicate that the business should be very liquid, but this is dependent on the high level of projected credit taken, which requires confirmation. Moreover, the profit projections look very ambitious when compared with past performance. A substantial improvement in sales is required. Much will depend on Wallace's winning back the lost business.

Additionally, a much higher gross margin than has been achieved historically is required. and although the first quarter's figures show some improvement in gross profit percentage, even this is not enough. The substantial cut in overheads that has been assumed looks ambitious too, although again there are signs in the first quarter that an improvement can be made.

There do not seem to be any on-off costs for redundancies, despite the fact that a significant cut in salaries is projected. The reduced stock and warranty provisions will need quality improvements if they are to achieved.

The debenture picks up good current asset cover for the bank. Two times cover is available, including one and a half times by debtors. Given the low bad debt record, this should be adequate security. On top of this, there may be some value in the plant and equipment not covered by hire purchase. Chattel mortgages would be needed.

Given the tightness in the projections, an interest cap or hedge for the borrowing should be considered.

This is a difficult decision. Although Wallace has the right background and there is acceptable security cover, the achievement of the projections looks very demanding. The bank could commission its own due diligence but, in the end, due diligence is still only a rather more informed opinion.

Overall it would be better if the proposition was re-engineered through the negotiation of a lower purchase price or a greater proportion of venture capital money compared with bank debt.

Case Study 7 – Northern Casting Co

Northern Casting Co is a division of a small public engineering company called Engineering Conglomerate plc. Two months ago, Engineering Conglomerate was placed into administrative receivership by its bank. The receiver, who is a partner of one of the major UK accounting firms, has kept the manufacturing businesses that make up Engineering Conglomerate trading while he tries to find buyers for them.

Northern Casting produces high-quality metal components, which are used in the brewing, machine tool, automotive and defence industries. It has a broad spread of customers, no one of which represents more than 5% of sales.

The works manager of Northern Casting, Peter Collins (48), calls to see you. He has maintained a satisfactory personal account with your bank for 20 years. With the help of some of the employees, he wants to purchase the business of Northern Casting Co. He tells you the following:

(a) The proposed new shareholders can raise £180,000 to invest in the venture.

(b) A price of £280,000 has been agreed with the receiver for the plant and stock of the business.

(c) The plant and machinery comprises machine tools, foundry and finishing equipment, which are currently under-utilized. The previous book value of the plant was £250,000.

(d) The receiver has sold the factory premises occupied by the business separately to a property company. The property company will grant the new venture a 15-year lease subject to five-yearly reviews at an initial rent of £120,000 per annum. However, because the new venture is unproven, the property company is insisting that a bank guarantees the payment of the rent for the first three years.

(e) The venture will be incorporated into a new limited company and be called Northern Casting Co Ltd.

(f) The receiver has carried out an analysis of the old Northern Casting Co. Division accounts over the past three years, and this has been provided to Collins, who has also produced projections for the new venture with the help of an accountant friend.

(g) There is a requirement for bank support as follows:

Overdraft   £300,000

Loan   £100,000 (five years, including one year repayment holiday)

Rent guarantee

Collins asks whether you can assist.

Northern Casting Co

Profit and Loss Summary

12 months	Actual Year A £000	Actual Year B £000	Actual Year C £000	Forecast Year 1 £000	Forecast Year 2 £000	Forecast Year 3 £000
Sales	1,454	1,510	1,219	1,650	1,800	2,000
Cost of sales						
Materials and subcontracting	(475)	(545)	(438)	(578)	(630)	(700)
Labour	(324)	(300)	(261)	(276)	(302)	(335)
Gross profit	655	665	520	796	868	965
Expenses	(489)	(435)	(390)	(622)	(629)	(631)
Profit before tax	166	230	130	174	239	334
After:						
Rent	–	–	–	120	120	120
Depreciation	27	27	24	16	16	16
Director's remuneration	–	–	–	30	30	30
Interest paid	–	–	–	35	26	4

Forecast Balance Sheets

	Opening position £000	Q1 £000	Q2 £000	Q3 £000	Q4 £000	Year 2 £000	Year 3 £000
			Year 1				
Current assets							
Cash	–	–	–	–	–	83	313
Debtors	–	344	357	370	383	397	441
Stock	130	130	130	130	130	130	130
	130	474	487	500	513	610	884
Current liabilities							
Trade creditors	–	–	30	62	64	66	73
Bank overdraft	–	275	213	142	9	–	–
VAT payable	–	12	12	13	14	14	15
Accruals	–	21	22	23	24	24	24
Tax	–	8	18	30	43	60	84
	–	(316)	(295)	(270)	(237)	(164)	(196)
Net current assets	130	158	192	230	276	446	688
Bank loan	(100)	(100)	(100)	(100)	(100)	(75)	(50)
Fixed assets							
Plant and machinery	150	146	142	139	134	119	103
Net assets	180	204	234	269	310	490	741
Financed by:							
Share capital	180	180	180	180	180	180	180
Profit and loss	–	24	54	89	130	130	561
	180	204	234	269	310	490	741

Accounting Ratios

	Year A	Year B	Year C	Opening Position	Year 1	Forecast Year 2	Year 3
Net gearing (%)	–	–	–	55.6	61.9	–	–
Current ratio	–	–	–	–	–2.16:1	3.72:1	4.51:1
Acid test	–	–	–	–	–1.62:1	2.93:1	3.85:1
Credit given (days)	–	–	–	–	85	81	80
Credit taken (days)	–	–	–	–	40	38	38
Stock turnover (days)	–	—	–	–	–56	51	46
Gross margin (%)	45.0	44.0	42.7	–	48,2	48.2	48.2
Net margin (%)	11.4	15.2	10.7	–	10.5	13.3	16.7
Interest cover (times)	–	–	–	–	–6.0	10.2	84.5

This case represents a simple MBO with no venture capital house involvement.

Collins has been a valued personal customer, and the bank would want to be positive if possible. The proposed investment of £180,000 looks quite substantial in terms of Collins's and the workforce's resources.

The shareholding structure will be important given the diverse ownership. It is possible that control of the business could be in too many hands, and there might be insufficient certainty of direction.

The composition of the management team will be a key issue. Collins should understand the production side, but who is going to look after marketing and sales? The finance function appears light. Collins had to use a "friend" to produce the forecasts, which suggests that there is no one within the business itself, and this must be a concern.

The price being paid for the business looks fair given the book value of the plant. On a P/E basis the price looks cheap at just over two times last year's profits.

Buying just the plant and stock avoids the risks involved in buying the business as a whole, such as hidden bad debts etc. It is possible that customer confidence has been damaged by the receivership, so it would be helpful to understand the strength of the current order book.

The financial analysis is complicated by the absence of audited accounts. The business was previously only a division of Engineering Conglomerate. Some sort of warranty covering the accuracy of the historical figures should be sought from the receiver.

Historic profitability has been good, with net margin always above 10%. There is a problem though, because the historic figures do not contain a full set of overheads. In future the business will be carrying additional costs for rent, interest etc., which are at a level in the first forecast year that would have wiped out the last historic year's profit.

The profit forecast for next year is predicated on a substantial increase in sales. Having said this, sales last year were well down on the previous year, perhaps because of the effects of the receivership – the reason needs to be established. It might be possible to achieve the sales volume, but the forecasts also assume a much higher gross margin than has been achieved before.

The overheads look conservative, but there have to be question marks over some other figures:

(a) The constant stock figure while sales rise sharply looks wrong.

(b) Will there really be no capital expenditure?

(c) Why can no trade credit be obtained initially but be available later?

As security the bank should be able to take a debenture. What would this be worth?

		£
Debtors @ 70% x £344,000	=	240,800
Stock @ 10% x £130,000	=	13,000
Plant @ 25% x £146,000	=	36,500
		290,300

To cover the peak borrowing of £375,000 plus the rent guarantee. This looks thin. Directors' guarantees would help, but these might be difficult to obtain given the diverse ownership structure.

Overall the proposition looks too naïve. It is difficult to feel confidence in the management or its plans. Security cover is also thin. The deal should be declined.

Case Study 8 – Diesel Machinery Ltd

Diesel Machinery Ltd is currently a wholly-owned subsidiary of Conglomerate plc, a large diversified industrial group. Conglomerate plc is in financial difficulties and needs to reduce gearing. It has therefore decided to divest itself of some of its non-core subsidiaries, including Diesel Machinery Ltd.

Diesel Machinery Ltd was formed 18 years ago as a distributor of diesel engines made by major manufacturers. Its main market (80% of new equipment) is the sale of engines as electricity generating sets, mainly used to provide emergency and standby electrical power. The remainder of sales are to meet specific customer needs; the company adapts engines for installation into customer products.

Two of Diesel's directors, Ian Foster (aged 46), the managing director, and Trevor O'Neill (aged 38), the marketing director, have expressed interest in leading a management buy out of the company. Both Foster and O'Neill have been in the engineering industry all their working lives, and have worked for Diesel for five and four years respectively. They have been given a great deal of autonomy in running the company but believe it has been under-resourced by Conglomerate plc. They also believe the business could be run more tightly, and have identified ways of reducing overheads by 7%.

Conglomerate has put an asking price of £2.5 million on the business, but Foster and O'Neill believe they can knock this down to £2.2 million and have produced financial projections based on this sum. By re-mortgaging their houses they can, between them, raise £125,000, which will purchase part of the equity of the company. They have found a venture capital house that is prepared to invest the balance in return for £250,000 of the equity and £1,825,000 of redeemable preference shares, provided that a bank can be found to provide initial overdraft facilities of £800,000.

The venture capital house has sent you a copy of the financial projections, as Diesel's offices are near your branch. You are asked whether you are interested in providing the required overdraft.

Diesel Machinery Ltd

Historical and Projected Financial Information

	Actuals			Projections		
Year to 30 April	Year A £000	Year B £000	Year C £000	Year D £000	Year E £000	Year F £000
Turnover	7,574	6,271	8,801	9.923	10,901	12,169
Gross profit	1,716	1,446	1,642	2,141	2,409	2,812
Profit before interest and tax	242	125	150	481	595	777
Retained profit	18	(181)	(97)	86	151	276

Accounting Ratios

	Year A	Year B	Year C	Year D	Year E	Year F
Gross margin (%)	22.7	23.1	18.7	21.6	22.1	23.1
Net margin (%)	–	–	–4.4	4.9	5.6	
Net gearing (%)	–	–	31	55	61	88
Current ratio	–	–	1.61:1	1.46:1	1.41:1	1.32:1
Acid test	–	–	0.84:1	0.87:1	0.83:1	0.77:1
Credit given (days)	–	–	72	83	79	75
Stock turnover (days)	–	–	67	57	55	54

Sales Projections

Year ending 30 April	Year D £000	Year E £000	Year F £000
New equipment	5,348	5,865	6,547
Parts	3,364	3,706	4,137
Servicing	1,211	1,330	1,485
	9,923	10,901	12,169

Balance Sheet

As at 30 April Opening position £000		Year D £000	Projections Year E £000	Year F £000
	Fixed assets			
147	Plant and machinery	103	59	23
	Current assets			
1,611	Stock	1,557	1,646	1,788
1,746	Debtors	2,257	2,369	2,513
3,357		3,814	4,015	4,301
	Current liabilities			
1,519	Creditors	1,777	1,947	2,144
422	Bank	698	727	905
10	Lease finance	8	7	5
132	Taxation	126	160	213
(2083)		(2,609)	(2,841)	(3,267)
1,274	Net current assets	1,204	1,174	1,036
(21)	Deferred tax	(21)	(21)	(21)
1,400	Net assets	1,286	1,212	1,038
	Financed by:			
375	Share capital	375	375	375
1,825	Preference shares	1,625	1,400	950
(800)	Revenue reserves	(714)	(563)	(287)
1,400		1,286	1,212	1.038

Some of the figures in these financial statements have been subject to rounding.

Diesel Machinery Ltd

Projected Cash Flow Statement

Year ending 30 April	Year D £000	Year E £000	Year F £000
Profit before tax	432	531	684
Depreciation	64	64	56
	496	595	740
Working capital changes Increase/ (decrease):			
Stock	54	(89)	(143)
Debtors	(511)	(112)	(144)
Creditors	258	170	198
	(199)	(31)	(90)
Other fund movements:			
Taxation	(150)	(143)	(175)
Dividends paid	(203)	(203)	(180)
Capital expenditure	(20)	(20)	(20)
Preference share redemption	(200)	(225)	(450)
	(572)	(591)	(825)
Net cash flow	(274)	(27)	(175)
Represented by movements in:			
Lease finance	2	2	2
Overdraft	(276)	(29)	(178)
	(274)	(27)	(176)

Some of the figures in these financial statements have been subject to rounding.

This case represents a simple MBO.

The fact that the bank does not know any of the principals involved is not unusual for an MBO, but the venture capital house would usually introduce the business to one of its regular bank contacts, so some caution is needed.

However, the size of the venture capital investment compared with the bank requirement is impressive.

The management's own commitment is significant in terms of their own resources. They should know the business well. Having said this, it has not performed well under their stewardship in the past. Moreover, if it has been under-resourced when part of a major group, then it is unlikely that the new owners will be able to address this issue quickly.

The main product is at the "heavy" end of the engineering range, and a large portion of new equipment sales are likely to be dependent on the construction market, which tends to be cyclical. This is less than ideal in the context of an MBO, where solid predictable cash flows are needed to reduce borrowing quickly. However, the parts/service element of sales should provide a more stable element of cash flow, and this represents 46% of forecast sales.

What is the attitude of the company's suppliers going to be in the face of their weakened credit covenant? The attitude of the engine supplier will be especially crucial, and needs to be determined.

Looking at the financial analysis, the historical track record of losses has to be a concern. However, it is profitability at the PBIT line that is the most important, given that the interest charge will be different in the new scenario and the business has been profitable at this level.

The projected sales performance looks demanding compared with the recent past. While the new equipment sales forecast might be explained by a cyclical upturn, the increase in parts/service sales probably requires the business to achieve an increase in market share. Why should this be possible?

The gross margin projections are in line with previous performance with the exception of the most recent year, so they should be achievable. The problem comes when gross margin and sales performance are linked. Sales increased in Year C, but this was only on the back of a gross margin reduction, and this does not augur well for the attainment of the future combined sales/gross margin targets.

Gearing looks acceptable going forward, but there has to be an issue in the fact that it increases as the preference shares are redeemed. In fact the venture capital house gets repaid quicker than the bank despite being nominally subordinate. It seems likely that the bank requirement will rise further in the years beyond the forecasts as a result of this process.

Capital expenditure is low compared with the depreciation charge, suggesting a potential short-term cash gain at the expense of a higher cash need in future.

The forecast assumptions look questionable in a number of areas, and thorough due diligence will be required to validate them.

The security position is apparently strong, as the debenture provides excellent debtor cover – over three times in the first two years. However, reservation of title could be a problem. Normally it is difficult to trace title through to debtors, but in this instance it may be possible because the engines are likely to have individual serial numbers. Having said this, the parts/service debtors are significant, and will not be affected by reservation of title.

In favour of the proposition is the relatively low borrowing requirement and good security cover. Against is the preferential exit by the venture capital house (although it should be possible to renegotiate this) and, more importantly, the questions over the forecasts. Due diligence is going to be crucial but if it is positive most banks would lend.

INDEX

V

W